JOCK STEIN
THE DEFINITIVE BIOGRAPHY

ARCHIE
MACPHERSON

Dedication

To Stuart and Scott

Published in 2004 by Highdown,
an imprint of Raceform Ltd ,
Compton, Newbury, Berkshire, RG20 6NL
Raceform Ltd is a wholly-owned subsidiary of Trinity Mirror plc

ISBN 1-904317-73-1

Designed by Fiona Pike
Printed and bound by Cromwell Press

CONTENTS

ACKNOWLEDGEMENTS

This book could not have been written without the exhaustive research and erudition of former librarian and football historian Pat Woods whose knowledge of the period covered in the book is second to none. I interviewed so many of Jock Stein's former friends, workmates and his colleagues in football from his player and managerial days that it would be difficult to list them all in appreciation. However I must mention Tony McGuinness for recalling many moments in his friendship with the Stein family. I am also grateful to members of Tony Queen's family who revived memories of the favourite Stein holiday island, Menorca. I am also indebted to those who sadly are no longer with us, like Tony Queen , but who in the past spoke to me freely about their times with the 'Big Man'. It was a special pleasure though to be led through the period of the coal-mining days of Stein with former miner Harry Steele and to hear the Burnbank tales of his upbringing from local historian Jim Wallace. From Stein's earlier playing days I was especially grateful for the contributions of his former Coatbridge team-mate Adam Maclean and the historian of Albion Rovers , Robin Marwick. William Walker who barely missed a game Stein played for Rovers renewed my respect for footballing loyalty. To Bobby Flavell and Jock Aitken , both formerly of Airdrie FC , my indebtedness for their conversations. Stein's Celtic colleagues, Sean Fallon and the late Bertie Peacock spoke enthusiastically to me of the early playing days at Parkhead. As always, Ernie Walker, former secretary of the Scottish Football Association , guided me with sensitivity and wit through the latter days of Stein's career. Relatives of the Gribben family, as if realising again what that name meant to the history of Celtic and the making of a legend , could not have been more helpful. Alan Herron, formerly of the Scottish Sunday Mail, who wrote profusely during the Stein era was a source of invaluable information. So also were those who gave unstinting attention to our general research. They included the staff of Airdrie Library, Hamilton Library, the Mitchell Library (Glasgow) and the British Newspaper Library (London). But it is his former players I have to thank most of all. They dug deeply. They unearthed memories in a manner which did not allow the obvious nostalgia to cloud their judgements which ranged from reverence to outright criticism. In deeply regretting the passing of Ronnie Simpson during the completion of this book, I nevertheless salute him and all the other Lisbon Lions and former players for expressing their views frankly to me. Without their candour it would have been a canvas without colour. I must also thank the patient and long-suffering tea-lady, my wife.

INTRODUCTION

Twenty-six thousand feet above the Pacific somewhere between San Francisco and Honolulu in the spring of 1982, Jock Stein awoke from a deep slumber in the aircraft seat beside me and began to speak. He preferred speaking to sleeping. He was loquacious by nature. He incited talk at times because he loved argument, dispute, contention, put-down punchlines – of which he was the master – and somehow had this arresting quality of always ending up with the final word. Only once did I see someone leave him mute and crestfallen, although that was when he was but a shadow of the footballing warrior he had been at his zenith.

As the engines droned on, he spluttered out of his sleep, looked quickly at me and then around as if he had become disorientated, adjusted himself so that he was sitting more upright and then after a few moments of silence he began to talk. In a low, husky voice bedevilled by the jet-lag that was drugging both of us after a long haul from Glasgow–London–Seattle–San Francisco en route to New Zealand, he began to speak about the incident just outside Lockerbie in the summer of 1975 that almost took his life. He had driven headlong into another car coming down the wrong side of the motorway and his Mercedes ended up a mangled wreck with he and his passengers seriously injured and near to death.

I have never grasped why this surfaced at this particular time, but from within his sleep he had been touched by a memory that seemed to be puzzling him. It was about nearly dying. I had never thought I would listen to something so deeply and intimately revealing, for normally he protected his privacy with the preoccupation of a Rottweiler patrolling his patch. Often you would think you were inching closer to some personal revelation, then he'd bring the shutters down with a clatter. The Stein domestic estate was protected by a high wall that stood in stark contrast to his public image of a man who had an opinion on virtually anything and who pronounced his views with the authority of an oracle. Even at his peak, though, he was deeply suspicious of the media and with one or two exceptions kept a strictly functional relationship with it. But here, now, was a mellower man, who should never have undertaken this particular journey anyway but was doing so out of a sort of political correctness, offering a brief glimpse of his inner self.

'They say I was nearly a goner,' he muttered. 'But all I can recollect is seeing a flower-box. I could see all these flowers with the different colours, all bright and kind of waving in the wind. Maybe I was passing over to the other side. I don't know why. Is that like being close to death? Maybe it reminded me of a flower-box I had known when I was a boy. I just don't know. I wasn't feeling anything, no pain or anything like that at that time. All I remember is that flower-box in my eye. It's strange, isn't it? That's all I saw. Makes you wonder about how you die and what's out there.'

I recall that as he said that he put out that large hand in front of him, as if to beckon the unknown mysteries of the universe. He then went on to say that he had lain back on his bed during the long process of recovery, assessing his life in a way he never had before and feeling that certain things weren't worth a shit any longer. He didn't say which.

It is not strange for anyone recovering from a near-death experience to take stock of life anew. But Stein opening up about it, even so slightly, was surprising, and it puzzled me. I had been attuned all my professional life to a different person. Nobody of my generation could ever dismiss from the mind the Stein who burst upon our lives as a dynamic, self-assured man who could lift your spirits with a jest or demolish you when he seemed to resort to an almost mean and vindictive mood. Stein of the great vision could be Stein of the explosive outburst. But the mix was compellingly attractive.

Of course, at the outset we knew something phenomenal was occurring, but little did we realise the extent of the revolution he was foisting on Scottish football. No alabaster saint could have managed that. That same aggressive Stein had renounced the sectarian divide, which still bedevils our land, and forced the famous rivals Rangers to examine their own future as a club weighed down by the illogical pursuit of success through religious bias. Had Stein never appeared on the scene, Rangers' transformation in that area might have been much slower. It was that Stein who took on the media so successfully in an age when it was perceived within Celtic that everything was processed to please Ibrox. He left you feeling that he was virtually writing the copy for some of the journalists. Nobody with only avuncular charm as a tool could have achieved that. It was the mature Stein who gave the impression of immortality, not in the now famous quoted context of Bill Shankly who attributed that to him after the Lisbon victory in 1967, but in rising from what most people thought would be a death-bed, with his car squashed beyond recognition.

INTRODUCTION

Now, just for that moment, he was but an old man sitting in an aircraft. It is easy enough to say so now, but I did feel that this lifestyle – flying between continents to see a third-rate national side, New Zealand (his opponents in the upcoming World Cup finals in Spain), just to indicate to the public through the media that he was taking his role as Scotland's national manager desperately seriously – was fast burning him out. It is difficult to appreciate the ageing process of someone whose image still burns youthfully and brightly in the mind's eye. In that respect he had always seemed quite indestructible. Now he looked and sounded appealingly ordinary and vulnerable.

But that was a fleeting impression. For in a way I felt a little bit as though I were sitting beside the tattooed man from Ray Bradbury's *The Illustrated Man*: the pictures on his body told different stories. Stein had no tattoos that I know of, and certainly not of King Billy on his chest as was widely rumoured at one time, but out of every pore on his body could stream a thousand stories relating to the most significant era in Scottish football and to the attitudes of a society in which his father never wished him well when Celtic played Rangers and his best friend shunned him because he signed for the Parkhead club. I was with a man who had really begun to alter people's perceptions on bigotry in such a practical way that it challenged the ineffectiveness of pious utterances from various pulpits. A consistently successful Celtic side under Stein put Celtic scarves into 'Protestant' school playgrounds where previously they would not have been found by tracker-dogs.

You could not properly put the current and future basis of Scottish football under examination without studying how this man from Burnbank in Lanarkshire transformed the landscape. He came on the scene as a journeyman playing for a humble club in a manner that showed little sign of emerging greatness. But that is part of what made him. Unquestionably there was good fortune to speed him on his way, from time to time, but essentially we are looking at someone who grafted hard at his trade and almost miraculously turned his respectable mediocrity as a player to his advantage. For Stein knew the game from the bottom up. He got inside men's heads because he was not as good a player as he would have liked to be, but in the process of understanding his own shortcomings he realised better than most what a player would best respond to.

Even though I did, during that trip, try subtly to get him back on to the subject of that car crash, he didn't take the bait. For when we arrived in New

Zealand he was fêted by the welcoming party, more for being the successful Celtic manager than the visiting Scotland official. This seemed to revive him. Mention Celtic to Jock Stein and it was almost as if he had been given a blood transfusion. He didn't live in the past, but he liked to visit it from time to time. We had an enjoyable if largely unproductive stay. But I was thankful for the whole tiring process of the journey out there if only for that intensely surprising revelation.

On the way home, he turned to me just before we landed in Glasgow. 'If this war in the Falklands gets any worse and Maggie puts the boot in, you get your two boys and send them to Ireland out of the way,' he said. 'Tell them to get the hell out of it. You don't want them fighting in that bloody war.'

Three years later, one of those two boys saw him collapse just outside the tunnel at the edge of the pitch in Cardiff. 'Are you all right, Jock?' he shouted from the enclosure just behind the Scottish bench as Stein was being carried away. The big man, eyes closed, couldn't reply. But his story will never be silenced.

CHAPTER ONE
A PLACE IN THE SUN

'Heh, you, get out of that sun!'
The voice pierced the marbled, immaculately tiled interior of the sumptuous Palacio Hotel in Estoril, Portugal, like a rifle shot. Jock Stein's 'Heh, you!' could turn legs to jelly, stop traffic in the street, clear buildings of starlings and make some of those he was targeting feel as if they were about to meet their Maker. This simple verbal tactic could be used to great effect, not just on his players but against members of the media who would count a Stein volley as one of their more memorable moments in life. On this occasion, though, he was singling out his reserve goalkeeper, John Fallon.

Now, it is difficult to avoid the sun in Portugal in the month of May. It is why people go to that country in the first place. To pick out our celestial source of light and energy for particular repugnance was to reflect Stein's obsessive application to the task in hand of winning a European trophy, which a few months previously would have been discounted by the rest of Europe as merely a figment of the imagination. Stein versus the sun along that coast was simply a preliminary bout to Stein versus Herrera, the Inter manager, later in that May week of 1967. On paper it seemed as if you couldn't beat that orb in the sky, but Stein was taking it on. His players were to regard sunburn as the stigma of disloyalty. On his command they were to try to keep out of the sun as if they were dodging a marksman with a telescopic rifle. Sun meant a sapping of the energy, and the Celtic manager was fearful that everything might come unstuck if even momentarily they were distracted from what they were there for – the winning of the European Cup.

As the manager approached Fallon the player bridled, although he also looked slightly perplexed because he wasn't outside but sitting in a lounge with the sun striking him through a nearby window. He moved promptly into the shade though. 'I told you before not to get into the sun, all right?' Stein added before turning away from us unsmiling, his face a stark contrast to the relaxation the decor was supposed to induce. He limped over to the hotel reception, then held court with some Portuguese journalists who had turned up on the doorstep and with whom he dealt patiently for a few minutes before walking away down a corridor, as if in search of someone else to prod into awareness of the serious task ahead.

Of course the place he had chosen for the squad's three-day stay could, in only three hours, have induced torpor in those who dropped their guard against the sensuous delights of the area. The Palacio, half an hour away from Lisbon, was tucked into a plaza just across from the esplanade and only a hundred yards away from a sea that during the entire trip operated merely as an expansive, motionless mirror to a cloudless sky. Inside the premises was a pool that might have been constructed by Busby Berkeley for Esther Williams. Around the interior grounds of the hotel were semi-tropical gardens that would have made an appropriate background for someone in a white dinner-jacket strolling along with gin and tonic or Dom Perignon in hand. In the 1930s, when the hotel was constructed, luxurious Hispano Suizas had filled the forecourt where now a football team bus made it difficult occasionally for the Mercs and Rolls-Royces to slide up to the front entrance. You could only conclude that this was a residence for wanton indulgence, not athletic preparation. It shimmered with class.

Yet that is why they were there. It reflected not self-indulgence but status. Stein had imbued in his players the need to think about their own capabilities rather than be obsessed by the talents of the opposition – any opposition. Step one was to house them like royalty. He had set himself the task of keeping in order players who certainly did not suffer from wild and extravagant habits (at least, for one or two individuals, not at that stage) but who nevertheless would have been less than human had they not been tempted by the surrounds to break his commandments. Still, as John Fallon would imply with his words to me – 'He could scare the shit out of you!' – disobeying Stein was a risky business.

Into this elegant spot for hedonists had come a group of West of Scotland lads more accustomed to the bracing breezes coming off the Firth of Clyde, at Seamill Hydro on the Ayrshire coast, and who could recognise the onset of hypothermia rather better than the dangers of bleaching in the sun. They had arrived by bus from Lisbon airport on Tuesday afternoon, 23 May, and after separating into twinned rooms and dropping off their baggage had gone for a short, casual walk with Neilly Mochan, their trainer. Half an hour later they had returned and, as politely as the dowager duchesses who used to vegetate there, taken tea and toast.

After the first light training session the players were allowed half an hour in the pool – half an hour was the very limit – then they were chased back indoors to a decking area where they began their solo schools in an area more acquainted with the rigours of contract bridge. Celtic captain Billy McNeill believes the card schools were good therapy. 'We were a team of bad losers,' he explained. 'We hated to lose at anything. So you got the same when we were playing cards. That kept the edge on us, for we played, we argued, disputed, huffed – we just hated losing. We were aggressive and cheeky and arrogant at times. Jock liked that. That's the feeling he wanted to breed among us. So there we sat, disturbing the calm, with the hotel staff wondering what the hell was going on. Don't underestimate what I say. All that was part of the preparation. Playing cards was about winning and losing, and as I say, nobody was a good loser.'

The following morning they leapt eagerly into the bus to take them to training in the Estadio Nacional. When they arrived they discovered that Inter were already in the toils of preparation, and it became immediately obvious that the Italians, who were accustomed to complete privacy for their normal training routines, did not like to be watched: they abruptly brought their training to an end, as if they had caught sight of a pursuing pack of hounds on their heels, cleared the field and made for the dressing-room. But when Celtic emerged to start their session the entire Inter squad was squatting on the sideline, ready to watch their every move. It might have been construed as an act of intimidation, or arrogance, and to an extent the Celtic players were certainly conscious of their presence, for the Italians stayed for the duration. But neither Stein nor his players blinked. Indeed, they felt they had attained a minor triumph at a time when any little incident might aid or mar morale.

'We had a training exercise which was a high-risk one for us,' full-back Jim Craig recalled. 'It could easily have gone wrong and we could have made a balls of it. It was that type of quick-passing, quick-sprinting one which could break down easily. We would line up in two rows about fifteen yards apart and the movement would start with the player at the end of one line passing the ball down to another at the end of the opposite row. He would kill it in one touch and send a long pass back to the next player at the end of the other row and then sprint to the end of the line. All it needed was one bad pass, one fumble, one deflection and the whole thing could end farcically, and sometimes it did, with Jock giving us a roasting. But, as if it was ordained on that particular day, it was perfection. The passes were crisp and accurate, and with Jock shouting encouragement and walking around us it was, I admit, very impressive where it could easily have made us look a bit foolish in front of the entire Italian team. I know it seems like a small matter but we did come back to the hotel feeling quite chuffed with ourselves. It was as if we had been inspired by the occasion. And in any case, to be honest, I think we were naïve about the whole business. For I don't honestly think that there was a single player who thought we could lose the final. By that I mean everything had worked out so well for us that season, so why not this final coming up? Yes, I know that sounds very naïve, but that's why we weren't tying ourselves in knots inside.'

Boredom was the only irritant, but it was encouraging some of the bolder players to slip out of Stein's view and resort to natural form. To achieve that you had to have the ingenuity and courage of those who hatched escape schemes in Colditz. For Stein always positioned himself strategically in a hotel lounge so he could see everything that moved: who came, who went. He was the predecessor of the security camera. You would see him talking to someone while at the same time sweeping an eye around the area taking in anything that moved. From where he sat in a lounge you wouldn't bet against him knowing, there and then, what the chef was doing with the coq au vin in the kitchen. As Mochan accurately observed about his sensory capabilities, 'He could detect a fiver fluttering down a corridor.'

But footballers are ingenious when it comes to escape routes, and one late afternoon after a training session Tommy Gemmell, Bertie Auld and Willie Wallace slipped out while Jock was engaged with some other business and took off in a taxi to the picturesque little fishing village of Cascais, where in an English pub they downed 'three or four pints of Watney's Red Barrel', as Gemmell put it to me, and then slipped back in. Such an intake of beer, even on the eve of the match, meant nothing to fit men, but the players knew it was a transgression that would have had them splattered to the wall verbally by their manager. On the other hand it did show that these three mercurial players simply could not resist the urge simply to be themselves. It was a fit of normality outwith the Stein purview that showed, in retrospect at least, that these men were not stiffened rigid by the formalities of preparing for the final of their lives. It was in fact a healthy breach of discipline, although to have argued that in front of Stein would have required a feisty lawyer.

Perhaps what it also demonstrated was that Stein had instilled in his players such a degree of self-belief that although they were going well out of bounds they knew it would have little detrimental effect on any outcome the following day. According to John Fallon, this was down to how Stein focused on matches. 'Jock never over-concerned himself with the other team. What he did was talk about us. Not them, but us. All the time. He wanted to din into us how we would play, and if we did, we'd get success. Now, who could have argued with him then, for we totally believed in what he told us. He got the results, didn't he? Of course sometimes he would say, "Any questions?" And I remember once when he did that Bertie Auld and Tommy Gemmell raised their hands and made one or two points. He just gave them a blank stare for a few seconds and then said, "I'm the manager and we'll do it my way." But he didn't dismiss what they said. For he was fly. He would definitely use us for input that way without admitting that there was any alternative to what he was laying down. To me he was like an old schoolmaster: don't ask questions, just sit there and listen.'

To break the monotony of their stay in the hotel, to distract them from the privations of having to ignore the luxuries around them, and to avoid the supporters who were now pouring into the area, some of them making tracks for the hotel to see the players, it was decided on the eve-of-match night to go on an organised walk. It turned out to be more eventful than they had anticipated.

They strolled along a country road in the direction of the villa of Scottish businessman Brodie Lennox who had established a home in Portugal years before. He had invited the players to come and relax away from the persistent eyes of media and supporters. When they arrived he gave them the run of the villa; they played snooker, then watched Spain playing England in an international match on television. Dusk had descended by the time they left, and what seemed like a simple retracing of steps became a nightmare. For Mochan decided to take a short-cut as he could see the sign for the hotel. Taking a short-cut in terrain you are not intimate with is the classic travellers-tale recollection of disaster, and Mochan's decision did not fall far short of that. They started by climbing a high fence, then set off in the direction of the hotel, only to come across a wall with a slope on the other side which would have intimidated a ski-jumper. The entire squad, about to play in the greatest match of their lives, decided to take it on, climbed the wall and dropped down the slope. It was only when they looked back up towards where they had come from that they realised the risk they had taken. It was an odd way to prepare for the great event itself, but there was not a twisted ankle among them.

On the morning of the game it was the Feast of Corpus Christi and all the Catholics in the party went to Mass, not out of gratitude for surviving the 'walk' the night before but as part of the observance of the Holiday of Obligation. They were joined in a local church by some of the supporters. Stein and the other non-Catholics remained in the hotel. After the service they had a short workout in the surrounding gardens, then a light meal. Bed for a couple of hours was the next stage for them all. Everything seemed to be perfectly in place. But nothing ever runs that smoothly.

To start with there was an upset to face up to when one player was woken abruptly from his afternoon slumber. Mochan appeared in Jim Craig's room and took the player aback with his sharp bark. 'Neilly, who very rarely swore, came marching into the room I was sharing with Tam Gemmell and asked me where my boots were. I pointed them out. It was then that he said, "We've just signed a contract with adidas and you're the only player in the effing team wearing Puma. I've got to go and get black paint to colour out the Puma flash and then I've got to find white paint to put in the adidas marks. You're an effing nuisance!" You could say a wee bit of the tension was getting through to him. So hours before kick-off he took the boots off me and went away to do his painting job. All I got out of it was some loss of sleep and newly painted boots for the game.'

By three o'clock that afternoon they had boarded the bus for what ought to have been an uneventful and relatively short trip down the coastline to the Estadio Nacional. But the Portuguese driver didn't know where the stadium was. After a while on the bus somebody shouted out to Stein, 'Boss, I think we're going the wrong way. Look at where all those cars are going.' They were lost. They managed to get the driver to turn round and follow the main line of cars and buses, but then they became jammed in the line of traffic and time began to slip away. As they started to fret a little, Bobby Murdoch, the midfield player with the immaculate passing touch, used his fine judgement to defuse the tension a mite by coming up with the natural and logical response to this. 'They can't start without us,' he announced.

There was, however, an advantage for them in this delay, for by the time they had arrived, examined the pitch and returned to their dressing-room there was barely time for them to be seized by stage-fright. They were now too busy for that. Bertie Auld felt quite nerveless and was even inspired by the normally mundane sight of jerseys hanging neatly on pegs in the dressing-room. 'What hit me firstly was the colour of the jerseys,' he recalled. 'Maybe

14

it was the sunlight pouring in. I don't know exactly what made it so, but the jerseys seemed like sparkling green and white like I have never seen them before. Just the same jerseys, you would think, but there they were looking as brilliant as I'd ever seen them. That made a great impression. You know how you put on your Sunday suit for special occasions? It was something like that.

'There was the usual banter about the dressing-room and then the Big Man came in just before kick-off. Now, he had a well-known habit whenever he walked into a dressing-room. He would lift his left leg and swing a pass at something lying on the floor – a spare lace, a piece of paper, a bit of mud. He would just lean back and swing at it like he used to do on the park. There was nothing in it other than maybe just a wee bit of nerves. Well, he did exactly the same that day. He came in, swung his leg at something on the floor and then opened his mouth, and I'll never forget what he said. It wasn't a team talk or anything like that. There was no great passion. But there was sincerity, and that's what made it so effective. He just said, "Right, lads. You've made history. Go out and enjoy yourselves."'

Then they had to face the long, dark underground tunnel before climbing up to the pitch. They went in order when they were called and lined up just as the Italians ambled up alongside them. They seemed to stand for an eternity there, longer than usual for some reason, and some of the players felt it getting to them. Bertie Auld remembers that the sight of the renowned Inter players sent a first shiver of apprehension through his mates. It was Jimmy Johnstone who made the first observation: 'Jesus Christ, they look like film stars!' There was a nervous laugh from one or two of the players but Auld confirms they looked impressive. 'They were like film stars. My God! You should have seen them. They were all dark-haired and it had all been slicked down like Valentino as if they had all been on the Brilliantine. The exception was [Inter and Italy captain Giacinto] Facchetti. He was blonder but big and handsome, a tremendous figure of a man. And they were all tanned and had been rubbed down with liniment or something for their skin was glistening and their teeth were glistening like pearls. Honest, they looked something special.'

The antidote to the sense of awe, which might otherwise have overwhelmed them, came instinctively to Auld. He started to sing. Not just anything – it was the Celtic song. 'Hail! Hail!' he began, and the rest joined in, the Italian players looking at them with some mystification as the chorus swelled into a kind of roar of defiance. The opposition, some of whom might have had more than a passing interest in grand opera, were learning that anything Verdi could do with an inspiring chorus so could a Glasgow comedian called Glen Daly, whose composition was now being called upon in that time of need.

The singing carried on unabated after the signal to march on. Up the steps they went, and as they did so an order was barked out to the man who would sit on the bench near Stein throughout the match, reserve goalkeeper John Fallon. 'We were coming out the long tunnel and I had just got to the top of the stairs when I heard Jock shouting: "Hey, John! Get that bench near the line before them!" So I had to sprint towards the bench he was talking about. When I got there I planted myself on it and I noticed that we were on the halfway line and the other one was further up. That might not have seemed an important thing. He just wanted to put one over Herrera, even if it meant just a few yards of difference in the benches. So when the Italians came up I was sitting there trying to look as if I was minding my own business. They tried to get me off it and called for the Portuguese police. I told them to get lost, in my best Blantyre manner of course, and the police took our side. "No, no! This is Celtic," they said, and the Italians were fuming. Now of course that meant I had done the donkey work, fought for the bench and Jock could just stroll up in a dignified manner as if it didn't matter where he sat. But he had stuck one up Herrera. That was his first victory over them. We were on the halfway line, they weren't.'

The players, strung out ahead of Stein as they made their way up the stairs to the pitch, might have been elsewhere, scattered to the winds, had 26 months earlier the man not made his return to Celtic Park as manager. Others might not have ended up with Celtic at all, as circumstances in virtually all of their cases could so easily have sent them in different directions. Their strong bonding now, on the verge of a supreme test of nerve, was almost miraculous given the nature of their haphazard coming together in the first place as a group of players. Billy McNeill, the captain, once told me that 1964/65 would have been his last season with the club had Stein not returned. 'I had made up my mind that it was time to move on at the age of 25 as I couldn't see anything positive happening at the club,' he said. Ronnie Simpson, when he was with Newcastle, had such a bad thigh injury he was told he might never play again. Bobby Murdoch had been thinking of moving to Australia. Bertie Auld would have stayed in England had Stein not changed chairman Bob (later Sir Robert) Kelly's attitude to him, and almost accepted an offer from Falkirk instead. John Clark, as a teenager, could have emigrated to England had his father not been killed tragically in an accident on the eve of their departure. Stevie Chalmers had contracted meningitis as a teenager when it was nearly always fatal, but fought back to recovery. Jimmy Johnstone felt like leaving the club even after Stein had arrived, as intially they were not hitting it off. Willie Wallace was thinking of emigrating to Canada had Hearts not agreed a transfer to Celtic at the time. For a whole variety of reasons they might not have made it to this point. But now, by whatever fatalistic intervention, the strands had been brought together in a dark tunnel in Portugal to form a group of lads quite unaware of how a simple climb up a few steps would change their lives for ever.

When they emerged into the sunlight the players screwed up their eyes and had to blink several times to adjust to the dazzling light of the stadium, as if the sun they had shunned for a couple of days was seeking revenge. Stein blinked as well. But he had much more experience of handling a change of light. He had started his working life doing exactly that, ascending daily to the surface from 1,000 feet underground in the pits of Earnock in Lanarkshire. A crucial part of the reward for doing so was simply survival. He showed his gratitude for that by never banishing those days from his mind. And if you did want to quiz him about it, he would sometimes start his story with how, frequently, down there in the dark, he would feed bread to the rats.

CHAPTER TWO
RISING FROM THE DARK

T he rats featured only at intervals, for in between feeding himself and
the rodents, young sixteen-year-old John Stein was earnestly fulfilling
his duties as a miner. It was inevitable he would go underground, following
in the footsteps of his father and other family members before him. It was
natural selection. Nobody thought otherwise. Burnbank, his home village,
wouldn't have existed in the first place had there been no mines. The entire
North Lanarkshire area was part of the crucible of Scotland's
industrialisation. But down there, 1,000 feet underground, they didn't
think of themselves as important cogs nobly oiling the wheels of industry;
their principal objective was simply to earn a wage and survive. D.H.
Lawrence's Walter Morel in *Sons and Lovers* encapsulated the miners'
existence in two simple sentences: 'You get used to it. You live like the mice
and pop out at night to see what's going on.' The very brevity of that has an
impact which conveys much of what Stein, as a young lad, had to cope with
in his formative years with the challenge of swapping daylight for the dark
as a way of earning a living.

He was born just before six o'clock on the evening of 5 October 1922, at
339 Glasgow Road, Burnbank, the only son of George and Jane. The house
no longer exists, having been pulled down to make way for new development.
Agnes Jack lived beside the Steins during the first part of his childhood. 'We
were neighbours there for years,' she said when interviewed back in 1965 for
the *Scottish Daily Express*. 'John was a wee curly-headed boy. They moved
when he was about twelve, and when he started work he went into the pits
like his father. There was nothing else for boys to do. They were hard days. I
remember the Depression and the soup kitchens. And how Mrs Stein lost
two of her girls: one died through burns, the other when she was a teenager.'

This bleak picture is markedly relieved by reference to the schools Stein
went to where he found not only solace in comradeship, for he was always a
gregarious personality, but also great satisfaction through his natural
inclination to kick a ball. He firstly attended Glenlee Primary, which was
itself a constant reminder of the nature of the land, for it had to be shored up
because of underminings and eventually had to be re-sited and replaced by a

modern school in 1964. When he was twelve Stein was moved on, for two years, to Greenfield School, which was for those who were not supposed to be gifted intellectually. But in truth, it would have been difficult for him to surmount the circumstances that made it an extremely remote possibility for working-class pupils to fulfil their true potential academically, even though the myth persisted historically around the Scottish parishes, and still does, that whatever the circumstances, if you had ability you would make it academically. Judging by the shrewdness, alacrity of mind in argument and the wide general knowledge he displayed at his managerial peak, which provoked the late John Rafferty of *The Scotsman* to say to me once, 'The big man will give you a conversation about any subject under the sun,' it is tempting to reach the impression that sitting in the classroom of either of those schools was an intelligent child whose abilities might have taken him on an entirely different route, with the right prompting. Jim Craig, his full-back over his most successful seasons, said quite candidly, 'My dental practice was near the SFA offices when he was Scotland's manager and I used to go up and have a lot of chats with him. We talked not just about football but about life in general. It was stimulating to say the least. Jock was not an educated person in general but he was a highly intelligent man. He would have sauntered through a university degree course.' But in the 1930s this lad o' pairts was unlikely to have progressed through the system to higher education because life was unfairer then.

His school teacher in charge of football when he was at Greenfield, John Gibson, a man who did so much to sharpen his appetite for the game, did not become starry-eyed about his pupil after Stein had become famous. Much as he admired what his former pupil achieved in later life, Gibson remembered his efforts in the team as modest. He might even have given Stein some tips on how to man-manage. 'I was like what John is now,' he said in 1965 just after Stein had won the Scottish Cup with Celtic in his first outing and had then become the temporary Scottish team manager. 'I was ruthless. I picked the best for my team and if they didn't stay in form they were out. John played at left-half for me and he wasn't the most outstanding player by a mile but he was a lanky lad and good enough. I never thought he would get so far.'

Stein's father had clear footballing ambitions for him, playing for Blantyre Vics then onwards to Rangers. The Vics and Rangers bedecked themselves in red, white and blue of course, and these were the colours that permeated George's vision. So in 1940, after playing juvenile and works football, when

Stein made up his mind to sign for Burnbank Athletic, who did not play in blue and were called the Bumbees because of their black and white colours, his father was offended, treated it like an act of treachery and tried to stop him. When officials from the club turned up at the family house with a bottle of whisky to pacify his father they were sent packing by an enraged parent who felt his son had been taken advantage of, having been made to sign under pressure on a bus coming back from a trial. The papers pertaining to that were thrown in the bin and he never did play for the Athletic; he went almost immediately to the Vics and the parentally-approved colours of red, white and blue. Although it is perfectly clear he had the greatest respect for his father, it is significant that Stein was already displaying that characteristic which he maintained throughout his life of acting with independence of mind and clear calculation. Here he was, setting out his stall in life with a first step he felt suited him regardless of what anybody else thought. That he had to submit eventually does not detract from the fact that this is the earliest evidence of Stein's indifference to custom and habit which prevented him, in the final analysis, of being sucked into the more sinister traditions of tribal sectarian thinking.

To the outsider, the sensitivities about colours of jerseys and the reasons that lay behind them would be bizarre. But not in Burnbank, where blue or green signified identities that took on cosmic significance in a village which was largely Protestant but with a Catholic fringe. The social fissure that separated the two tribes fell just short of the creation of ghettos but caused a natural gravitation to certain areas. The majority Protestant population would use Burnbank Cross in the heart of the village as their meeting point, either to have a blether, to slip lines to the bookie, to nip in to the surrounding pubs for a 'hauf and hauf-pint', or to watch the Orange Walk pass through on the 12 July; the Catholics congregated socially further down the street at Glenlee Street corner where the 'chapel' was, a place locals from either side called Pope's Corner. Gatherings here mirrored exactly the social intercourses that were going on around the Cross, except of course on the 12 July. Mixing in a formal way was out. Unless your very life depended on it, and then only after deeply profound consideration, would you dream of wandering into the other area and drinking with the other kind in one of their pubs. Such divisions both in separate schooling and in the self-regulated zonal areas perpetuated the ignorance that lay at the heart of bigotry.

Stein's family were staunch Protestants and his father a fervent Rangers man, but there is not a shred of evidence to suggest they nursed hatreds for the other side, and certainly there was no association with the Orange Order, although later Stein, it has been claimed, became a Mason. He did admit to me, in later years, that he felt uncomfortable having anything to do with the secret society in his capacity as a public figure. But it would be foolish to think that a young man brought up in such an environment would not be affected in some way by the frenzy of sectarian feelings, very much as the fall-out from a nuclear cloud seeps strontium-90 invisibly into the bones. So it would be naïve to think he had no views at all. What we know of him seems to indicate that he never got in the thick of it, that he kept himself to himself in these matters, and, if not treating the whole thing with disdain, he was at least identified by his peers as being somehow different.

Former miner Harry Steele went to the same school as Stein. He played football with him, palled around the cinemas and dance halls with him, chased girls with him, played bowls with him and drank beer in places where, despite constant temptations, Stein stuck to his soft drinks. 'I've had a good laugh listening to all the things said and written about Jock when he was famous,' he said. 'They talked about him being a hard man; a "tyrant" somebody called him. He was never a hard man in Burnbank. Not once did I see him take his jaiket aff to have a fight with anybody. Not once. I took the jaiket aff manys a time for a punch-up but he never did. And there were plenty fights. You fought with your hands; there was no dirty fighting like you might have now. And there was plenty between Catholics and Protestants, but not just that. Saturday nights coming out the pubs you had to watch yourself. There was a lot of drink taken. You should have seen the fights then. And of course when the Blantyre Celtic played the Vics the Protestant boys would come down from High Blantyre and the Catholics from Low Blantyre and some of the bloody mayhem that would go on after these games was unbelievable. Now, I was in the Orange Lodge myself and played the flute in the local band, but all the time I was with Jock I never heard him saying anything against Catholics, and by God there was plenty said about that, for all his pals were Orange. Aye, he and his faither were Rangers men, of course, but that was all. I tell you, Jock never really had a bad word to say about anybody. If you ask me, knowing Jock as I did, and watching and reading all about him, when he went to Celtic as the manager and was supposed to be the hard man I think he was just putting on a uniform. You know like the polis do when they are on duty. Jock put on his manager's uniform.

Underneath all that I cannot believe Jock really changed. He was a quiet sorta fella and you'd never see him losing his temper.'

To those of us recalling Stein hoving into view over the horizon and limping towards us garbed in his black coat, venom in his eye and about to unleash a verbal volley in our direction, Harry certainly paints a contrasting picture. But other witnesses vouch for what he says. Jim Wallace, the local Burnbank historian, knew the twenty-year-old Stein when he himself was a youngster. 'Jock was the kind of lad who took time out to speak to the kids. A lot of adults don't bother with young kids but he would spend a lot of time talking about football with us. He knew my father well because they were both heavy gamblers, and whenever I went up to the Cross to see my father, when they were there putting their lines on with the bookie, Jock would talk to us and tell us jokes. My recollection is of a modest young man who really was a bit shy.'

'I tell you,' Harry Steele recalled, 'Jock liked a night out with his pals at the dancing. But sometimes when you went looking for him he would be up the fitba' park teaching the kids how to kick a ball. He would spend hours with them. And even when he was playing with the Rovers he would play with us on a Sunday in some of the pub games between the different social clubs. He wasn't supposed to, but he did, and he got stuck right in as if his life depended on it.'

The challenges underground in the mines must have furnished him with insights into and sympathies with how men behaved, and he soon learned that whatever bitterness existed on the surface in the name of religion, underground the hazards of working obliterated the need to enquire about what school anybody went to or what might be the significance of anybody's surname. The omnipresent threat of death concentrated minds. For example, in a three-month stretch during the period 1942–3, seven men were killed working beside Stein in the Bothwell Castle pit on the other side of the River Clyde from his home village, the pit where he was to finish his mining career. But on the surface, political lunacies continued to exist to perpetuate the sectarianism. For it was the strategy of the Duke of Hamilton's factors to ensure that one pit was predominantly Protestant and the other Catholic, a policy that itself encouraged specific local concentrations: Burnbank was largely Protestant, Bellshill Catholic, Larkhall Protestant, Blantyre Catholic. So there is virtually nothing you can analyse about the background to Stein's growth through puberty to manhood that is not to some degree affected by the stand-offs of one community with another, most often benignly suspicious but not infrequently violent.

Stein became one of the shamelessly exploited when he followed his father into the mines only a few months after leaving school. He had gone to work in the local Stevenson's carpet factory for a few months but that was in his anxiety to get out of school and earn some money to supplement the family's meagre income, even though his parents had apparently wanted him to carry on with his schooling. Nothing came easy in those times, for people suffered real hardships. Industrial disputes in the mines were rife, and the year before Stein was born, during the long strike of 1921, it is recorded that 9,000 meals a day were provided by the Burnbank soup kitchens. When he was nearly four, during the General Strike that was prolonged by six months in the mining areas, the *Hamilton Advertiser* recorded that in Blantyre 'day in day out men and women can be seen busily engaged in trying to procure coal and sticks from the colliery bings and some of the men are able to augment their limited means by selling bags of both to make a few extra shillings'. So it is no wonder a lad sensitive to the uncertainties of that world would want to go out and earn a wage packet as soon as he could.

His respect for his roots in the mines never diminished. His life-long friend Tony McGuinness recalled that during the miners' strike of 1984–85, when he was driving and would see a lorry at night trying to break the strike by going through a picket line with coal to Ravenscraig steelworks, he would turn on his full beam to try to dazzle them. And on another occasion around that same period, when he and I were travelling together in his car, at 90 miles an hour I may say, to a football forum in a hotel in Fife, the old loyalties to his kith and kin in the industry surfaced pointedly when he spat out his disgust about Arthur Scargill. 'He's nothing but an egotist. He's just pulling them into the mire. If they had left all this to Mick McGahey he would have had the whole thing sorted out by now.' He had deep respect for Scotland's communist miners' leader, which was mutually returned. For in his twenties, when in his early days with Albion Rovers, in the second week of a strike, Stein handed over money to McGahey which represented what he had earned playing for Rovers that week. It wouldn't have been a fortune, only a few pounds at the most, but the magnanimous gesture is one the trade unionist never forgot, and it indicated that while Stein had not been overtly political in his early days, throughout his life he would hardly ever be seduced away from his attachment to the working man, despite his success. By and large he might have been described as nearer in spirit to Keir Hardie than Tony Blair.

The pull of mining was inevitable, and before long examining the warp and weft of the carpets gave way to the snorting and hooves of the pit ponies at the Earnock Pit. He worked with the ponies to start with in conditions that were superior to other local pits, but he had to move in 1943 when the Earnock coal-seams were being worked out. He went with his Burnbank colleagues across the river, almost opposite David Livingstone's birthplace, to work in the Bothwell Castle Nos. 1 and 2 pits, and then in 1948 to the Priory Pit nearby where the hot but dry conditions of Earnock gave way to a damper and wetter workplace. 'Jock's main job was to send the empty hutches along to the coal face where we were working,' Harry Steele explained. 'We would send them back full and he would organise emptying them out and send them back. He had his wee benefits. Where he was he didn't need to move to get his food. The canteen would send down his rolls and ham to him in the lift. He got warm rolls, we got none. But he also knew all the train drivers, because he was playing with Albion Rovers at the time, and when we were on the wee puffer that took us back to Burnbank it went past his row of houses at Earnock. Well, they used to slow down to let him off there while we had to sit and get off when it stopped at Burnbank station further on. He seemed to have this knack of talking people into helping him out.'

Sometimes the bookies did too, and sometimes they didn't. For it was at Burnbank Cross that Stein developed what truly could be described as a lifelong addiction to gambling. In those days it was quite illegal to gamble with street bookies, but that did not deter the men in the area from indulging heavily. Stein, from his teens, spent many days there because he was close to the local bookie Mick Mitchell and helped to gather in the lines that were being put on. Of course, they had to have a young boy as a look-out for the police. But that ploy did not always work, and with a regularity that was almost yawningly predictable to everybody the police would swoop upon the gathered flock and hike them off to the station, where after a decent interval of an hour or so the bookie would turn up and, with great panache and not the slightest iota of social stigma for anybody, bail them all out. Back they would go to their pitch until the next round-up, and the hypocrisy of it all continued.

Jim Wallace feels it is a safe bet that Stein would have been part of one of the police's culls, for every able-bodied male in the area almost felt it carried a macho significance to have been pulled in. 'He and my father bet on everything. Even football. I suppose he wasn't supposed to as a player, but he did. There's no doubt he had a weakness for it even then. But as opposed to that he wasn't a drinker. Now, it was a hard feat to be teetotal in Burnbank. If you consider the population was only about 3,000 yet there were around 20 pubs in the village, you can work out that drink could be a real menace. Saturday nights in particular could be dreadful for families with many a woman in terror of what would happen to her when the man came home drunk. Many a one took a right battering. But in the middle of all that, and with all his pals heavy drinkers, he never indulged, never.'

Stein's renowned teetotalism did not seem to spring from some superior moral position, for he mixed with heavy drinkers socially all his life and, although from time to time he would ridicule those of us in the media who wandered back to team hotels after a heavy night out, there was no tone of sermonising about it. So perhaps it was his early observation of the excesses of drink around Burnbank that influenced his own lack of inclination to follow suit.

Neither did he succumb to the established views on how you should court and whom you ought to marry. On 3 October 1946, he married twenty-year-old Jean Toner McAuley in Gilmour Memorial Church Manse, Hamilton. He had met her in a chip shop in Cambuslang when she was fifteen and he was four years older. They went together for some five years before they wed and he was devoted to her and the children they eventually reared. All that on paper seems simple, but not in Burnbank in the 1940s. For Jean was Catholic. The heavily drawn fault lines normally meant that you married within your own faith; crossing over in any shape or form, and particularly in marriage, required a degree of moral courage that seems ridiculous now but then could mean being shunned by a whole community.

Harry Steele knew the risks. 'If you wanted to go out with a girl or a boy from the other side,' he explained, 'you couldn't be seen walking down the main street with her. You would have to walk her home round the back streets even if it was a really long way round, just to be safe. That happened to both sides. If you were going regular with somebody from a different religion, most parents would end up saying, "Get rid of them. I don't want you to be seen with them again." That was the common response. It took some nerve for most people to mix. And of course if you "turned" and left your own religion and went over to the other side, you were out in the cold. You were finished with your own community. If it happened to one of our boys they would never come near us at the Cross again. They would know better.'

'Turning' seems such an innocent word, but in the West of Scotland, changing your religion as the result of a marriage could be seen as an act of betrayal. Nothing of the sort happened to the Steins when Jean 'turned', rather than her new husband. The idea of a 'mixed' marriage caused him no anxieties, and was a forewarning of his sanguine attitude to other decisions he would make which were to offend even more grievously in his home area.

He had, of course, already risked a family rift by at first opting for the Bumbees as his first local club, but in eventually playing for Blantyre Victoria he began fairly quickly to establish a name, if not a distinguished reputation, in the junior game. The Vics might ostensibly have been seen to be a conduit to Ibrox, but paradoxically it spawned two Celtic managers and a chairman: Stein himself, Billy McNeill, and Sir Robert Kelly. But Stein gave no early indications that he was of the right stuff for football at its highest level. He was useful and dependable, and tough when required. The *Burnbank Gazette* reported on 3 October 1941, 'At last Friday's meeting of the Central League, J. Stein of the Vics was suspended for fourteen days for a field offence.' As players in those days in junior football could get away with offences that would now be construed as crimes against humanity, being suspended for a whole two weeks suggests that Stein's unspecified offence put him up there with some of the toughest in junior football, and that he was no pushover. In a game against Yoker, for example, on 22 August 1942, the *Gazette* noted that he scored his first goal for the club with a header, in a match whose tone could be deduced from the report that a linesman had to be sent off during the game! There is scant reference thereafter, except on Saturday, 3 October when the *Hamilton Advertiser* rather baldly stated, 'Kirkland was a big success at centre-half and simply walked through the game. On the other side of him Dunn and Stein were exceptionally strong support.' Not enough to set the pulses racing, you would think, except for one occasion.

On 1 August 1942 the *Gazette* reported that the previous week Blantyre Victoria had held a very successful five-a-side tournament. There was never anything exceptional about such pre-season entertainment, although in those days it was taken seriously enough by the players. But this was different. War was raging. A couple of teams were unable to attend because of a shortage of players. 'The difficulty was overcome,' the *Gazette* tells us, 'with Matt Busby

(Hibs and Scotland) raising an Army five bringing the contestants back to the original six teams … The Vics [with Stein] obligingly decided to play the Army five, beating them 2 goals to nil.' Nothing more is reported. Would we be playing fast and loose with history by taking that bare report and making the assumption that two of the greatest football managers of all time, who would go on to win unique battles on the continent, met for the first time in contest that day? That Blantyre pitch could perhaps make the modest claim that the playing fields of Eton had no exclusive boast to inspiring men to future European triumphs.

CHAPTER THREE
A ROVER

On 14 November 1942, William Walker, a clerk at Coatbridge's railway station, at the start of a lifelong devotion to Albion Rovers, queued up to watch visitors Celtic play his beloved club at their home ground Cliftonhill. It was a dull, cold day; a raw wind whipped through the streets of that industrial town like a climatic reminder of the austere times of the early 1940s. By the time he had settled himself on the terracing, roughly ten minutes late, William had already heard two eruptions from the crowd. Celtic were two up. Not long after that they were three up, and William felt he was in for a gruelling afternoon, especially as he was surrounded by exultant Celtic supporters making light of a war environment which that day had seen a Fuel Communiqué issued by the government advising housewives to make economies in view of the importance of coal, and recommending the sharing of fires with friends and neighbours. By way of alternatives, watching your favourite team triumph could fire the bellies just as effectively. But William was not of a mood to share a blazing coal fire with any Celtic supporters, and feeling down at the mouth his uncharitable frame of mind blanked out the thought that the nation the following day would be celebrating the success of the recent Battle of El Alamein with the ringing of church bells. For what was even more perplexing was the sight of a new, lanky figure out there on the field, in central defence. William had never seen him before, and he seemed, in his gangly state, to be just short of invisible since his defence had been broached several times with apparent ease. The lean figure was simply listed as 'Junior' in the press coverage.

Neither William nor the Celtic support could have realised, as an easy victory seemed to be heading Parkhead way, that they were in at the start of one of the most illustrious careers in British football. For at the end of a game that saw an amazing Rovers fightback to 4–4, the young unknown and unnamed centre-half signed an autograph outside the ground. It read: 'J. Stein'.

'I saw virtually every game that Stein played in for the rest of his career at Rovers,' William said. 'Yet in that game he didn't register with me to be honest.' The game didn't register much with Stein either, for in later years he was to admit to a questioner that although it was his debut on a new stage, against one of the strongest teams in the land containing famous names such as Jimmy Delaney, Bobby Hogg and Willie Miller, he couldn't remember anything about the match except the score. The *Sunday Post* noted that while 'Rovers had a trialist in their raw, lanky junior centre-half, the ponderousness of his counterpart John McPhail cost Celtic two goals'.

It was not exactly a report that alerted the country to the birth of a star; it was more like an entry into a ledger noting that a small credit had been added to an account. I suppose the reporter in later years, re-reading words like 'raw' and 'lanky', with a certain looseness, and relating it to the giant Stein became, might have ranked himself with the Hollywood scout who dismissed a young man called Astaire with the opinion, 'Can't act. Slightly bald. Also dances.' But what Stein had done was help Rovers, then at the foot of the table, overcome adversity, and even though he was simply a triallist hiding under the dreaded pseudonym of 'Junior', a name more historically associated with 'hopeless cause' rather than scintillating brilliance, he had not disgraced himself and he had done nothing to discourage the Rovers management looking on. Although he had not yet signed for the club and his future was still unclear he would have enjoyed the *Sunday Post* report of that match headed 'Celts Fiddled, Rovers Burned!'

The manager of Rovers in 1942 was a major-domo figure called Webber Lees who ran the club with a dominance Stein would experience on a much grander scale under Bob Kelly at Celtic. He had a reputation for having an eye for young talent. He had brought Stein in to train with the club a few weeks earlier, and that first game against Celtic convinced him he had an asset. Rovers were trounced 4–1 in their next league game but that did not deter Lees from acting quickly to sign Stein. Three weeks after that debut against Celtic the *Airdrie and Coatbridge Advertiser* noted, 'On Thursday evening [3 December] Manager Webber Lees secured the signature of John Stein, of Blantyre Victoria, and he will be included in the Coatbridge side against St. Mirren at Cliftonhill Park today.'

Moving to Coatbridge to play his football did not mean a quantum leap to a completely new environment. This was still North Lanarkshire, where the social structures were simply replicated from one community to another. The same sectarian feelings prevailed, although different in scale from his home village of Burnbank. Irish immigrants from both sides of the religious divide, working in the iron and steel industry, set up stall in different parts of the town, which became Protestant and Catholic enclaves and which produced the usual suspects: Orangemen and Sinn Fein sympathisers. It was making Coatbridge a microcosm of Scottish sectarian hostility. Rovers suffered from all that. For the centrifugal pull of the Old Firm – whose grounds in Glasgow were, even in those days, a relatively short travelling time from the town – meant the club would always be denied the dimension of support they deserved for a local club, hoping to draw substantially on a population of 44,000 at that time. Of course they never did, and Stein would have been as aware as any that the Celtic support, who later would pay homage to him, were simply passers-by at Cliftonhill. As an indication of the strength of the pull of the Parkhead club in the area, when Stein later played for Celtic in the Coronation Cup final at Hampden, against Manchester United in 1953, an incredible total of 57 double-decker buses left from a single famous pub in the west end of the town, Phil Cole's, to support the team. With the Rangers support in the surrounding areas just as substantial, the small, unglamorous stadium of Cliftonhill, raised on a hill facing south towards the 'dark satanic mills' of the Phoenix and Clifton Iron Works of Whifflet, existed as a no-man's land where attended those supporters who were either untainted by the endemic intolerance within the town or would be proud to call themselves hopeless romantics and would not mind those outsiders who might accuse them of being 'saft in the heid'.

The Rovers played in blue, and that would certainly have pleased Stein's father. In a saner society the colour spectrum would not have mattered, but in later years, when Webber Lees had gone, and in an effort to appease those who felt blue was just too politically insensitive, the colours were changed to red and yellow. So, as in Blantyre with the Vics, Stein filled the same colour of jersey, but there was a difference: with the Vics he had played most of his games in the old-fashioned left-half position; in his eight seasons with Rovers he played all his games bar one as a centre-half. And it was with Rovers that his technique and his personality evolved.

In one game against Rangers shortly after he had joined he was being given a rough time by big Jimmy Smith, a tall and powerful forward who was built like a brick wall. Stein simply returned it measure for measure. Eventually he went heavily into the tackle on Smith, who turned and snapped at him, 'You're only a boy, behave yourself.' It might have deterred others – after all, the Ibrox players always considered they carried a special aura which had to be deferred to – but Stein, even though he had more than a soft spot for the jerseys he was playing against, took the warning as benignly as a young lion cub being offered raw meat. He clattered Smith again. The next time the ball was in the air between them, Stein afterwards said, he knew what was coming but just couldn't or wouldn't get out of the way. Smith went straight through the ball as if it wasn't there and butted Stein in the face. His nose snapped. Underground at the Bothwell pit after the event Stein turned up proudly proclaiming that his nose was broken, as if it were a trophy, and boasted about the incident to the men around him, all of whom were Rangers inclined. You can only imagine it was to demonstrate that any latent sympathy from boyhood he had for the club wouldn't intrude on his on-field single-mindedness. Adam McLean, who played centre-forward for Rovers, was certainly aware of Stein's fondness for Ibrox. 'The Rangers result was always the first one he wanted to know when he came off the park,' he said. 'He was a Rangers man at heart all right when he was with the Rovers, but it never affected how he played them. In fact he was a big-occasion man. He was a better player when he was up against the Old Firm. But always when he came off the park he wanted to know how Rangers had got on.'

At the peak of his managerial career with Celtic there was a background hum within the Rangers community that it would be only a matter of time before he underwent a Damascene conversion, left Parkhead behind and went west to Govan to his true spiritual Protestant home. But if he was demonstrating then, in the 1940s, when parental and environmental influences were much stronger on him, that he was certainly no slave to traditional loyalties when he pulled a jersey over his head, the thought of a tormented Stein in later life, torn between the old faith and the new power he had established at Parkhead, is risible.

In that first year with Rovers he was clearly enjoying his regular place in the side, which was cemented by the fact that he was a miner – a reserved occupation during the war. For like so many other sides, Rovers were finding it difficult to field the same eleven players in consecutive games. Eighteen of their players were in the Forces, and from game to game they would have to make as many as ten changes in the side, calling on triallists, players on loan and getting commanding officers to grant leave to certain players. In the midst of this selection turmoil the young, gawky centre-half was becoming the only regular and he began to assume the status of brigadier when in fact he was only a private. For he had a distinct handicap: his right foot and a football shunned each other as much as they could.

'He really didn't change much from when I first saw him until he left the club,' William Walker said. 'That isn't being critical. It's just that you got the impression he went out to do a job and got set about it. Nothing flamboyant. And of course you could tell very quickly what his limitations were. One was his right foot. He couldn't hit a barn door with it. That's why he even described himself as just having a left foot and a right knee.' The origin of his kneeing-of-the-ball technique lay with Rovers. In an interview he gave later in life, Stein claimed that his particular idiosyncrasy had been developed with the help of the South African player Dougie Wallace, particularly when both had gone to Llanelly in Wales to play. But Adam McLean feels Jock was suffering from a lapse of memory about that and that he practised this odd skill at Cliftonhill.

Over the next four years, up to and beyond the end of the war, as Rovers with their part-time players on the then statutory wage of £2 a week fluctuated between the occasional surprising victory and outright thrashings – they finished fifteenth in the Southern League in 1942/43 – Stein's personality began to unfold. As if working underground for a living wasn't hard enough he was having to sustain the pain of regular defeat at the weekends, which might have discouraged the faint of heart. In fact the body armour and rapier wit that were to stand him in good stead in later life were beginning to be forged.

'They were playing at East Fife one day and it was awful,' William Walker recalled. 'Stein and the rest were being given the runaround. There was one group in particular on the terracing who were giving Jock a hard time. He couldn't touch the ball, but they would be shouting things like, "Away you go, ya mug!" It just went on and on until Jock couldn't stick it any longer, and when he got the chance over at the touchline he belted the ball right into them and shouted so loud everybody could hear it, "I'm a mug? You're the mugs for payin' to watch me!"' Perhaps an overworked line, but it offers just a hint of Stein's ability to use a razor-sharp tongue to humble the toughest.

He was clearly a football student, though, not just a pedestrian player eking out a humdrum existence in a poor team. Adam McLean, the striker and local boy who scored a winning goal for Rovers on his debut three years after Stein arrived, noticed the centre-half's restless curiosity about the techniques of football as soon as he joined the club. 'There I was sitting after training on the first day and this lad starts to quiz me about certain players in the league and juniors he had seen and whether a certain player kicked with the right foot or the left. And I don't mean in the religious sense, I mean he would sit and analyse. It was Jock. The only time I have ever come near anything like this kind of depth of analysis was when I trained with Bryn Jones of Arsenal when I was in the Army. But in Scotland I'd never heard this kind of detailed analysis before.'

Stein was obviously spellbound by a game he wished he could have played better than he actually did. But there was another practical reason for his interest in other players and the development of the team: he was slowly becoming the de facto manager of the side. He spoke more about tactics than ever Webber Lees did to the players. In Adam McLean's words, 'He picked the team. He could wrap the manager round his pinky. Lees just did what Jock wanted him to do.'

And his obsession with the game was supported by a native cunning that began to surface in Coatbridge. Adam McLean's view is that 'cunning' is perhaps not strong enough a word, and that 'devious' might be more appropriate. 'We all agreed terms with the club after being promoted to the First Division in 1948, to sign on for £9 a week. We would have liked more but Jock assured us that it was the best we could get. There were some mutterings about what we ought to do about it but Jock kind of pacified us. Then, and I can't remember how, somebody got hold of his pay docket and discovered that he was getting £10 a week. We couldn't believe he would do something like that and for a while there was some animosity in the dressing-room. But he was a powerful personality with a great tongue in his head and he just rode that situation out.'

That personality seemed to have been brought into play in February 1947 when Stein and the others demanded a specific bonus for an important cup game at Dens Park against Dundee. The request was rejected, and what happened next is not easily forgotten by the Coatbridge people who travelled in big numbers for the match. 'Jock didn't try a leg,' William Walker claimed. 'Not just Jock but all of the rest of them, but particularly him since he was the leader. You wouldn't have believed they could have been so poor. I'll never forget that. The fans were enraged. I don't think things were ever the same again with Jock. It didn't matter what kind of explanation anybody at the club gave, it was fixed in the fans' minds that the players couldn't have cared less.' But Adam McLean, who played centre-forward in that match, hotly disputed this version of events. 'I couldn't have tried harder,' he said. 'And Stein would never do such a thing. He hated a beating, hated going down.

Supporters just easily forget that Dundee were a great side and were by all accounts a lot better than the Rovers. No, Stein was a born trier. That sort of thing wasn't in him.'

But public perception is difficult to dampen down, and to this day that performance is marked down as a black day for the club. What probably had influenced expectation was that Rovers had surprisingly beaten their fierce and traditional rivals Airdrie in the previous round (3–0) when for perhaps the only time in their many duels Stein got the better of his on-field nemesis Bobby Flavell. The Airdrie centre-forward was one of the best Scotland ever produced in that position. Among his many claims to fame, including playing for Scotland at Wembley, was the fact that he also played alongside the great Alfredo Di Stefano with Millionarios in Colombia. Flavell was always one of the quickest on a park. 'Jock was a tough player but never dirty or anything like that,' Flavell said. 'He had a weak side, the right side, and I tried to take him on there, and sure enough I could get the better of him and annoy him. I think he would have kicked me if he could have caught me, but I was too fast for him.' Except, of course, in that Scottish Cup game when Stein blotted him out of the game. Sadly it was a duel between them that went beyond the grave. When Stein was going through a decidedly sticky and unsuccessful spell as Scotland manager a tabloid newspaper asked Flavell for his comments on Stein's tactics. They splashed his criticisms, which came over as a hatchet job. When Stein died and friends asked Flavell to attend the funeral, he declined. 'I would have been a hypocrite to have gone after what I had said about the man,' he said.

Throughout the eight years he played for Albion Rovers, Stein continued to work underground at Bothwell Pit. He seemed to have worked out a shift-pattern with his boss that suited his football commitments. Night shift, for instance, was definitely out on a Friday. It was particularly important for himself and the club that he was at peak fitness for season 1948/49 because Rovers had been promoted to the First Division for only the fourth time in their history. With numbers on the shirts for the first time, they lost their opening three games in a row, and even though they did push Celtic to a 3–3 draw at home in front of a 25,000 crowd in one of their earlier games, the season was a disaster and an embarrassment for Stein personally as the conductor of the defence: Rovers conceded 105 goals and won only three out of 30 games. They went straight down again, of course.

He was becoming disillusioned with his lot, even with the challenge of the top league they had been promoted to. And he was suffering recurring groin injuries that were keeping him out of the team too frequently. He was also being dropped more regularly, and was probably fortunate to miss a game at Tynecastle on 2 April 1949 which the *Airdrie and Coatbridge Advertiser* described as 'a miserable afternoon' as Rovers were decimated by Hearts, 7–1. The discontent became obvious in the dressing-room, especially when to his and everybody else's surprise Rovers turned down an offer made for him by Kilmarnock, with whom he might have carved out a profitable career. That irked him.

It was about then that he began to listen to others, like his team-mate Dougie Wallace, telling him of greener fields elsewhere. Wallace, acting as a go-between, persuaded a representative from the Welsh non-league club Llanelly (as it was then called before an upsurge of Welsh nationalism brought about the spelling change to Llanelli) to come and speak to Stein. They did not need a silver-tongued lawyer to make the case; it could have been done by pigeon-post for all Stein cared, for he was in the mood to depart. And that he eventually did, without the club initially getting a penny for the transaction, even though he was still officially a listed Rovers player for the forthcoming season. He left Scotland the same year that the Stone of Destiny was purloined from Westminster Abbey by a group of Scottish nationalists before being recovered. Stein's crossing of the border happened to be illegal as well.

CHAPTER FOUR
JOCK WHO?

L lanelly was Celtic's Crewe Junction. Not an exotic spot in its own right, not a major metropolis, only historically significant to Celtic for the switching of routes of one man from a minor line to a major one which changed the course of the club's history – but for that reason the small Welsh town remains alluringly pivotal when examining both club and man. In fact, the town mirrored some of the industrial characteristics of parts of Lanarkshire, with all their attendant problems. When Stein arrived there in 1950 to play full-time football for the first time in his life they were closing the old tinplate mills and shutting down the docks for the anthracite coalfields. Wales was in industrial transition; the town's future was uncertain. But the people seemed no more than his own kith and kin as he blended easily with the working-class ethic of an area from which pretension was largely absent. When, on his first night away from home, he asked his landlady Lizzie Williams in Mansell Street for a bath she directed him to a tin one hidden under a table. Not surprisingly she reported that Stein was at first surprised but finally amused by that. He was always fond of lolling in a bath, especially when he could open his lungs and sing through his extensive repertoire of ballads. The tin bath would not have curbed his enthusiasm. He had hardly expected sophistication, but the very homeliness of his basic but snug digs created some comfort for a young man split from his family for the first time.

The pits in Lanarkshire were now simply a memory that certainly did not recur nostalgically, for without casting any aspersions on the trade he had left behind, he made it clear to all that he was glad to be out of them. After all, for the first time in his life, at the age of 27, he was a full-time professional footballer, albeit in a league that merited only scorn in the upper echelons of British football. That scorn, however, was tinged with not a little apprehension because there was a healthy tradition of non-league clubs overcoming the odds against more prestigious opponents in the FA Cup, Yeovil Town and Colchester United being just two examples. This sort of success fed the ambitions of the chairmen of various non-league clubs, and Llanelly was no exception. The club itself had just been elected to the Southern League as a hoped-for preliminary to gaining membership of the

Football League. After all, Colchester and Gillingham, two Southern League clubs, had just been promoted to full Football League status. The logic that motivated the club stemmed from that precedent, and from the fact that the chairman at the time was reporting that Llanelly FC had never been in a better financial position.

But there was a certain amount of bitterness in the background, as reflected in the *Airdrie and Coatbridge Advertiser* which on 15 July 1950 accused Llanelly of pulling the 'Bogotá trick' on Albion Rovers – a reference to the flight of the former Airdrie forward Bobby Flavell to Colombia without compensation to his previous club. This reflected the view at Rovers that the club had been badly short-changed. Still, everybody had accepted the reality of Stein's departure. He had turned down Rovers' offer of £4 a week for Llanelly's £12 (the famous Rangers captain George Young at that time was earning only £12 a week, and that close season was holding out for more). Stein's exit from Scottish football might have gone smoothly for him had an article in the *Scottish Sunday Express* of 3 September not alerted both clubs and the respective football associations to the basic illegality of Stein's move. It referred to the 'Strange Case of the Vanished Centre-Half'. They, like others, were wondering where this kenspeckle player had disappeared to and in pursuing the matter revealed to all and sundry that FIFA had established a regulation in 1946 in Luxembourg which stated that any player leaving one association to play in another had to have a clearance certificate from the previous authority. This Stein did not have. Rovers reported Stein to the Scottish Football Association who then passed the information on to their Welsh counterparts, and Stein was then deemed a sort of *persona non grata*. Clearly he had been completely unaware of the regulations concerning such transfers, but he also knew that now he had to toe the line. So did Llanelly. Stein, quite innocently, had already been playing for the Welsh side for several weeks, so Llanelly were told to stop selecting him until the matter had been resolved. Rovers, with the bit between their teeth, declared they would agree to the move only after appropriate compensation.

On 16 September Llanelly played an important FA cup-tie against Ebbw Vale. Despite the game's significance in terms of the desperately needed financial benefits accruing from progress in the competition, Stein did not appear, much to the surprise of the local media, who had been impressed by his early contributions. He had travelled that same day back to Coatbridge to make a settlement with Rovers, reported to be around £750, and returned with the appropriate documentation to legitimise his move. While he was in Coatbridge he sat prominently in the stand and watched his former colleagues lose 3–1 to Stirling Albion at Cliftonhill. Despite that, and the fact that his departure had been something of a local *cause célèbre*, the *Airdrie and Coatbridge Advertiser*, which had been critical of him for leaving the club, made no mention of his presence, nor of the settlement. It was as if he was being airbrushed out of existence. Obviously being a non-person in Coatbridge can be a prelude to fame. (Interestingly, the local Llanelly paper the *Star*, identifying the new player as 'John (Jock) Stein, aged 27, six feet and 13 stone', reported that Charlton Athletic had also shown an interest in the same player but had not been able to agree a fee with Albion Rovers.)

Stein's original connection had been principally through his former Rovers colleague Dougie Wallace, portrayed over and over again on the Scottish club scene as a troublemaker and rabble-rouser in the dressing-room. As a player-coach in the Welsh town, and knowing they needed to strengthen the squad after promotion to the Southern League at the end of season 1949/50, Wallace had recommended to the Llanelly manager Jack Goldsborough that a trip to Scotland would not be a waste of time. Goldsborough had then set out on a cull of Scottish players. Aside from Stein, he later netted Neilly Fleck from Dundee United, Davie Mathie from Motherwell, Bobby Jeffreys, formerly of Aberdeen, and Lachie McInnes from Albion Rovers. They were all by that stage hardened Scottish pros who, lumped together, might have been described as 'Have Boots Will Travel, Inc.'.

If they could have been called a Scottish mafia, then there is little doubt who the *capo di tutti capi* would have been, for almost immediately Stein made his presence felt when he was made captain shortly after joining. In his first game he got the result that was a splendid overture for any stranger coming into town. In his May 1965 account of his introduction to the town in, Jack Webster of the *Scottish Daily Express* reminisced with steel-worker Kelly Evans, who himself had played for Llanelly 700 times between 1919 and 1936 and who might have been suspicious of these foreigners but was in fact bowled over. 'We had been in the wilderness for a long time,' Evans said, 'but then John Stein arrived and it was time for a new spirit. We were going into the higher grade of football, the town was football crazy, as it had not been for a long time, and in John's first game the team won 7–1. He was not a brilliant ball player and some people said he had only a left foot, but he was

just the real good solid player that we needed here. He was such a favourite.'
The *Star* newspaper of the time reported on 26 August that 'Stein followed
the Scottish pattern that is sometimes mistaken for slowness. It takes a quick-
thinking player to exercise that perfect control and coolness that deceive an
opponent.' What he was proving was that despite shortcomings in some
technical aspects of the game he was superb in the air and few could outjump
him. This proved to be invaluable in one of the most important games he
played. It was in October 1950, it was an FA Cup tie aginst Merthyr Tydfil
watched by 13,000, and he scored with a resounding header in a 5–5 draw, a
match chronicled as one of the most remarkable in the club's history and
which led to a victory in a replay (2–1) and Stein hearing a rousing chorus of
'Sospan Fach' being raised in celebration by the supporters.

It was certainly a different tune from those triumphalist songs he had
heard around Lanarkshire, but if it seemed to be chiming in a new era of
prosperity for him and the club then it was wholly deceptive, for other
circumstances were beginning to take toll of his new-found confidence.
Llanelly lost to Bristol Rovers in the next round of the cup, but only after a
morale-destroying second replay. Then the club's 1951 application to join the
Football League was rejected, leaving only himself and Dougie Wallace as
full-time professionals. Stein was staring at a dead end. Rumours began to
surface about the financial viability of the club itself, the worst among them
being that the club's finances were being mismanaged and books doctored.
Speculation abounded; even the attraction of a tin-bath was no consolation.
Dissent over wages and bonuses set in so much among the players that Lachie
McInnes refused to return to the field for the second half of a game against
Bath City. Over and above that, Stein was to learn that a big club, thought to
be Wolverhampton Wanderers, had made a bid for his transfer and that it
had been turned down (Wolves were in fact to pursue him all through his
later career). He was not able to mask his disappointment and his form began
to reveal evidence of a man wondering if he really had made a major mistake
moving from Scotland. In one match against Merthyr Tydfil, the Southern
League leaders, Stein was involved in a mêlée which saw punches thrown and
resulted in him being ordered off, fined £2 and suspended for 28 days.

Many a footballer has had to face up to such low periods, but there was
something more unsettling in the background. His wife Jean and daughter
Ray had stayed on in Hamilton for a short period, but the separation was
making them miserable, so they moved south to join him and Ray was sent to

the local school. But they had only been away from their Lanarkshire home for about eight weeks when Jean had to take a call telling her the house had been burgled. It was not as if she had left a palace behind. It was a humble council house. But possession of such in an age of housing shortage was a considerable asset. Stein wasn't even there when she took the call for he had travelled with the team to Hastings for a game. Jean was distressed and confused, and felt intensely homesick. She confronted her husband when he returned on the Sunday and made it clear she wanted to go back to Scotland, whatever else he might have in mind. His wife's distress, her homesickness and his growing disillusionment with the way things were now working out with the club pressed heavily on him, and when she insisted he approach his manager to tell him that they all wanted to go back home, he relented. Stein had already talked to Jack Goldsborough who, being a civilised man, accepted the inevitable, that his most respected player was going to leave the club and 'go back hame'. When Goldsborough asked him what he was going to do, Stein told him he would just quit football and go back to the pits. To all intents and purposes he had given up. It was back to the pits, the bookies, the banter round the Cross, and possibly the terracings, where he might go and watch the Vics or the Rangers to while away his time. He was edging towards obscurity.

Billy McNeill, who was to become the greatest of all Celtic captains and the manager in succession to Stein, has often described the history of Celtic as a fairy-tale. Anyone with any doubts about that needs to picture a dejected Stein mentally packing his bags, feeling like the bankrupt whose investment has turned sour, bracing himself for heading back to a lifestyle he thought he had left for ever, and then to picture a man 500 miles away at about the same time who used to sell coal with his horse and cart around the village of Baillieston just outside Glasgow, and who just happened to let slip from his lips one day the words 'Jock Stein'. It was where it was said, and to whom, that made all the difference to Celtic's history.

Jimmy Gribben became a Celtic scout in 1940 after a career in junior football in a rough-and-tumble era. It was, he used to tell his family, like taking part in a commando raid: on the final whistle it was a case of 'grabbing your clothes and making a run for it to get out of the way of trouble'. So respected was Gribben within the game that Bill Struth, the distinguished Rangers manager of the 1940s and 1950s, would have a 'wee hauf' of whisky ready for the Celtic man when he came with the team to

Ibrox. In an age of discontent within the Celtic community Bob Kelly turned to Gribben for advice.

It is not entirely clear what had been retained on the retina of Gribben's mind's eye about Stein. Adam McLean, Stein's Rovers colleague, has his own view: 'I remember one night we played a reserve game at Celtic Park. Celtic had fielded [John] McPhail at centre-forward and he was a handful, as you would know. Well, Jock never gave him a kick at the ball. He out-headed McPhail, who was good in the air. All right, it was just a reserve game, but the way Stein played that night he must have caught somebody's eye.' But perhaps even more significant was a game played by Rovers at Celtic Park in January 1949 when they played for an hour with only ten men. They were well beaten in the end, 3–0, but it could have been worse and their defensive performance received wide praise, the *Sunday Post* identifying Stein as one of the 'heroes'. The *Sunday Mail* noted that 'pivot Stein, along with Muir and English, looked as confident as if the score had been reversed'. That game would possibly have registered on any football shrewdie like Gribben. Equally he lived only half an hour away from Coatbridge where Stein played his home games, and it is likely that he saw him more than once or twice in a season.

We have no clear idea how long it took Gribben to respond to the chairman's request to seek out a player who would be required merely to be a useful stand-by player. But then he mentioned the name. They had a slight problem though, for they did not know where Stein was at that time. Even Gribben had lost his whereabouts. But it did not take them long to discover that he was in South Wales. They made an approach to Llanelly for him.

Stein was never to forget Gribben's influence on his life. When Celtic won the Scottish Cup in the 1965 final against Dunfermline he gave Gribben the trophy to carry into the Central Hotel for the post-match celebrations. And on the return from Lisbon with the European Cup in 1967, Stein pushed his way through the crowded Celtic Park foyer to make sure Gribben, in the boot-room, would be the first to have a close look at the trophy.

In an interview in 1958, the famous Scottish journalist Hugh Taylor revealed Stein's feelings on first hearing of Celtic's interest in him: 'I thought they were kidding me when the news was broken. I just didn't believe it. Celtic, after me? It was laughable.' Taylor added to that by summarising the feelings within the Celtic support: 'The Celtic fans were not what you would call delighted with the transfer. Some of them had not even heard the name

Jock Stein. Others declared he was too old!' An interesting but wholly fanciful interpretation of the signing was made by the *Glasgow Observer and Catholic Herald* in its piece, tucked away under an item on Boy's Guild football. 'Those who have seen Johnny [sic] play can vouch for his ability and experience,' it read, 'which should prove a decided asset to Celtic.' But they also stated, 'John Stein of Llanelly, the former Albion Rovers centre-half, realised his ambition when he signed for Celts on Tuesday.' Ambition to play for Celtic? They obviously hadn't heard of Burnbank!

The news of his December 1951 signing for Celtic was greeted by two distinct groups of people with almost the same degree of incredulity. Firstly there were the boys from Burnbank Cross whose sectarian solidarity was as unflinching as it had always been. They found it hard to comprehend. Had Stein turned up at the Cross blind drunk and ranting against the evils of gambling, it would not have caused as great a stir as the news that he was about to don a green and white jersey. As Harry Steele admitted, Stein became an outcast. 'He lost a lot of pals overnight when he signed for Celtic. "Turncoat" was about the kindest thing they said about him. After a wee while his name just wasn't mentioned at the Cross. And although he was in and around Burnbank for a long while he never came back down amongst us to stand and have a blether.'

In one of his quieter and more reflective moods in the middle of his career as Scotland manager, Stein told me of one reaction. 'I came back to the house to see my mother and I went into a bedroom to change clothes. I was in there taking my time and my best pal I had grown up with came in to talk to my mother, as he always did, because he was close to the family and spent a lot of time with my mother and father. He didn't know I was in the house. My mother told him that I was home and was in the next room and to go in and see me. "John has been asking about you", she told him. He never said anything. He just turned and walked out and never spoke to me again.'

To watch Stein deliver that anecdote, in an almost languid manner as he lay back against a leathered couch late at night in a small hotel in Elgin, was to appreciate that for all his apparent hardness, for all that he was trying to recount a story in a deceptively casual way, the incident had pained him deeply. But life socially would never be the same again, and it is not difficult to conclude that one of the driving forces for the rest of his life in club football at Parkhead, and especially when he became manager, was to wreak revenge on those who had turned their backs on him by making Celtic great. For instance, I watched him at the final whistle of the Scottish Cup replay against Rangers at Hampden Park in 1971, waiting close to the dug-out to interview him, and as Celtic won 2–1 he gave a little skip and jig towards the tunnel with his fists clenched like a man dancing on the grave of his past loyalty.

Then there was the Celtic supporters' reaction. To understand how they felt you have to understand the state Parkhead was in at that time. Since the war the club, which enjoyed massive support, had struggled to win anything. They picked up the Scottish Cup in 1951 with a goal by John McPhail against Motherwell, which I witnessed myself from the schoolboys' enclosure. That was their first major trophy since they had won the league title in 1938. They then went on that same year (1951) to win the Festival of Britain St Mungo Cup, beating Aberdeen in the final. But they had lapsed into recurring mediocrity. A measure of their inadequacies and the disillusionment of their supporters came in season 1951/52 when for the first time in 80 years they lost a Scottish Cup replay, on this occasion to Third Lanark who had beaten them 2–1 at Cathkin. This underlined not only an apparent lack of ability but the almost spiritless surrender of the only major trophy they had won in fifteen years, outside the St Mungo Cup. It represented staggering underachievement for a club that moved whole armies around the country in its support. Even worse was the fact that they were no longer the major challengers to Rangers, having been replaced by Hibernian: since the end of the war the pendulum of success had swung between Ibrox and Easter Road where the Famous Five Hibs forward line was playing the kind of football Celtic themselves had always aspired to.

When Stein joined Celtic, the club had a league record that made their aficionados wince when they were forced to consider it. They were in twelfth position in a sixteen-club league with a record of ten points from eleven matches (three wins, four draws and four defeats). The pain became almost unbearable, dissent grew thick on the ground, and the supporters wanted a positive and creative sign from the board that they knew what they were doing and where they were heading. What they were being informed about now was that the club had signed a little-known player from a little-known town in a little-known league in a country that was addicted to a game where the ball is shaped like an egg. It was not an acquisition likely to win friends and influence people. If there was incredulity at Burnbank Cross and its environs, then you might say that on the other side of the sectarian divide many of the Celtic support were stricken with increased anxiety and were struggling to make sense of it all.

It is certainly true that Celtic had made it clear they wanted a defensive signing simply to supplement a back line that was being depleted by injury and in any case had hardly inspired confidence. Nevertheless, to have gone down the route of dipping into non-league football for recruitment seemed to suggest that Celtic, unlike others, were under the impression they were still subject to post-war austerity measures. Rebellion loomed, as Bob Kelly acknowledged to the *Daily Record* in an interview he gave on 1 February 1965, long after the Stein dust had settled and the move had brought glittering prizes. 'I brought him back from the wilderness of non-league football in Wales,' Kelly said. 'In fact the club was almost boycotted because I bought Stein. I was proved right.' And the word 'boycott' would not have been used lightly by the Celtic chairman, for he was one of the major figures in Scottish football of the twentieth century and was sensitive to any current of opinion about his club, whether from within his own support or outside it.

But a combination of circumstances had brought Stein to Celtic; it wasn't simply the masterstroke of a visionary. The burglary in Hamilton had deeply unsettled the family in exile; Jimmy Gribben had an obviously unique memory bank; players fell injured just as Stein was hanging up his jacket to train with the reserves. In this light his arrival at Parkhead appears to have been a massive stroke of good fortune – or, as others might have it, the result of divine intervention. Whatever interpretation you make of Stein's move, it is indisputable that Bob Kelly became a mightily relieved man. Of course in terms of the possible boycott to which he referred it would not have gone unnoticed among the Celtic support that they had just signed a Protestant from Burnbank, which would be the nearest the club could get to importing directly from the Shankill in Belfast. Whether that might have lain at the root of the unrest is not at all clear. It certainly would not have inspired elation at first, even though there was an honourable Celtic tradition of holding the door open to players of any faith: they already had Protestant players in the shape of Bertie Peacock and Bobby Evans, for example. It was more likely that while his origins would not have been treated lightly, the supporters were simply resenting the fact that Stein seemed a cheap option.

The manager who greeted Stein and was pictured beside him as he signed on was one of the most self-effacing men in Scottish football, Jimmy McGrory. His constant geniality, the gentle and polite manner with which he seemed to exist within the maelstrom of Old Firm politics and his dignified bearing stood in sharp contrast to the autocratic Kelly. When you met McGrory inside Celtic Park, nursing his pipe constantly like a life-support system and invariably greeting you with a broad smile, and didn't know who he was, you could have mistaken him for some pleasant grandfather who had been sent in to wait for a ball to be autographed in the dressing-room. According to Sean Fallon, the Celtic captain at that time, McGrory's team talks hardly evoked the tone of the Gettysburg Address. 'It's going to be a hard game today, lads,' was about as much he could summon up.

So Kelly was the dominant figure, even when it came to selecting the team. John McPhail, years after he left Celtic, told me that in those days there was a specific ritual when it came to away games. 'What would happen when we were away from home is that Bob Kelly and Jimmy McGrory and maybe another director or two would go into the toilet in the dressing-room and shut the door. We would all sit around waiting for the team announcement. Out they would come, and Jimmy would read out the names. That was it. Just the names read out and then you got on with it. There was one day when I knew in my bones I wouldn't be playing. It was a cert. I had been playing badly and I was putting on weight. Well, that day, to my utter surprise, Jimmy read out my name in the team. I noticed then the chairman hadn't come out of the toilet and I discovered later that he was answering the call of nature for he had something wrong with his stomach that day. The team Jimmy read out wasn't the one they had selected in the toilet. He made a mistake naming me, and since the chairman wasn't at his elbow there was nobody there to correct him. I had stripped off like everybody else and was out on the park before Bob Kelly realised it. Celtic won that day, by the way, and I got to play because of the chairman's diarrhoea. I know it sounds incredible now, but that was the way the club was run in those days.'

Stein was discerning enough to know that all was not right with his new club, but nothing would have stopped him from snapping up the offer of a change of life. It is certainly true that his share of good fortune, at the expense of others' misfortune, was at particular stages of his life highly significant. Such it certainly was a couple of months later for Princess Elizabeth when she learned in her room in the Treetops Hotel in Kenya that her father King George VI had died and she was now the Queen.

CHAPTER FIVE
A CROWNING YEAR

On 20 May 1953 they closed the gates at the Celtic end of Hampden Park before the Coronation Cup final kick-off. There were 117,060 inside but thousands were still locked out, suffering the anguish of the disadvantaged and downtrodden, for many of them had travelled hundreds of miles to see the climax of the competition and could not be accommodated in their traditional east-end terracing area. The throbbing expectation of the Celtic legions, both inside and out, on this pleasantly sunny spring evening was spiced by a sense of bewilderment that a team that had had such an undistinguished season and had watched their great rivals Rangers lift a league and cup double could actually have reached the final of this unique competition – featuring Manchester United, Arsenal, Newcastle and Tottenham Hotspur as well as the normal opposition from Scotland of Rangers, Aberdeen and Hibernian – celebrating the coronation of the young Queen Elizabeth.

That day the huge crowd saw Celtic led out by the man about whom there had been controversy, both inside and outside the dressing-room, on his arrival at the club but who had become in an amazingly short space of time as integral to the spirit and organisation of the team as the four-leaf clover was to the Celtic insignia. Jock Stein's captaincy coincided with an opportunity to embellish the Celtic history book with a deed that would be the permanent reminder of their ability to surmount even their own apparent inadequacies and stoke the legend, within their vast community, that they were simply destined to be a major force in football. This single game seemed to wed Stein to the remorseless force of fate that would culminate in the famous Shankly proclamation about him in Lisbon in 1967.

He helped shape it himself through sheer hard work. Stein had signed on 4 December 1951 for £16 a week. Four days later, because of injuries besetting the team, he made his debut against St Mirren, at home on a miserably wet day that produced an attendance of 20,000 – 10,000 down on the previous home game (put down, of course, to the weather). He came through that game solidly without mishap. The *Sunday Post* reported, 'Jock Stein made a quiet debut, attempting nothing spectacular.' However, the

Sunday Mail report on that game suggested that the team announcement had caused a stir: 'First there was a whistle at the announcement that Jock Stein would play at centre-half, and when the crowd heard that John McPhail would be at outside-left they were nothing less than astounded.' We are left to conjecture about the meaning of the whistling at Stein's name, although since many simply had never heard of him before, it was probably down to sheer surprise. However, Cyril Horne of the *Glasgow Herald* spotted something worth noting: 'For more than an hour this tall, well-built player staked a claim for a regular place in the first eleven. Before he not unexpectedly tired late in the game he displayed confidence in himself and appeared to radiate confidence amongst his defensive colleagues, and his clearing in the air and on the ground was accurate as well as lengthy. Stein is naturally a left-footed player however, and had Stewart been alert he would have made the centre-half's task much more difficult.' Getting akin to a seven out of ten from an experienced and distinguished writer was not a bad start.

Given that sort of press recognition he might have suffered from over-exuberance in the next game at Methil against East Fife: he suffered a concussion after clashing with the opposing centre-forward, was off the field for fifteen minutes and returned to play the rest of the game shakily, as nuisance value, at outside-left as Celtic went down 3–1. He recovered for the next match in which they beat Motherwell 2–1 and would have taken satisfaction out of a 4–3 away win at Pittodrie against Aberdeen in the next. He certainly gave no indication of the state of bewilderment he justifiably could have been suffering after making the transition from the valleys of Wales to Glasgow's east end without a pause for breath. On New Year's Day 1952 he played in his first Old Firm match, which did not go well for him. Celtic, playing at home, were beaten 4–1 by Rangers. There was no victory for the side for the next four games, but his wife Jean, who recorded her delight at being back among her ain folk, was unaware of her husband's difficulties at Parkhead for she also acknowledged later that Stein never brought his problems back home with him.

Even in such a short space of time Stein was, by dint of personality as well as the steadiness of his play, becoming simply unassailable in that position for Celtic and had created a niche for the rest of his career. Still, at the start the man from Llanelly was not having an easy time with some of his well-established colleagues. What was distinct about him, though, even to those who were reluctant to welcome him to their bosoms, was the quality of leadership he showed as he established himself as a talker and organiser on the field. This was becoming clearer to Kelly and McGrory, who were inclined to turn a deaf ear to the murmurings about Stein around the dressing-room. The two who were most suspicious of Stein's attributes were John McPhail, who initially felt the new player was surplus to requirements, and particularly Charlie Tully from Belfast, who simply did not like Stein to start with because of his Protestant background. Both were firmly established players and favourites on the terracing, and they seemed disinclined to recognise the embryonic leadership qualities in this new man. Stein greatly admired Tully as a player but detested his attitude; Tully's fondness for the social whirl did not sit well with Stein's dourer Presbyterian work ethic. Throughout his career Stein hated men who did not give 100 per cent. He had immediately recognised that football with Celtic had to be part sport, part devotion to a cause. Sean Fallon reported that Stein, while acknowledging Tully's superb qualities and his popularity on the terraces, felt that the Belfast man was too much of a maverick. 'When you were playing in a match and Charlie never tracked back to help you in defence and you never saw him much,' Fallon said, 'then you knew he had had a good night out on the Friday.'

It's not of course unique to have dressing-room resentment when a new player comes in, especially if he has decided views on the game. As Stein had had that experience, and as he was by nature opinionated, he preferred the company of those who could banter with him on the same level and who loved to analyse the game. He found a kindred spirit in Bertie Peacock, the Northern Ireland international, and Fallon himself. These two players personified much of what Celtic's playing tradition was. Peacock was a Protestant from Northern Ireland and Fallon was a Catholic from the Republic of Ireland who had started out as a Gaelic footballer. Stein liked them both in equal measure. Fallon was as tough as teak and had an honest, bold-chested approach to the game that sometimes could look raw and uncultured but would be ignored by the opposition at their peril. Peacock certainly had a more darting elegance to his game which was in stark contrast to Fallon. This trio formed a formidable clique in that dressing-room which with the added patronage of Bob Kelly, who liked all three for various reasons, meant they would be inseparable and influential. And influential is exactly what Stein always wanted to be. The three of them would take off to Ferrari's Italian restaurant in Glasgow frequently and chew the fat over long lunches.

Stein interspersed this socialising with cultivating his relationship with various Glasgow bookies. There is no evidence in his whole career of his trying to shake off the addiction. He enjoyed the horses in particular. Hardly a day passed in these early days when bets were not being slipped to bookies. It was about then that Tony Queen, the Glasgow bookie, just starting up his business and a fervent Celtic supporter, began a lifelong relationship with Stein which of course was almost terminated near Lockerbie when he was a passenger in Stein's car in the serious crash in 1975. Queen was as Glaswegian as Sauchiehall Street and he was one of the handful of people to whom Stein, in the intensely political cauldron of Old Firm politics in Glasgow, could unburden himself with a complete degree of trust. Any time Queen talked to me about Stein he simply called him affectionately 'The Big Barra'. He could talk back to Stein without too much fear of a backlash, and especially when he had had one or two drinks he would use his dry wit to show he was not in awe of Stein's massive stature. This was the kind of genuine off-field friendship, at that time, which also kept the new player in touch with the feelings of the Celtic support.

So although not everybody in the dressing-room warmed to Stein, these were simply minor abrasions compared to the basic fact that he was back in the West of Scotland footballing environment fully appreciative of his good fortune at getting a new start in life with a famous club and determined to make full use of it. But in that first season, 1951/52, it didn't quite seem so. He played twenty times without stirring the imagination of either the supporters or the press and Celtic finished in ninth place as Hibs won the championship. Nobody, not even Tony Queen, would have bet on what would happen in the following season, nor on the club honour that would come Stein's way.

Sean Fallon was the Celtic captain at the start of the 1952/53 season. It was his responsibility to choose a vice-captain, and he opted for Stein. That status, though, was not to last long. For on 20 December Fallon injured his arm at Falkirk, and though he played on – typical of his enthusiasm and toughness – it was later discovered that he had broken his arm in four places. Stein, as next in line, took over the captaincy and was never to relinquish it until he finished his playing days at Celtic. Again, someone else's misfortune at the club had seemed to be to his advantage. As Tony Queen used to say to him, 'If you fell intae the Clyde you'd come out with a trout in your mouth.'

His appointment as captain didn't suit everybody. After all, they had hardly accepted him as a player when he had arrived. Jimmy Mallan, a sturdy defender, initially treated Stein as if he were a scab. 'What the hell have they brought you in for? We have plenty of centre-halves.' Charlie Tully, who from time to time sprinkled gold-dust on Celtic's style with audacious dribbling and passing, felt the tradition of the club was being compromised, and after one heavy defeat against Rangers at Ibrox had let frustration get the better of him and had bluntly stated in the dressing-room just after coming off the pitch, 'There are too many Protestants in this team.' This enraged the others and there was almost a fist-fight about it, but Sean Fallon, whose brusque physical play on the field belied his pleasant and calming demeanour off it, was able to rise above it all and quell any violent backlash. 'I was fed up pointing out that we couldn't do without Protestants,' he said. 'There were always those lads in Celtic teams and great players – Bobby Evans and Bertie Peacock for instance – and Celtic were not a club that would put up a bar to anybody. Yes, there were some in the team who didn't like what I was doing with Stein, but it proved to be right. I just liked what he said about football. He knew the game inside out and he talked simple common sense about it. And I knew he could look after himself. He was able to shrug off any conflicts we had and get on with the game. Then I had the problem with my arm when I broke it. I had been friends with Bertie Peacock and I had to take him aside and say that I was making Jock captain in my absence and that his time would come some day for that position, as it did. So the big man became captain and it was a decision that I knew Bob Kelly wouldn't interfere with. For by that stage the chairman, who ruled the roost all right, had got on good terms with Jock and liked him a lot, so whatever anybody else was whispering about the captaincy, nobody would defy Bob Kelly.'

Not even Stein, who was once severely censured, along with Bertie Peacock, by the chairman who had heard from some 'spies' that the two players had been seen drinking the night before a game, when in fact Stein was on lemonade and Peacock had had only one beer. Apart from anything else that would have alerted Stein to the grapevine that existed within the Celtic community, who understood Kelly's views on morality and became eager whistle-blowers. It is a system he fully exploited himself when he returned there as manager. And at that time, as he and his mates were struggling on the field, the chairman was as much the butt of the frustrated Celtic supporters as some of the players were. His widely accepted hands-on role made that inevitable. Kelly would sit centrally in the directors' box listening to the abuse hurled at him by supporters as Celtic went through one slump after another, staring straight ahead with a stoicism that had a Mount Rushmore resilience to it. Thus, this highly principled man who demanded the highest level of conduct both on and off the field was watching in some agony like anyone else as Celtic lapsed into recurring mediocrity.

But then came an unexpected turn of events that was to make Kelly's seat in the directors' box much less like being placed in the stocks. It started in what might have been an inauspicious way. Celtic made a signing from Middlesbrough in May 1953. He was Neilly Mochan, the 'Celtic daft' player who had played previously for Morton and who was to become one of Stein's closest friends and working colleagues. Bertie Peacock, with the benefit of hindsight, admitted how important that was. 'Now we were only in the Coronation Cup because we were Celtic and we could pull in big crowds, which is what this tournament needed. That's the only reason. We didn't deserve it in terms of football for we'd had a terrible season. But you know, the funny thing about that is that we felt we had nothing to lose. We were all so glad to see the back of the league and cup that we were all looking forward to this. We never thought of winning it of course, but we really weren't worried about how we would play. We just didn't give it a thought. I'm not saying we were all relaxed, but we seemed to go into this feeling refreshed. And we had this new player who looked really on fire. You know Jock always referred to this final as the "Neilly Mochan final".'

For the supporters there was a certain irony in their participation in this tournament to provide a Scottish sporting tribute to the new monarch, because finding a royalist sympathiser on the Celtic terracings would have been like discovering an eskimo hunting for moose in the Kalahari Desert. Indeed from time to time the playing of the national anthem at various games was received by their support as a rebuke to their own Irish republican sympathies and they counterbalanced it with their own ditties. That in itself would provoke a reaction at Old Firm matches and trouble would ensue as the other tribe, not slow to respond to perceived provocation, gladly joined in with royalist fervour. But there was also the irresistible challenge on this occasion to grab, and hold permanently, a trophy that had more significance to their arch rivals on the other side of the city, where the Union Jack and the new Queen's portrait were emblems of the club's supposed ascendancy.

Stein led the team on to Hampden Park on 11 May to play Arsenal, the English champions, in the first game. The cognoscenti gave Celtic little chance, but Arsenal were not up to it the way a refreshed Celtic were. Accustomed to being held in awe by most opponents, the Gunners were driven back for most of the game by Celtic's aggression which was helped by the backing of almost 60,000 supporters. Had Swindin in the Gunners' goal not had one of those daft days when he seemed to get all parts of his body to different shots, there would have been many more than the single goal of the game, which was scored by wee Bobby Collins who from afar always looked as if he could fit into Stein's hip-pocket.

The warning of a clear and present danger to Manchester United had been posted, but even if they had been absorbed by the English side prior to the match it had little effect. Celtic were two goals up after 53 minutes through Peacock (first half) and Mochan (second half). There was a late spurt by United when Jack Rowley notched a goal with thirteen minutes to go, even though he had met a rugged centre-half and had to change position. As W.M. Gall of the *Scottish Daily Mail* put it, Stein 'was a bit hard at the outset on Saturday on Rowley, who never quite recovered from a leg injury and latterly went to outside-left'. But that goal had been too late. Celtic, simply a trickle for the previous nine or so months, were now beginning to look like a flood.

Rangers, Aberdeen, Newcastle United and Tottenham Hotspur fell by the wayside in the other ties, so it was Celtic versus Hibernian in the final. This was the same Hibernian team that under the enlightened stewardship of chairman Harry Swan had travelled extensively throughout the continent absorbing the nuances of European skills. They would be Scotland's first representatives in the invitational European Cup where they reached the semi-final. They had massacred Manchester United in a testimonial match in September 1952, scoring seven against them. Stein was to be faced directly by the man who had a penchant for dramatics just as time was being called. He had been dubbed by the media 'Last Minute Reilly' for having scored two very late equalising goals against Ireland and England. The other players around him either had dribbling skills par excellence or could terrorise through sheer shooting power, the left foot of Eddie Turnbull in particular. This formidable unit had won three post-war league titles during a period when Rangers constantly threatened to place the rest of Scottish football under the spell of their Iron Curtain defensive attitude with the long ball punted upfield by the man who Stein once admitted was his all-time favourite Scottish player, George Young. The agonising factor was that Celtic had been merely bystanders in all of this. Now they were going to face off with the club whose football they largely admired and respected. Whatever style they might be aspiring to, Celtic under Stein wished to rediscover that most basic of objectives – winning.

'You know,' Bertie Peacock said, 'I had a look around at the huge Celtic support and I didn't want to spoil their day. If there was anything that kept driving me on it was the fear of losing. That can really motivate players you know, and I think it was affecting us all like that. To have come all that way and then lose out on it. It was unthinkable.' Losing certainly did not go through the mind of Stein, who initiated the move that brought Celtic their first goal and in effect began the man's career-long association with the winner's rostrum. Almost on the half-hour he made a simple but accurate clearance to Willie Fernie (selected to replace the injured Charlie Tully) who in turn played the ball into the path of the new man Mochan. With his right foot, which is the one people thought was only for standing on, he drove into the net from about 25 yards. It was one of those strikes whose distance increases according to the passage of time; it is still mulled over by men who were boys at the time and claim to have witnessed it. It doesn't really matter. Legendary moments win imaginative recruits, and the fact that it burns vividly in the collective mind of successive generations of Celtic supporters underlines the significance of the goal and Stein's attribution when later he held the cup in the boardroom and told visitors, 'Here it is – Mochan's Cup.'

Stein himself went through that game with the customary unflashy performance. Importantly, he tamed Lawrie Reilly. According to Cyril Horne of the *Glasgow Herald*, 'Stein gave Reilly not even a semblance of a chance to prove he was a saver of lost causes.' Behind him in goal was a man who was not rated highly even by the Celtic support, John Bonnar. But that day he proved the old maxim 'Cometh the hour, cometh the man'. He chose to stifle the best that Hibs could throw at them. Gordon Smith, on the right, tried to exploit Bonnar's smaller than average height for a keeper by tormenting him with a stream of crosses but he dealt with them capably; on top of that came his constant shot-stopping as Hibs in the second half bombarded the Celtic defence and stretched the nerves of both supporters to the extreme. With four minutes to go and only one goal behind, it looked as though Hibs had equalised. The correspondent for the *Edinburgh Evening News* reported, 'His [Turnbull's] lob was perfectly flighted, [Bobby] Johnstone rose and with a turn of the head sent the ball speeding for goal. It carried the stamp of the equaliser until, in the last split-second, up shot Bonnar's hand to divert the ball over the bar. Johnstone – unluckiest of all Hibernian forwards – could be excused for throwing up his arms in despair; and, as the players sorted themselves out for a corner-kick, his disappointment did not prevent him from sportingly patting the goalkeeper on the back.' Celtic defended the corner, swept downfield, and from a pass by Bobby Collins Jimmy Walsh smashed in Celtic's second. The game was won. The Coronation Cup was theirs. Years later, Willie Ormond did not reflect the sporting acceptance of defeat by the rest of the team, who unreservedly shook hands all round at the time, when he told an interviewer that 'Celtic were a poor bloody lot' and lamented the fact that his team 'couldnae get one by that bugger Bonnar in 1953'.

Although there would be dramatic dips and rises for him during the rest of his playing days, that match can be put down as a marker on Stein's progress from the ordinary to the superlative. As he climbed the steps to receive the Coronation Cup, any vestigial doubts among the Celtic traditionalists about his value were swept away. The final act of his apostasy was now complete: the Burnbank 'bluenose' had become the Celtic victor.

CHAPTER SIX
CAPTAIN COURAGEOUS

In the Broadway musical and Hollywood film *Chicago* there is a show-stopping number called 'Mr Sellotape'. It is the almost plaintive *cri de coeur* of a man who is indispensable to so many around him but paradoxically is never noticed all that much. He binds, he sorts, he covers, he mends, but with little attention paid to him. It is a song that might have been written for a centre-half with a good left leg, a remarkable right knee, a tackle that did not err on the side of caution and a soaring power in the air, all of which for the next couple of years was basic to Celtic's defence. But if you study newspaper reports of that era, Stein was given scant attention. Match reports are not peppered with his name. Reading some, you would have thought he wasn't there at all.

As Celtic began to consolidate on their Coronation Cup win, Stein's name only occasionally merited a mention, and then in the perfunctory way of those who have suddenly awakened to his influence and rather guiltily pointed it up. Of course the entertainers in the side, especially the flamboyant Charlie Tully, the folk-hero and rapidly weight-gaining John McPhail, and the effervescent right-half Bobby Evans, were footlight performers with much of the rest a supporting chorus. They were the stars in a side that had renewed its self-belief. Certainly over the following two years that famous half-back line of Evans, Stein and Peacock tripped off everybody's tongue mechanically, as if they were a well-known legal firm to whom you referred in time of need. They became virtually inseparable. Yet the very fact that Stein was sandwiched between the other two seemed to further camouflage his unflurried effectiveness.

Still, the largely inconspicuous job he was fulfilling was certainly winning respect from his peers. Above all, he was commanding it not only in the dressing-room but in the boardroom too, where chairman Bob Kelly was now beginning to feel that in bringing Stein to Parkhead he had just backed an outsider who had won at 200–1. Kelly was born and raised in Blantyre, which is but a short stroll from where Stein was brought up, and their affinity as salt-of-the-earth men from virtually the same parish meant they were at ease with each other despite Stein's clear deference to the chairman. And the very facts that his player had been a miner and Kelly was fond of the mining community, from which many of the Celtic support emerged, gave him added reason to pull this man closer into his confidence. They talked the same sort of language and preferred plain speaking to waffle. Both men could carry that plain speaking into shatteringly direct bluntness and could cause men to tremble with but a sharp look. The mutual respect between the chairman and Stein was hardening because he had demonstrated he was not just a hired hand for the club but had also quickly developed a love for it and the supporters. Then again, he knew how to handle chairmen. His team-mate at the time Bobby Collins didn't need to be a student of wildlife to arrive at this conclusion about Stein: 'When that big fox Stein goes into the woods all the other foxes run out.' He was laying the foundations for a later partnership that would be unrivalled in Scottish football. Stein and Kelly, the Fox and the Lion, could apparently hunt well together for the spoils.

They certainly both went after Rangers with a shared hunger. In his first Old Firm match Stein had suffered the indignity of playing against ten men but losing 4–1. That in itself was a reflection of Rangers' domination of the period. But there was now a post-Coronation Cup confidence about Celtic and they went to Ibrox on 19 September 1953 in a more resolute frame of mind, earning a 1–1 draw. This was a game played in monsoon conditions, which did nothing to dampen the militant tendency in the crowd, for when a police officer tried to haul down a Union Jack at the Rangers end at half-time, a riot ensued. The fighting provoked a charge down the pitch by mounted police with batons drawn and order was restored. Stein was learning that to survive these fixtures you had to play hard but keep your nerve and not lose control under any provocation.

But nobody expended more energy to beat Rangers than Stein. And he had very personal reasons for that. A special one was his father. On a trip to Athens in 1982 to watch one of Scotland's upcoming World Cup finals opponents, Russia, play Greece, we sat blethering in a hotel about Old Firm games he had been in. 'You know,' he told me, 'whenever I was going out to play Rangers my mother, if she was around at the time, would say, "Good luck, son. Have a good game. I hope you win." My father never did. He never wished me good luck when I played against the Rangers. He couldn't bring himself to do it.' When I asked him if his father would actually have wanted him beaten, he put his hand to his mouth as if he was going to bite his fingernails to cloak that defining smile he could produce to emphasise something, and said almost wistfully, 'Aye!' So, unlike many others there, whenever Jock Stein pulled on the green and white hoops he was trying to prove himself to his own private, personal audience of one.

That incentive was clearly at work at Celtic Park on New Year's Day 1954, for Celtic won that match 1–0 as a result of a Mochan goal half an hour from the end of the game, in front of 53,000. The significance was that it was their first official Ne'erday victory over Rangers in the Scottish League since 1938 and it was a game in which the new all-weather white ball made its Old Firm appearance, much to the displeasure of Rangers, whose stronger players preferred the traditional sodden mass of leather. Celtic's adeptness with the lighter ball, w hich favoured more skilfull play, led not only to that victory against the old rivals but to a healthy position in the league: on 20 February they were in second place behind Hearts, albeit by seven points. It was their highest position in years, and with the team showing sterling fighting qualities the impression was that under Stein a major renovation was underway.

He himself showed that he would lead by example, and in a crucial game against Hibs at Celtic Park on 7 November of that 1953/54 season, with Celtic reduced to ten men after Tully had been carried off in the 35th minute and after going behind to two goals in two minutes by Lawrie Reilly, Stein, with the instinct of the gambler, pushed himself into attack. With only seven minutes left he created a moment that inspired the *Sunday Post* to head its report 'The Glorious Grit of Stricken Celts' and which saw Stein not in his Mr Sellotape mode but demonstrating the true grit of a Rooster Cogburn with eyepatch. The paper noted that it was a 'Boy's Own Paper Finale'. For, as Celtic with their ten men strove to equalise, John McPhail got his head to a cross, nodded the ball across goal and, as sports writer Jack Harkness observed, 'Up went another head to guide the ball home. Suddenly we noticed that the owner of the head was none other than Jock Stein. Up spurring the lads on, the skipper had risen to the occasion.' The match finished 2–2, and it was Stein's first ever goal for the club. Even though he was to score only one more in his Celtic Park career, this one mattered a great deal in retrospect for it helped Celtic maintain their unbeaten home record. That was crucial, for their away record at that time was deplorable by comparison (they lost seven in all that season). This was much more obvious leadership to the onlooker and it showed that Stein, who barked and bawled his way through that match, was not to be dictated to by events but would take a hand in shaping things himself.

Hearts were Celtic's major rivals in the league that season, but after trailing the Edinburgh side for much of the season the turning point came on 6 February 1954 when, after a controversial 3–2 defeat at Tynecastle where it was alleged that Jimmy Wardhaugh of Hearts fouled the Celtic keeper George Hunter by pushing him over the line for the winner, Celtic put together a sequence of results in which they won nine successive league games, five away from home, scoring 32 goals and conceding only four. This left them requiring a win at Easter Road on 17 April to achieve something that had been denied them for sixteen years – the league title.

On the day of that game the *Daily Record*'s Donald Bruce, as if suddenly realising Stein's importance, commented on Stein's selection to play for the Scottish League against the Football League later that month and said that the player had been 'a wonderful inspiration to the fighting Celts'. Celtic stamped their authority on the match when Mochan scored in exactly 60 seconds – the fastest goal of his life, and one from which Hibs never recovered. Another by him and a goal four minutes from time by John Higgins secured the much sought-after title. Two days later in the same paper, Tom Nicholson noted that Stein had performed 'outstandingly' during Celtic's 3–0 victory over Hibs that had secured the first leg of the double. Stein never varied in his opinion throughout the years that winning the league was the top priority, even though Celtic had attained a formidable reputation as a cup side. So he had steered them to the prize they wanted most of all, and with interest still alive in the Scottish Cup he was now within touch of helping to create the club's most successful season in 40 years.

Celtic disposed of Motherwell relatively easily, 3–1, in the Scottish Cup semi-final replay after a tight 2–2 draw. The final against Aberdeen, on 24 April, drew 129,926 to Hampden. It was the biggest crowd Stein and others would ever play in front of. He mastered the situation. He was to be faced by one of the trickiest centre-forwards of the day, Paddy Buckley, who as a darting, piercing player with quick acceleration punished slackness at will. However, the *Glasgow Herald* on 26 April reported that the threat had been nullified because 'Stein of the fairy-tale career employed all his resources of positional sense to counter-balance his disadvantage in pace and Evans, in particular, was frequently present to assist his centre-half'. But the paper also noted that it had been a 'rare lapse' by Stein when he headed a ball away weakly and allowed Buckley to score an equaliser in the 52nd minute, only seconds after Celtic had taken the lead. Then Sean Fallon's winning goal in the 63rd minute brought Celtic the victory they thoroughly deserved because of their superiority on the day. Yet within the *Herald*'s praise of the 'fairy-tale career' man is contained a hint of the possible decline of someone stretching with effort to his very limit. When you read 'counter-balance his disadvantage in pace' and 'Evans ... was frequently present to assist his centre-half', you feel as if he was beginning to find advancing years handicapping him. Stein had not arrived at Celtic as a youngblood but as a man with the 'auld heid'. Such players, of course, do have limitations, and at the age of nearly 32 even the shrewdest use of the grey matter in that 'heid' cannot shield a vulnerability to injury. As a player he was now in the final phase of his career.

As a football thinker, however, he was not yet out of elementary school. But he was being helped. For despite the image of parochial autocrat Bob Kelly readily conveyed when dealing with the minutiae of work within Celtic Park, he certainly believed in footballing education. With the honourable exception of Hibernian, compared to some others in Scotland, who wanted to see no further than their noses, he was a veritable Thomas Cook. His decision to send his entire playing staff off to Switzerland to take in the World Cup finals in 1954 as a reward for their most significant season in half a century could be seen as evidence either of a deep-thinking visionary or a healthy pragmatist. Whatever the case, it followed a pattern, for the Celtic players had already been sent to watch the England v. FIFA and England v. Hungary matches at Wembley, and I think it was these visits that made the greatest impression on Stein. He never forgot the Hungarians. Neither did any of us. But unlike us, at least Stein was in a position through the years to pursue the hope that he could field a team which would bear comparison with them. The green and white hoops of Lisbon were not shaped precisely on the model of the cherry shirts that had swarmed all over England thirteen and a half years before, but Puskas, Hidegkuti and company put a gleam in Stein's eye and an ideal in his sights that stirred his imagination, and that in itself was to rub off on anyone who put on boots for him at any stage.

As for his visit to the World Cup finals, he had many teams to watch, but he probably learnt more about mismanagement through witnessing Scotland's witless preparation for the event which saw Andy Beattie, their manager, resigning after they were beaten 1–0 by Austria. They were subsequently annihilated 7–0 by Uruguay, after which defeat Stein had to offer sympathy to two of his Celtic team-mates, Willie Fernie and Neilly Mochan, both of whom played in that disaster. But I doubt if Stein was really surprised by the fiasco surrounding that event. After all, the idiosyncratic handling of football matters was being perpetrated on his own doorstep in the east end of Glasgow by the very man with the honourable intention of sending his players on educational trips, Bob Kelly. And it was in the 1954/55 season that it was demonstrated to Stein more dramatically than at any other time that direct interference from boardroom level on team matters could simply be another form of self-immolation.

Celtic started on the right path on 18 September by beating 2–0 at Parkhead a Rangers side without its famous centre-half Willie Woodburn, who had been suspended sine die, but despite such early successes, and despite finishing the season with three more points than in 1953/54, they could only finish runners-up behind Aberdeen. Stein suffered an indignity in the highly charged Ne'erday game against Rangers at Ibrox when he carelessly headed a ball into the path of Derek Grierson whose touch to Billy Simpson brought the first of Rangers' goals in their comprehensive 4–1 win. (Simpson, the man from Belfast, was to be quite accidentally involved in a later game in shaping the rest of Stein's career.) Apart from that and a few lesser significant lapses, the same Mr Sellotape was out there for the rest of that season holding his side together to less than universal acknowledgement. But the disappointment of failing narrowly to win the title was but a frisson compared to the devastation and controversy caused by their defeat in the Scottish Cup final in April 1955.

This Celtic–Clyde showdown was to find its own particular niche in the history books for several reasons, not least because it was the first final to be televised live. The man who later commentated with me on the Lisbon final, Kenneth Wolstenholme, came from London to cover the match, which was transmitted, it has to be said, in a kind of grainy Mack Sennett black and white. (Bob Kelly would not have allowed the game to be covered live if he had been able to get his way. At that time he was beginning to develop a pathological hatred of television, and as if to confirm his fears, the attendance, massive by modern standards at 106,234, was smaller than it ought to have been.) Celtic should have had the cup won in the first half-hour of the game when they swamped the Clyde defence. Bobby Collins was demonstrably the most influential player up front, and like all wee men who perform like that he had the crowd backing him, like a favourite jockey leading the pack. He was also throwing his small but sturdy frame around and was particularly heavy on one occasion with Clyde's South African goalkeeper Hewkins. That was significant for what was to occur later.

Jimmy Walsh scored Celtic's goal in the 38th minute after the man with the long, elegant stride, Willie Fernie, had set him up on the edge of the penalty area. And that seemed to be that. Celtic scoring first in a cup final at Hampden was customarily a precursor to inevitable celebrations and a trophy presentation. But the television audience around the land was to be privy to one of the most bizarre goals ever scored at Hampden. For Celtic, after that opening initiative, suddenly looked like a team that had either run out of steam or were mentally preparing for after-meal revelries at Ferrari's. Clyde not only handled them competently but pushed the Parkhead side into a more subdued defensive mood. They suffered for that. Two minutes from the end of the game Clyde were awarded a corner-kick on the left of the Celtic goal. It was taken by the tall, erect, strong-backed inside-forward Archie Robertson. In Celtic eyes never has a corner looked so innocuous and turned out to be so lethal. Even Robertson himself admitted to the apparent shortcomings of his effort. 'I didn't mean the ball to go so near the goalkeeper,' he confessed. 'The wind must have caught it.' Well, this was no ordinary wind; the 'Hampden Swirl' had a mind of its own. John Bonnar in goal, who despite his shot-stopping heroics in the Coronation Cup final was not flawless when it came to cross-balls, followed the ball carefully with his eye, but true to its nature the wind bent the path of the ball at the last second and Bonnar's touch on it was no more than a gesture of farewell. The ball slipped through his fingers into the net for the equaliser. There was no time left for Celtic to win after that. Not just Celtic supporters but also the media and Kenneth Wolstenholme left the stadium in a state of near disbelief that the cup had been snatched away so late and in such a manner.

But what had occurred thereafter was to trigger in Stein's mind the need for inviolate managerial control over a team. Those next few days before the replay, particularly the team announcement for the game just before kick-off, preyed on his mind in the days leading up to his decision to go back to Parkhead as manager in 1965. He never forgot it. For, as he admitted to me long after the event, what happened next was a shambles. Collins was dropped. Mochan, who had scored nine goals in seventeen league matches that season, was kept in the stand. Walsh's position was changed unaccountably from inside-left to the right wing. McPhail, who had played centre, was moved to inside-left and Sean Fallon, famed for his rumbustious style, was brought back after a long spell of injury to lead the line. The changes were in themselves odd, but the dropping of Collins in the light of what was to happen was simply a provocation to the Celtic legions. The wee man had certainly indulged in uncompromising challenges in the first game and it was clear that Bob Kelly had taken a dim view of his demeanour, so Collins was not to play.

Stein never said an unkind word about Bob Kelly, that I know, but he as much as admitted to me that he had witnessed manager Jimmy McGrory being starkly ignored, ridden over and eventually, in terms of the loss of the replay, ultimately humiliated. It should be pointed out that Stein, when he came back as the club manager, treated McGrory with the greatest respect, even though he was simply an ancient retainer waiting for retirement, and Stein called him 'boss' until the day he died. Harry Haddock, Clyde's cheery and mobile full-back captain, read out the Celtic team in the Clyde dressing-room with astonishment and with a renewed feeling of confidence.

It was not misplaced. On a miserably wet evening, with only 68,831 in attendance and Hampden minus the television cameras, Tommy Ring scored the only goal for Clyde seven minutes after half-time. He had won his team a cup only to be greeted with outrage and indignation from his Celtic-supporting brothers, who refused to have dinner with him the next day. For Celtic it was a seminal evening, for they were not to win the Scottish Cup for another ten years. Stein did not dismiss the shambles but registered that evening as part of his education. But if he felt uncomfortable then, the blow might have been softened a little by looking back over his shoulder at his 'what-might-have-been' past. It could be seen in a report in the *Daily Record* positioned alongside that of a description of the replay with Clyde: on that same evening his old club Albion Rovers were playing in front of a mere 172 souls at Cliftonhill in a B division game against Brechin with gate receipts of just over £10. After paying the referee and linesman's fees, Rovers were left with eleven shillings, and they needed £150 to cover Brechin's guarantee. Sympathetic though Stein might have been to their plight, it also offered him another reminder of how fortunate his lot was now and that the Crazy Gang antics of the Celtic management were still preferable to an existence near the poverty line.

Recognition and a kind of absolution from that particular replay downfall was coming his way, for significantly the James Kelly (Blantyre) Supporters club made him their Player of the Year days after the final – as the *Daily Record* of 29 April put it, 'for recognition of his yeoman service to Celtic'. So here was the lad from the other side of the tracks in his home area finally being accorded full Celtic identity; Burnbank Cross now seemed of a distant age. That night in Blantyre he met a man for the first time who was to be his escort around much of the footballing world when he was both Celtic and Scotland manager. Tony McGuinness got to know Stein better than some of his players and remembers that night in Blantyre well. 'They presented Jock with a big fridge, which cost a lot of money in those days. I took a liking to him because he seemed a straightforward man and there was something about him that drew your attention when he spoke. Sincerity? It's easy enough to say these things, but I think that's what it was about him. And yes, we knew his background, so I think to be honest that made it a bit special that he was a Celt now.'

Stein himself addressed that point when he wrote a message to the Celtic Supporters Association in 1955 informing them, 'I cannot, like other Celts, claim that Celtic was my first love, but I know it will be my last and most enduring …' He had revitalised their community by steering his players to the winning of the Coronation Cup and the Scottish Cup and League Championship double. He had overcome resentment and intolerance, not just in his home area but within the heart of Celtic Park itself, and triumphed. But in pitting his body against Mother Nature he had no chance.

CHAPTER SEVEN
A STAR IN THE EAST

The distinct Stein limp became indissoluble from the personality which emerged from the shadows of a player declining in power into the glare of his rise to the dazzling peaks of managerial success. Only at times did it seem a pronounced hobble and that was when emotion was getting the better of him, in either elation or rage. But it was more a constant suggestion of the vulnerability of a man who, either in a tracksuit or in that favourite navy-blue overcoat he wore so often, could look quite immune to the process of wear and tear that afflicts most of us. The images of him skipping disjointedly on to a pitch to congratulate a player, hirpling up the tunnel at Celtic Park chasing Jimmy Johnstone, walking away from his car after a long journey as if his leg was in a clamp, rising from a chair, shoulders hunched, as if to get better leverage with the weakened foot, trudging lop-sidedly out of a press conference, advancing on you with intent, his feet in a curious staccato beat – they all keep company with memories of his triumphs and failures, like an identifying watermark.

The problem was his ankle. In a League Cup game against Rangers at Celtic Park on 31 August 1955 he injured it after a quite accidental collision with the Ibrox forward Billy Simpson. This was the beginning of the end for him as a player. He missed seventeen matches but came back to play against Partick Thistle on 17 December, looking reasonably comfortable as the side he captained again won, 5–1. But then came a long period of recurring problems with his ankle during which he would miss some games then return for another but eventually break down. All this was debilitating, and in the 2 January game against Rangers at Celtic Park in 1956 his apparent slowness allowed the bullish centre South African Don Kichenbrand, dubbed correctly 'The Rhino', to beat him for pace and score the only goal of the game. He played in only twelve competitive matches that season out of a possible total of 51. Then came his last game in the hoops. It was a friendly in May 1956 in Coleraine, Northern Ireland, the home territory of his great friend Bertie Peacock. It was there that the ankle gave out for good. 'It didn't look serious at the time,' Peacock recalled. 'He just went up for a ball, landed and rolled over, holding the ankle in the penalty area. There had been no contact, it was just in the landing. Something seemed to go. I can recall he was in considerable pain and of course he had to go off. I never ever thought that I would be seeing him for the last time in a Celtic jersey.'

On 10 June, two weeks later, the *Daily Express* reported that Stein was going into Glasgow's Royal Infirmary for an operation to remove a bone nodule and reported that the Celtic trainer Alec Dowdells, about to leave for Leicester City, 'expressed the hope that this operation would be a cure to Stein's troubles, making him 100 per cent for the start of the new season'. They tried everything, as Stein told the same newspaper himself. 'My ankle has given me a lot of pain since my operation, and I have been brought back here to see if the trouble can be located. I used to have to train hard at the start of a season to get my weight down, but with the pain and the lack of sleep during the past two weeks I have already lost a stone and a half.' He was kept in hospital for a week for observation and then was sent home. Celtic decided he wouldn't be allowed to start training again until they were satisfied his ankle dilemma had been solved.

Peacock recalled that Stein and his wife went from hospital down to Blackpool for a short break – the start of an expected recuperation. It was while he was there, Peacock said, that the ankle began to irritate and pain him until he could stand the aggravation no longer. He was compelled to push a finger down between the ankle and the plaster-cast which had been put around the joint. Hardened though he was to various injuries, even Stein was shocked, for all he could feel was a kind of mush. The ankle had become septic after what had been considered a routine operation intended to solve his problems (his wife Jean later claimed this was due to dirty stitches). Even at that stage he told people he feared the worst. He was correct. 'I don't know what the correct medical description was,' said Peacock, 'but he used to say simply that the ankle had frozen. Just like that, frozen. He couldn't move the joint. It was finished. You can imagine how he felt about that, a big man who could still have gone on and played more football – you just never know. And now his playing career was over. It's hard for anybody to take. But him, well, we're talking about one of the great captains who was so in love with the game he could hardly bring himself to sleep. It was his whole life. No, I wasn't surprised in the least that he overcame all of that and became a great manager because he was such a strong personality. But I can tell you at that time he was worried about the future for himself and his family.'

But there was no way that Bob Kelly would have allowed Stein to be cast into the wilderness. In the summer of 1957 he offered his 34-year-old former club captain a post as reserve-team coach, which in any case had seemed to be one of the reasons he had been brought to Parkhead in the first place. Stein, knowing that he couldn't kick a ball again in earnest, eagerly accepted. But even as he did so his thoughts were on management, somewhere, anywhere. His ankle still bothered him but he was no cripple.

He threw himself into his new appointment with relish. Posterity lends that job much more significance than it seemed to have at the time, for it coincided with the emergence of young men at the club who were to be called Kelly's Kids and who immediately fell under Stein's spell; names like Paddy Crerand, Billy McNeill, Bobby Murdoch, John Clark – largely the kernel of the side that would reach Lisbon in 1967. John Clark, the reserves coach's first ever signing, for a fiver a week, in fact claims that Stein made him the first ever groundstaff boy in Scotland. He also emphasised the bonding effect Stein created. 'He didn't just train and coach us, he was one of us. We were young lads who thought the world of him. Before he had a car we would all walk from the ground up to Parkhead Cross and get buses, particularly Billy McNeill and myself, since we were both from Lanarkshire. Many is the time our bus would come first but he wouldn't allow us on till his bus had arrived, since he said he was the boss. He would leave us standing there, laughing his head off, and sometimes we would have to wait for half-an-hour or so. Then he got his first car, a Hillman I think it was, and he would drop us all off, one by one, on his way home to Hamilton. That was the start of many car journeys with a man who if he hadn't been a football manager might have gone into Grand Prix racing. To take a car journey with Jock was an experience, I tell you.'

Paddy Crerand was beginning to be at serious odds with the club over the way it was run, and he too made the point that Stein's coaching was a revelation. 'He used to take low benches and place them round the touchlines. And you had to try to fire long passes and get the ball underneath them. He did that over and over with me until I was getting a high pass mark for it. And he would vary the training and have it all done with the ball in small groups and talk about the game with you and explain what it was that made players tick. He used to say, "If I tell you to do something and you go and do it, and then you go on and forget the next time, the problem is with yourself. You've got to grasp what's said to you right away or you have a problem. Think about the game." And he would concentrate on getting every player's strength fine-tuned. For example, he would make sure we all put the right crosses in for Billy McNeill to use his head. Over and over again. And look what that brought the club eventually. But what were the first team getting in training at the same time? Damn all, by comparison. Lapping, a kick-about, and then they'd go away back home. It was a joke. It is a damned shame that because of all these old fogeys with their traditions about background, Jock was allowed to leave. Those old fogeys at Parkhead should have appointed him manager before letting him leave.'

Stein was not simply confined to the training ground; he was in charge of a bunch of young players who loved to go out and play for him in reserve competitions. And in the spring of 1958 he assumed his winning ways again, this time in the Reserve Cup final, a two-legged affair with Rangers. Celtic won the first game at home 3–1, then went to Ibrox and thrashed Rangers 5–1. Shrewdly, Stein had managed to get into his team some experienced first-team players who responded promptly to his guidance. Winning had to go hand in hand with development and nurture. The two games were watched by a total of 40,000, which alone was sufficient reason for him to plan strategically, for even reserve games in those days carried the bonus of prestige. You could call that his first managerial cup win. All it did was stoke his desire to apply his skills at a higher level.

But there was one factor he construed to be a major and impassable blockade to progress within the club: he was a Protestant. He would have to move on. His wife Jean, in more diplomatic language, admitted as much to writer and journalist Ken Gallacher in 1988: 'He was more or less told by the chairman that he had gone as far as he could with Celtic, coaching the second team … I know the old chairman used to suggest that he had simply let John go out for experience and that it was the case that he would go back to Celtic, but I don't think that was right. John didn't think so either. He thought Sean Fallon was going to be the next Celtic manager. And he wanted to be a manager himself and nothing was going to stop him … I think he thought that the fact that he was a Protestant meant he would never be manager of Celtic. That's why he made up his mind to try elsewhere.'

It would not be strictly accurate to say that Stein harboured no resentment about such an attitude, even though he seemed to accept these things with little show of offence. For of course he was conscious of this factor all his working life with Celtic, and in the final analysis, although we saw nothing other than a man possessed when it came to the Celtic cause, he knew that his religious background would never leave the consciousness of some of the Celtic board, even at the moments of his greatest triumph. He himself admitted as much to friends; he even strongly hinted that it lay in the background when eventually he left the club for good. He hid his feelings about that, but they were there nonetheless, and he was street-wise enough to know that, sad though it might be, the rigidity of tribal thinking was something he could do very little about. His gratitude to Kelly for having salvaged his career, and the bond he had struck up with the Celtic supporters, sublimated the feelings he had about certain other individuals whom he believed never fully accepted him because of his background. There is no evidence to suggest that as he headed off he was setting a distant sight on returning to Celtic as manager, and they had given him absolutely no reason to believe that that was a possibility. It is much more likely that he felt he was finished at Parkhead for good, until his success in Fife later began to stimulate his imagination.

His eagerness to move out heightened when he learnt that Partick Thistle might be interested in taking him to Firhill as manager after the tragic death of the previous incumbent Davie Meiklejohn, the former Rangers player who, in August 1959, Stein had been alarmed to hear, had collapsed in the stand during a game and had died on the way to hospital. But that position fell to an ex-Ranger, Willie Thornton, then manager of Dundee.

He had the ear of someone else, though. The man who claimed to have been a key player in the move to Dunfermline was Jim Rodger, who was the worker bee of Scottish journalism. 'The Jolly', as he was called, flitted from phone to phone, from office to office, from chairman to player, from player to chairman, from editor even to Prime Minister, gathering enough pollen in the process to turn Scottish football chat and gossip into news that could be spread honey-thick over his various newspapers. He was an ex-miner, like Stein, and that affinity seemed to engender trust so that confidences could be filtered through each other. Rodger definitely attracted Stein throughout his career, and, as I was to discover in later years, when Stein was after the Scottish team manager's job the Big Man used him effectively as a contact and whisperer. Rodger did not mind irritating other people who thought him a skilled sycophant. He usually got what he was after.

So it's safe to conclude that calls were made by Rodger to whet Dunfermline's interest in Stein. Rodger, creating his own story as it were, made it clear in the *Daily Record* that Stein had not applied for the job but had been invited to attend. The Celtic coach had to travel to Dunfermline to be interviewed as there were two applicants. The other was Danny McLennan, a former Rangers player. The interviews were held in the offices of solicitor Leonard Jack, who later joined the board and became chairman. Solicitously, Stein was handed a voucher for a cup of tea in the town's Carousel Restaurant while he waited for the other candidate to be interviewed. On the same lines as discovering that George Raft was originally cast as Rick in Casablanca, you have to wonder what it would have been like had Danny McLennan got the post. However, on 14 March 1960, the 37-year-old Stein walked into East End Park as a manager in football for the first time.

We have to note how he concluded his first statement to the press: 'I was told there would be money to spend and that I would have complete control.' Where have we heard that before, and will again? It also indicates that the interview, if such you could call it, was not a one-way process, that he knew the measure of the task he was to take on and that he was setting out his own terms before accepting. After all, Dunfermline were, at that point, third from bottom in the First Division and only two points from the basement itself, and their previous manager, Andy Dickson, had stopped believing that he could save the club from relegation. It was not an appetising prospect for anybody.

But what Stein had also done was to investigate the financial status of the Pars. In his first statements he offered the customary blandishments about the playing staff, about how he respected them, and then added even more significantly, 'The shareholding had been tidied up by Leonard Jack and his influence made it certain that there would be a Board of Directors with a continuing policy. I saw a future.' This gave early indications of a man who was thinking beyond the dressing-room to the important alliance that had to be struck with any boardroom and chairman in order to make the job viable. His fervour to coach and to manage was being properly constrained by his constant need to know, wherever he was to go in the future, that he had a solid financial basis on which to work.

He made that easier for himself by being immediately successful. For by another huge coincidence his first game was against Celtic. Just as his debut day as a professional in senior football had been against them, in the wake of a famous desert victory, so Stein was able to get out of his players, on his debut day as a manager, an El Alamein-style response. For Dunfermline blasted Celtic with a goal after a mere ten seconds. It was his first managerial goal and his fastest ever. Scored by a big, rugged centre-forward called Charlie Dickson, it indicated that Stein had them coming out of the dressing-room like hounds to the hunt. George Miller, who was to be his captain eventually and who went on to manage the club but who was injured for that match and didn't play until Stein's next game, was in the dressing-room before that Celtic tie. 'He was bouncing about the place,' Miller recalled. 'The enthusiasm was unbelievable. There was nothing much he said except about how we had to keep in about them. It wasn't a time for too many tactics but he told us about some of the Celtic players and what to watch for. But that wasn't the most important thing. The previous manager, Andy Dickson, was a perfect gentleman, but he was a mild man. This new figure amongst us was going about as if our lives depended on it. The effect was that good players just became better players.'

Dunfermline won the game 3–2, the Stein acorn had been planted, and even on the barren ground of provincial mediocrity the growth was to be beyond the locals' wildest dreams. For on the back of that victory, their first in four months, came an astonishing sequence of six wins out of the last six games, which saved the club from relegation. Even back at Celtic Park, so soon after his departure, they must have been musing over this achievement. But these bare statistics reveal nothing of the emergence of Stein the plotter and schemer, who eventually from some of his opponents would draw descriptions of him that might have been applied to Machiavelli or indeed Auld Nick himself. He revealed this side in his own words to a Dunfermline historian when describing the circumstances surrounding a crucial game four weeks from the end of that 1959/60 season. 'The important match was the one against Kilmarnock,' he said. 'We were due to play the league game against them on the day of the cup semi-final. Because they were involved in that tie against Clyde I rearranged the game with Willie Waddell of Kilmarnock. We were to be idle on the Saturday and I planned to watch the reserve game. Kilmarnock would either be high after winning, low after defeat or worried about a replay. Anyway, we would play them on a Monday night while their concentration was low. I wasn't popular with the Dunfermline officials for going for a Monday-night game but my decision turned out to be right as we defeated the cup finalists 1–0.'

That sort of thinking was far removed from the mere drilling of players on a training ground. This was his first basic, untutored and instinctive foray into the managerial mind games for which he would become famous – or, as his opponents might say, infamous. Now, for a fledgling manager to outwit the ferociously proud Willie 'Deedle' Waddell on the matter of when to play a game, which Stein perceived correctly to be to Kilmarnock's disadvantage, was no mean achievement. I can even now visualise the glee Stein would have felt in making Deedle, a blue-shirted hero of his in the past, his first psychological scalp. For he had inflicted on Kilmarnock, who were in the running to win the title, their first defeat in 21 games. Stein had got his players on a roll and for the first time in their careers they were witnessing a man clearing the dressing-room of everybody bar the players twenty minutes from kick-off, and then delivering an accurate and uncanny breakdown of the opposition. Although in modern terms there is nothing unusual about that, in 1960 he was breaking new ground for those brought up in a kind of DIY footballing environment.

Survival that season brought about renovation. Stein went into the market to get players he thought would be the kind to consolidate the club's position as a First Division team. That was his first priority. Stability and status, not the yo-yoing effect of constant relegation and promotion. He went to England and bought defender Willie Cunningham and winger Tommy McDonald. He made other signings, but these two constituted the main building blocks of the club around whom a hardened team would emerge. And it worked. From tottering on the brink of extinction when he had arrived, Stein, by the end of his second full term in 1961/62, had pushed his club into fourth position in the league with only Dundee (the winners), Celtic and Rangers in front. The club's league statistics when he took over the job had read won 4, lost 13, for 51, against 66; at the conclusion of that second season under him they read won 19, lost 10, for 77, against 46. They were no longer caving in at the first pressure. They simply dared not show that weakness.

Their newfound confidence was making them feed voraciously on cup games in particular. His inspirational team-talks saw the players battle their way to their first ever Scottish Cup final when, on 5 April 1961, they disposed of St Mirren after a replay in the semi-final. Their opponents at Hampden would be Celtic, and from the moment that was confirmed his plotting started. His first major move in trying to win the cup was off the field. In a swoop that upstaged Celtic, Stein moved quickly to book the Seamill Hydro Hotel on the Ayrshire coast as his base for the game. This beautifully sited establishment had for so long been used by Celtic over the years, especially before finals, that you might have thought the club owned it. To have the audacity to snap up this accommodation from under the noses of his former club was a bit like someone pre-booking the Royal Box for the night of the Royal Command Performance. There was nothing Celtic could do about it, for, of course, the staff knew Stein well from his days at Parkhead. This was all part of the strategy of surrounding his players with the trappings of footballing excellence, the comfort and the luxury giving them the feeling that they had well and truly arrived.

But he also knew that the players from the provinces, faced by a huge Celtic crowd, might be overawed. Miller remembered how Stein dealt with that. 'He told us in no uncertain manner that Celtic were not a great side at that time and that they were deceiving themselves about their own abilities. He broke down their team for us, one by one, and went through what they were like and told us frankly that apart from a couple he thought were quality we could match them man for man in every position. He knew them inside out. It was all believable. That's the point. He wasn't making it up with some false talk. It was fascinating.' However, Willie Cunningham, who was to be one of the most consistent of Stein's players in his time at East End Park, and who became manager in succession to him, noted something else. 'I think he had a special feeling for Celtic,' he said. 'There was a tinge of affection there. When we went through for the game and I heard him speaking to people from the West you could tell he had a special regard for the club. He wanted to beat them all right, make no mistake about that. He was too professional for anything else, but there definitely was a tinge of Celtic about him.'

The first game, on 22 April in front of 113,328, was not memorable. The pattern overall was certainly of Celtic's aggression and the Fifers' organised resistance. Eddie Connachan in goal was making saves that were simply a preamble to the heroics that would follow four days later. Crerand dominated in midfield but his supply to the men in front of him was being wasted as Willie Fernie and John Hughes, up front, irritated the Celtic support with mazy runs that lacked finality. As the game progressed Dunfermline saw more of the ball, but the Celtic defence of MacKay, McNeill and Kennedy were largely unperturbed.

Celtic's chances in the game were distinct, but not so that the Pars defence ever looked like succumbing. When centre-half Jackie Williamson sustained a bad injury just before half-time and soldiered on for a while, only to hobble painfully and have to be taken off twelve minutes from the end, even then

Dunfermline stood solid. They might even have 'pinched' the game in the very last minute. George Peebles suddenly thrashed a ball towards Frank Haffey from 30 yards. The unaccountable was never far from the actions of the Celtic keeper, who allowed the ball to squirm from his grasp; as it slipped towards the goal-line and what would have been a certain Dunfermline victory, that splendidly alert full-back Jim Kennedy swept it away for a corner. Celtic must have known, even from that one incident, that they had a goalkeeper who was in need of counselling and rest after his Wembley trauma, for, as Scotland goalkeeper the previous Saturday, Haffey had had to shoulder a great deal of the blame for a humiliating 9–3 thrashing at the hands of the English. The fact that the Celtic management did nothing about that for the replay was to prove a bonus for the Fife club. The goalless draw probably made Celtic even hotter favourites to win the cup, for very seldom would they slip up at the second time of asking. But Stein knew that any feelings of being overawed had been dealt with by the first match and that his pre-match assessment of Celtic had been clearly absorbed by his team.

The weather had turned sour by 26 April. The crowd reflected that – 87,866. Rain drove into faces as it swept in from the west. Hampden looked grey and dour. The game was to be about attrition, not fluency. Replays in midweek anyway are but second-hand products and can never generate the same sense of occasion as the Saturday. Except, of course, the cup was at stake, and even performing on a drab stage would be worth the effort. With the normal disadvantage of playing in front of a vast multitude of Celtic supporters, Stein kept emphasising the need to think about the players against them, that they were not all that special. He moved George Sweeney to left-half to replace George Miller, who had moved into the centre-half position, and that player dogged the footsteps of Celtic's long-striding forward Fernie. This was man-marking with a vengeance. Connachan, in the Dunfermline goal, made some good stops early on but that was nothing compared to the last twenty minutes of the game. For in the 67th minute 22-year-old Davie Thomson scored for the Fifers when he sent Peebles away on the left; Thomson ran into the penalty area, bent low, met the same player's cross and scooped it into the net.

What followed was a siege as gripping as any ever seen at Hampden. For Celtic, realising the game might be slipping away from them, rained down shot after shot on Connachan. He stood up to it as if he were facing a dam bursting. He threw himself around the goal-line, he clutched, he palmed, he tipped, he smothered; in one particular instance he miraculously stopped a 25-yard Crerand shot that sped through a ruck of players and could only have been seen at the last second. Just after that, Hughes burst through on his own with only the keeper in front of him, but to his obvious disbelief saw Connachan save by throwing himself to the side to parry the shot. That was the save which really turned the game. For just as if it were part of the scenario of a drama that saw courage rewarded by divine intervention, Dunfermline scored again two minutes from time. Alex Smith pushed a ball through the middle to the powerful Charlie Dickson. It was over-hit, it was a goalkeeper's ball, but on the other hand it wasn't. Haffey fumbled it, and not only did he allow it to drop at his feet, he somehow managed to bypass the ball as well, allowing the astonished Dickson simply to accompany it into the open net. Dunfermline had won the 76th cup final in their 76th year.

The white-coated figure who dashed on to the field at the final whistle to hug his players was now both a local hero and, almost overnight, a national figure of substance. Ninety minutes had changed Stein's status. Bob Kelly, by now president of the SFA, was in the presentation area, where his wife handed the cup to Dunfermline captain Ron Mailer. Kelly, dignified as ever, must have gone through this process deeply wounded inside, yet alert to the now inescapable fact that the run-of-the-mill player he had brought from Llanelly as a useful reserve was indeed a born winner. In his gracious way he told the *Scottish Daily Express*, 'It's no loss what a friend gets.'

Stein threw himself passionately into the celebrations. Never did he hug a goalkeeper so much in such a short space of time as he did Eddie Connachan, a miner like himself who only gave up his job shortly after the final (by and large Stein was allergic to goalkeepers for they seemed to bring rushes of contrasting emotions to his head, as we shall see). The *Scottish Daily Express* the following morning used a headline that was too temptingly alliterative to avoid and which was to become a compositor's hardy annual and a journalist's off-the-shelf cliché – 'Stein's Stunners'. Now he was about to put them into the export business.

CHAPTER EIGHT
UNA GRANDE FORMICA

Europe was decidedly to Stein's taste. He took the Dunfermline Athletic club chef to cater for his side's nutrition when they went to play Vardar in Yugoslavia in the Cup Winners' Cup in November 1961. Such an arrangement was unheard of. But if that was unprecedented, and a lesson to others in the science of football preparation, none of them were prepared for a blood-bath of a game which many of the players were glad to survive without serious injury. They went down 2–0 on the night, but as they already had a lead of 5–0 from the first leg Stein had made another impressive start in a new environment. And now, as a young, successful manager, he would rarely be out of the sports pages. For the rest of his career he would excite comment and gossip and never be short of offering his own opinions. For he had made his imprint.

Stein clearly had special qualities, and others began to assume he was a candidate for any managerial job coming on the market. Reports that Hibernian of Edinburgh were looking for a new manager to replace Hugh Shaw, who had been 40 years with the club, fourteen of them as manager, had made Stein the 'talk of the steamie' around the time of the winning of the Scottish Cup. His name kept cropping up in dispatches concerning that post without a direct comment on the matter from him. But he did later confess to Joe Hamilton of the *Scottish Daily Express* that he turned down an offer from Newcastle United, just after the 1961 Scottish Cup success, of a £4,000-a-year job – double his Dunfermline salary – for he had felt a 'moral obligation' to stick with a club still flush with success. He added, more pertinently, that his wife and children were very fond of the town and nicely settled in a 'luxurious bungalow' near East End Park. But he did say, interestingly, 'A man wants to get on. It's not the money that interests me. It is advancement in football.'

But Mr Ubiquity, Jim Rodger of the *Daily Record*, was able to reveal in his paper on 15 November 1961 that the Dunfermline board, in the wake of Shaw's resignation, had refused to release their manager from the recently signed five-year contract. Hibs had offered Stein a ten-year contract at initially £3,000 a year. Rodger then revealed that Stein 'had pleaded with the

Dunfermline directors for his release' and was 'disappointed that he cannot take the plum post at Hibs'. What Rodger knew and the Dunfermline board didn't was that on a trip to Easter Road for a reserve-team game against Hibs, the Edinburgh club's chairman Harry Swan had offered Stein the job 'out of the blue'. Then, at a later date, Stein watched a Fairs Cup game Hibs were involved in, sitting beside Swan again, obviously in close harmony. Robert Russell observed in the *Scottish Daily Express* of 17 November that 'All day yesterday rumours were that the conversation between the two concerned matters other than bingo and bagatelle ... Dunfermline fans still feel the "Stein-For-Hibs" moves have not finished.'

They most certainly were not. Neither Swan nor Stein would make any comment on their meeting. But you have to wonder if Stein, reckless though he may have been in making his association with the Hibs chairman so public, actually felt that he could simply put the matter on ice in the knowledge that thawing it out speedily would always be an option. That seems to have been the case, for the public discussion of the matter became so intense that on 21 November Stein issued the following statement, which reads like the preamble to a departure: 'I have informed the Board of Directors of Hibernian Football Club that I am remaining as manager of Dunfermline Athletic. I hope to consolidate the progress the Club has made in the past year and to forge ahead with the plans for the future with the co-operation of the Board of Directors. I hope to justify the faith placed in me and I will do my very best for the Club and the town.'

In many ways it was not the best time to leave. Dunfermline were in full flow in a European tournament. He was riding high personally with players who would run until they dropped for him. And a European tie in Budapest, home to the Magic Magyars of 1953 and therefore Stein's spiritual football capital, was looming against Ujpest Dozsa in the quarter-final of the Cup Winners' Cup. Time was really on his side, and what he in fact was revealing through his official statement was a high degree of self-confidence. Not only would he not have allowed the controversy to upset him, it would have acted as a stimulant to him. He loved intrigue anyway and always would. His visits to Easter Road indicated that he was taking an active part in designing his future. Now he had to shape his players for a task at a higher level than they had ever faced.

Only 18,000 turned up in the huge Nep Stadium on 13 February 1962, largely because it was bitterly cold, and frankly the name Dunfermline held no great allure for a city that had been host to some of the best clubs around Europe. However, any doubts that might have existed about their right to tread the same hallowed turf as the Magyars were dispelled very quickly, for in keeping with Stein's ability to get players to forget the overture and get on with the performance Dunfermline scored after only 40 seconds, through Alex Smith. If that were not temerity enough in this citadel of innovative football, the Pars went two up in eight minutes when 30-year-old Tommy McDonald scored a second. Overall, McDonald turned in a performance that was described lyrically by John Mann in the *Scottish Daily Express*: 'He was tremendous, teasing and tormenting the Magyars with a display of ball-juggling that not even much-capped Janos Gorocs could match.' Ujpest, as if they suddenly had the measure of these upstarts, then began to assert themselves, and in the space of one minute, just on the half-hour, pulled it back to 2–2. At the end of the night the scoreline of 4–3 for Ujpest showed that deficiencies in defence had almost been compensated for by Stein's exhortation not to be inhibited in attacking. Here was the template established for much of his work abroad in the future.

For the return leg 24,717 tickets were sold and only just over 600 didn't turn up, which made the actual attendance just over 200 short of the crowd record of 24,377 set against Rangers in a third-round Scottish Cup tie in 1958. But this was also a show game. Other managers and officials poured into Dunfermline for it, and there was an unprecedented overspill from the press-box. It was one thing for the Old Firm to make some impression in Europe, but it was a rare opportunity to witness a provincial side attempting to humble a respected footballing name. In fact they were caught by the sucker punch when the brilliant seventeen-year-old Ferenc Bene scored the only goal of a game Dunfermline dominated for long periods. Stein was disappointed but not depressed at going down 1–0. He had anticipated the nature of the game but had hoped for the break which proved just beyond his side. 'If there is any glory in defeat I think we earned it tonight,' he said. 'I thought our tactics, in the first half particularly, worked very well and that George Miller was the best player on the field. In fact I wouldn't swap any of the Dunfermline players for those of the big-reputation Hungarians. But we are learning all the time at this game and for a first attempt at a continental tournament Dunfermline have done very well. There will be a next time.'

Of course there was, the following season in fact, when a Greek side pulled out of the Fairs Cup competition and Dunfermline – who had not qualified directly for Europe, although Stein had inspired them to climb to their highest position in years in the Scottish First Division, fourth position at the end of season 1961/62 – were asked to fill the vacancy. They accepted the invitation willingly, but in the first round they had to face the wealthiest team in England at the time, Everton, nicknamed the 'Bank of England' side for having spent over £250,000 on their current side. The winner of that game in the group system they had devised for the competition would play either Valencia or Celtic. So the incentive was great. There were four Scots in the English side, all internationals: Alex Parker, Jimmy Gabriel, George Thomson and Alex Young. That did not soften the impact of the two sides clashing, for it turned out to be the most controversial match of Stein's career to date.

Let *The Scotsman* of 25 October 1962 lend us something of the flavour. It began, 'This Inter-Cities Fairs Cup between Everton and Dunfermline was disgraced before a 40,240 crowd by all the startling scenes we have come to expect when Continental teams are involved. Method was abandoned in favour of muscle. The referee, who appeared to have things in hand in the first half, lost control in the second and should have sent off at least two players … At the final whistle, as the Dunfermline manager Mr J. Stein and a number of his players made their way to the tunnel leading to the dressing-room, they were showered with orange peel, bits of newspaper and other objects by Everton supporters.' Even after the game the Dunfermline team bus was attacked and a bottle smashed against its side as it drove away.

Part of the reason for the collapse in discipline on the field and the resultant anger on the terracings was the controversial goal scored by Everton and the Dunfermline players' resentment about it. In the 25th minute Billy Bingham took an inswinging corner which Stevens headed towards goal. Willie Cunningham got his head to it but it shot up, hit the underside of the bar and bounced down. The Irish referee ruled that the ball had gone over the line, to the consternation of the visiting players, who to this day have never accepted that. Of the rather condescending way in which his players had been treated as they entered Goodison Park in the first place, right through to that incident, Stein commented afterwards, 'I think they thought that this was the arrival of the "country hicks". With Willie Cunningham playing so well at the back and a tight defence, the only danger was at the corners. At half-time I made sure the players would let the Everton stars know they would be sorted out at Dunfermline.' When a Burnbank man talks about 'sorting out' somebody he is not referring to guiding a person through a crisis. It has a darker connotation.

But something of more lasting significance had happened in the game, and it was centred on the role of Willie Cunningham. *The Scotsman*, in the same report, described him as 'a floating defence man'. We now call that a 'sweeper'. Cunningham himself admits he approached the game with grave reservations. 'I had an argument with Jock about what he had asked me to do,' he recalled, 'lie in behind the other defenders and keep a look-out for breakthroughs. I told him I didn't want to play that role and we had a right barney about it. But as usual he was proved right. I strolled through the game, and Everton, who hadn't really come across this, couldn't penetrate as they thought they would. We didn't call it a sweeper but that is what it was and it was the tactic he wanted to use more and more in any European football. It really frustrated Everton. As far as I'm aware he was the first to introduce that into the Scottish and maybe even the British game.' It is interesting to note that Stein and Cunningham were having their own philosophical discussion on defensive tactics long before the manager went off to Italy to study Helenio Herrera's *catenaccio* techniques.

So Stein the innovator had simply whetted the appetite for the return leg. Everton drew a 25,000 crowd to East End Park a week later for they were packed with some of the giants of English League football and were sitting at the top of the First Division. They were beaten more comprehensively than the 2–0 scoreline suggests, with goals by Miller and then Harry Melrose in the last couple of minutes. They had been 'sorted out', in fact, but in a manner befitting a team that had simply outwitted and outplayed its opponents on the night. The performance certainly lent Stein enough confidence to tell the West of Scotland press that his team going to Ibrox for the next game on the Saturday against Rangers couldn't lose. In those days that was considered outrageous insolence. Telling people he could not lose at Ibrox? Was this a young upstart who had got too big for his boots? Or was he something special? He was outrageously correct. Dunfermline drew 1–1, and Stein's stock continued to soar. Were they watching at Celtic Park? Willie Cunningham thought they were. 'I told him often enough, "You're going to end up back there wearing green and white." He never squashed that altogether. All he would do is just burst out laughing and walk away. You really had to think something like that was in his head.'

With the added success of consolidating his club's league position and exorcising the spectre of relegation, which had taken up almost permanent residence in the stadium before his arrival, he could afford to prepare properly for his next European venture, against Valencia, the holders, on 12 December. They travelled to Spain appreciative of the opportunity to have a break from the gathering Scottish winter. But that was the only satisfaction as they were routed 4–0. The return leg at East End Park, however, was one of Stein's classics.

Everything we learnt about Stein through the years while following him throughout Europe was summarised in this one game. He seemed to be pitting his wits against the opposition manager, the referee and the weather. It was the all-encompassing Stein who, when you saw him at any vital game but more especially in European matches, seemed to grow physically before your very eyes, to be everywhere, sorting this and that, fussing, nagging, snarling, quipping. This is what everybody got that night. Firstly the game was played in such cold weather and on such a hard pitch that it is a wonder it was played at all. Willie Cunningham recalls that Stein was on top of the match officials from the moment they arrived at the ground, and that by his very presence and the way he talked to them he convinced them that the concrete-like pitch was perfectly playable. 'You felt the referee couldn't possibly cancel the game the way Jock went about the business of impressing them that everything was all right on the pitch,' said Cunningham. Valencia protested but they were overruled, and the match went ahead. Having got that out of the way, and having stood around glaring at the Valencia officials while they made their protest as if he would run them out of town if they tried to moan any more, with his sense of adventure he made the remarkable decision to give sixteen-year-old Alec Edwards and nineteen-year-old Jackie Sinclair their debuts in a game you might have thought was purely for the hardened veterans. Not so according to Stein, who in the dressing-room convinced his players the challenge was not beyond them.

What followed was one of the most remarkable nights in the history of European football in Scotland. The Fifers became the first British side to 'down the swashbuckling senors', as Tommy Gallagher reported in the *Dundee Courier and Advertiser*. Three goals inside the first seventeen minutes set the Pars up for an astounding 6–2 victory in which young Sinclair scored twice. Stein had got a game played that ought not to have gone ahead; he had bewildered the opposition by throwing on players they had never heard of; he had projected that sense of intimidation he had used on everyone off the pitch on to the performance of the players themselves.

Only an emerging giant could have achieved that. And now, with the aggregate score fixed at 6–6, the stage was set for a play-off in Lisbon.

Only 1,000 people turned up in pouring rain in the Portuguese capital on 6 February 1963 to see Valencia knock Stein's men out of the competition by a single goal scored by a left-back who hadn't scored previously that season. It was an anti-climax, for sure, but Stein was on the steepest of learning curves. Unfortunately, the tournament turned out to be a financial disaster for the club. Their share of the gate from the Lisbon match was £3 10s, which hardly covered the cost of the bus from the airport. The agony was prolonged because Valencia went on to win the trophy.

Dunfermline, though, finished safely in mid-table at the end of the season, and Stein moved into his last spell with the club with his ambition burning ever more fiercely, in tandem with the continual speculation surrounding his future and the failure of Walter Galbraith at Hibs to win any confidence with his board. It did not prevent Stein from increasing his education with a trip to Italy in November 1963 and a visit to the man who seemed to have assumed a kind of footballing papacy, Helenio Herrera. The idea was the brainchild of one of Scotland's most perceptive journalists of the time, Drew Rennie of the *Scottish Daily Express*, whose paper financed the trip which Stein made in company with Willie Waddell, manager of Kilmarnock, and his trainer Walter McCrae. The newspaper had sent out a young reporter, George Reid, later to be a nationalist MP, MSP and Presiding Officer of the Scottish Parliament in Edinburgh, to sound out Herrera with this idea. It was he who had reported that Herrera was so impressed with Stein's energy, in the way he bustled around the training camp or hurried off to see a horse race and was never at peace, that he described him as *una grande formica* – a big ant.

The 47-year-old Argentine had assumed a Peronist stance in Italian football. As he himself told any visitor inspecting his vast array of personal files on players, 'I'm an absolute dictator here!' It is that above all which impressed Stein. He saw much that was new in terms of the variety of training and the need to use strengthening and deep-breathing exercises to 'toughen up' players, and listened avidly to Herrera talking about sudden attacks from deep by up to eight players, which in a nutshell was 'counter-attacking', and about the use of the attacking full-back, epitomised by the great Facchetti. But it was the dominance of the manager or coach which stayed in his mind. For the three principles by which Stein clearly wanted to live in terms of his management of men, as was proved in later years, were control, control and control. He also added to me many years later that he had to be cautious about adopting methods or attitudes which simply didn't suit the sort of environment he had to work in. The Italian player was of a different breed and lived in a different world to the British player, where a George Best and a Jimmy Johnstone were subject to the pressures of, say, a deeply ingrained booze culture. They required different handling. Herrera had established a sort of monastic isolation for his players. That was impractical back in Scotland where the beer-mat was more prevalent than the prayer-mat. So Stein did not return with a dossier of sophisticated tactical ploys, as some might have imagined. He came back with renewed confidence in the way he wanted to project his own personality.

Stein's public successes were obvious, but his internal club skills would also have been passed down the grapevine, and at Easter Road in Edinburgh patience had run out on the manager Walter Galbraith. On 27 February 1964 Scottish newspapers reported that Jock Stein would be allowed to leave his post at Dunfermline at the end of the 1963/64 season. The sense of desolation around the area was palpable. George Miller experienced it. 'Of course it was no surprise,' he said, 'but even then it was hard to take. This man saved this club. He just didn't save it, he made it feared. Can you believe that? In four years from being a laughing stock we could claim the Scottish Cup, practically unbeatable at home in the league, great victories in Europe, a packed ground, coaches and managers coming from all over to watch us. We were midgets and he made us ten feet tall.' There were no reports of sports editors overcome with shock at the announcement either, and it didn't take them long to speculate on where Stein was heading, for only two weeks after that Dunfermline statement it was announced that Galbraith had left Easter Road for good. It was, of course, a remarkable coincidence.

A few weeks later, on 28 March, Stein took Dunfermline to Hampden to take on Rangers in a Scottish Cup semi-final. A goal by Davie Wilson of Rangers just before half-time was sufficient to knock them out of the cup. On 30 March, the day after he had met quite openly with the new Hibs chairman Willie Harrower, it was revealed that Stein was being allowed to leave the Fifers with immediate effect and would be joining Hibs as manager. It all seemed like a carve-up that bore the stamp of a production by J. Stein. So that game at Hampden had been his last with Dunfermline.

The Rangers supporters, streaming out of the ground in jubilation, would hardly have noticed the slightly hunched figure limping from the dug-out and then up the tunnel at the end of the game. But in the not too distant future they certainly would. For sooner than anybody could have possibly anticipated *una grande formica* was to return to haunt them for a generation.

CHAPTER NINE
A CAPITAL INTERLUDE

Stein did not convert Easter Road into Camelot, but his residence in the capital was so short and successful that you could describe this phase of his career as 'one brief, shining moment'. Hibernian was what he had wanted, at least in the interim. They were a club with a big support base, substantially more money to hand than he had been accustomed to in Fife and with a not too distant history of renown. He had had enough of the hard grind of provincialism. It had certainly provided him with memorable occasions and had toughened and honed his managerial skills, but, as he would tell Willie Cunningham, 'There comes a time when you know you can't get any more out of yourself.' It is a working regulation he might well have misplaced in his last couple of years as Celtic manager.

All this had happened so conveniently that it is not difficult to work out that Stein had been on top of the situation from the outset, and perhaps had dictated some of the manoeuvres. Only two weeks after the Dunfermline directors had agreed to release him at the end of the season, Galbraith had handed in his resignation. There had been gathering desperation in Edinburgh, for just before the time of Galbraith's departure Hibernian were twelfth in a league of eighteen and had never been free from the anxiety of relegation. Morale had sunk so low throughout the club that after a spell during which they seemed destined for the drop, had taken only one point from three and were being beaten at home by Airdrie, a solitary spectator decided to protest. When a ball left the field of play and landed at the top of the terracing, he grabbed it, walked to the wall behind him and kicked it out of the ground in disgust. The police were not amused. They arrested him. But the Hibs chairman Harry Swan was not unsympathetic, asked for his release and then gave the man a complimentary ticket for the next game on the grounds that unlike some players, at least the man knew what he was doing with the ball. This single act was enough to spare the chairman from uttering those words of gallows humour, 'I have every confidence in our manager.' After that single gesture by the chairman, Galbraith knew his time was up.

As Stein looked westward, as he undoubtedly often did, even when finding a daily short-cut from his bungalow in middle-class Queensferry

Road on the west side of Edinburgh through the tenemented grey streets of Leith to Easter Road, he would not have failed to notice that Celtic were about as resplendent as a painted ship upon a painted ocean. They had won nothing major since their famous 7–1 rout of Rangers in the League Cup final of October 1957. It is inconceivable that the man did not now harbour a much more realistic hope of getting back to Parkhead to sort this out. For he was no longer the stout Protestant lad who had helped the cause but could go no further within the club; he was now a managerial winner.

Pat Stanton, one of the most intelligent and elegant of players ever to grace the Scottish turf, was a young eighteen-year-old at Easter Road when Stein arrived, but already playing in the first team. Broadly speaking, he felt that the impact of change was like transferring from the Deadwood Stage to the Royal Scot. 'He didn't walk in, he blew in,' Stanton recalled. 'What most people didn't know was that he knew me well as a player and had tried to get me to sign for Dunfermline when I was a juvenile. So I had a head start on most of the other players to be honest. But there was something else that was so different. We had never seen it before. I know it sounds nothing nowadays, but none of the lads, even the older ones, had ever seen a manager do it before. He wore a tracksuit.'

Of course, he had been similarly attired at Dunfermline, and this new style was less sensational publicly than Mary Quant's mini-skirt, which was emerging as both a practical garment and a symbol of the swinging sixties. But it was beginning to dawn on the media that a cultural change was taking place and that Stein was leading by example in a manner that would be as momentous throughout training grounds as the new hemline coming out of Carnaby Street was in the high street. Over at Ibrox and Celtic Park, if Scot Symon and Jimmy McGrory respectively ever attended training sessions they were dressed as if they were preparing for church – jacket, collar and tie, coat, soft hat. They were several degrees distanced from the turmoil of training and in effect had no input. Stein was a participant who would come off a training ground, hair awry, heaving his frame along as if he had just crawled through a barbed-wire fence in a muddy field. The age of the tracksuited manager was now upon the land.

Stanton was to form a solid defensive partnership with John McNamee, whom Celtic had regarded as surplus to requirements and who was snatched up by Stein as his first signing. In midfield he had two ball artists: the neat and creative Pat Quinn and the remarkable Willie Hamilton. But splendid though they were, they were both under-achievers. Had Hamilton not been afflicted by that serious environmental disorder in Edinburgh of there being too many boozers and betting shops, he could have been one of the players of the century. He particularly shone in a Summer Cup play-off game against Dunfermline, mesmerising the opposition in a manner that had Stein drooling afterwards about one of the great talents. In later years he used to talk about him as if he was grieving over the misspent youth of his own son. Pat Stanton recalled his adoration. 'When I had gone to Celtic in 1977, as a player, after Jock had been there for some years, we were sitting around in the dressing-room one day and just talking about players that he liked through the years. Up came the name – Willie Hamilton. Roy Aitken, the Celtic captain at the time, asked, "Who was he?" Jock acted as if Roy had missed something special in life. "Think of Kenny Dalglish," he said to Roy. "Think of somebody just as good as Kenny, and that was Willie Hamilton." And then he went on at length about how he could do this and that with the ball and could use both feet with equal ability. And of course he wasn't exaggerating. Under Stein I witnessed what he could really be like. The Big Man brought out the best in him.'

Before Stein's arrival, Hamilton's ability to last 90 minutes was seriously in question. Now, he and the others around him were reinvigorated. On 25 May 1964, the day after that aforementioned play-off game, Tom Nicholson of the *Daily Record* wrote, 'There's not a brain in Scotland today quicker to spot the chink in an opposing defence than Hamilton, or quicker to exploit it with passes of such perfection that a goal seems an inevitable result. He's the sad example of the brilliant individualist who doesn't conform or refuses to fit into the pattern expected by clubs.'

That report more than hinted, in its conclusion, at the fairly wide knowledge in Edinburgh that Hamilton did not toe the line easily and that he had a lifestyle that would have made George Best seem like Mahatma Gandhi. Rumours of his excesses were rarely exaggerated. Jimmy O'Rourke, who was just emerging as one of Hibs' best players over the following decade, summed him up thus: 'Willie was paid on a Tuesday; by Wednesday he was skint, everything gone.' Indeed, at that juncture he already had a transfer request handed into the club which is typical of a player who feels the world just doesn't understand him. Stein therefore had on his hands a player with touches of genius who was already showing a fatal awareness of how to dig his own grave. But he needed him and was willing to go to extra lengths he would not consider for others. If he wanted to make sure he didn't go on a binge before an important game he would actually put Hamilton up at his own house on a Friday night so that he would have an alcohol-free zone for at least 24 hours. O'Rourke recalls seeing Stein giving Hamilton a 'bung' just inside the tunnel one day after training. 'There's a tenner,' he heard Stein saying. 'Now don't be asking me any more this week.' As Hamilton walked away and Stein saw that he had been observed and overheard, and knowing that the players would assume the tenner would end up in the hands of a bookie since Hamilton was an inveterate gambler, the manager simply said to them, 'He takes chances. And if you don't take chances during the week, how can you take chances for us on a Saturday?' That explanation of the therapeutic value of gambling might not have impressed a jury in a court case; it simply meant that Stein knew he had to keep this player in the mood, not by denying his habit but by feeding it. He was also painfully aware of what it was like to lose in a betting shop himself.

Hamilton was the difference between a skilled team and an exceptional one and was to the fore in the Summer Cup. In the first leg of the semi-final at Kilmarnock, which Hibs lost 4–3, it was Hamilton's influence that kept the scoreline within manageable proportions for the return leg, and he duly stole centre stage again with a performance that tantalised Kilmarnock, led by that fearsome duo Willie Waddell and Walter McCrae, into a 3–0 defeat. The *Sunday Post* on the following day, 31 May, did not need to seek too far for a headline and picked the statutory one: 'Stein's Stunners'. More lyrically, Hugh Taylor of the *Daily Record* stated on 1 June, 'The air's electric again at Easter Road,' and went on to assert that the golden era of the Famous Five had been recaptured: 'Confidently I predict that Hibs will once again be a power in the land, a team glittering with skill and power, tenacious, inspired by outstanding artists. Already Jock Stein, the Merlin of football, has proved he's got that certain something and the magic he wove at Dunfermline has rubbed off on Hibs.' Things seemed to be going so well that Hamilton withdrew his transfer request.

However, the momentum of this creative drive was halted by a plague. The typhoid outbreak in Aberdeen that summer prevented the final from being played until August. It was a final that was to go into three games. Hibs lost the first leg 2–3 after twice coming back. Then, before a 28,000 crowd at Easter Road, they won 2–1 after extra-time. Stein, with only minutes left, had switched winger Jim Scott with centre-forward Stan

Vincent, which led to Vincent's winner, and it sent Stein's stock soaring again. They lost the toss for venue for the third game but went to Pittodrie and played well above Aberdeen's standard, winning 3–1. It was Hibernian's first trophy in ten years.

On a personal level the word was now out that Stein could hack it anywhere. Of course the winning of this cup was not as notable as anything he had achieved at Dunfermline, but it was the continuation of triumph and the fact that in the capital city, where he received greater publicity, he had revived one of the great Scottish clubs and looked like restoring them to their proper status. Down in the English Midlands the chairman of Wolverhampton Wanderers was putting Stein's name in a notebook as his board began to assess the failing powers of their famous manager Stan Cullis. Over at Celtic Park, deep-rooted reservations were beginning to mellow.

An episode then occurred which might be called the Curious Case of the Veteran Goalkeeper. It involved the man who was to become the most famous of all Celtic goalkeepers, Ronnie Simpson. The player had started his senior career with Queen's Park in a match against Clyde at Hampden in June 1945, which I witnessed myself as a schoolboy. He seemed as sprightly when he finished his career as that day when he first appeared on the scene. He had gone south to Newcastle and returned to Scottish football with Hibs as a 30-year-old, which in those days even for a goalkeeper was considered in the veteran category. It was clear that Stein did not look too favourably on him. Simpson could only look back on his first dealings with the new manager with regret. 'I made the mistake of going in once and asking for more money. We had heard about what some of the Motherwell players were getting and although I was a part-timer working for an oil company I thought I deserved more. So I asked for a £2 rise. You would have thought I was threatening to rob him. His reaction was quite frankly astonishing. He just dismissed me. In fact he told me I wouldn't be picked in future, now that I was holding out for more cash. But hold out I did. No more pay from him and I wasn't going to play anyway. It was a massive fall-out. When I think back on it, I probably was just as perverse as I thought he was because I just turned up at Easter Road for the wages I was due and I didn't even train. I was being too stubborn, but it was a reaction to the way he had just dismissed me. And I had been told anyway that he was looking for another goalkeeper to sign. So I dug in. Every time I came in for the wages he would have a go at me, but he would also say, "You're being a silly laddy. We're offering facilities for you to keep fit and you're ignoring them. It won't do you any good." I suppose I should have listened to him, but I was so annoyed at the way I had been treated. I didn't play, I didn't train.

'Then one day he said that Berwick Rangers had put in an offer for me and that I had to meet their manager. The man came to see me one night and as we were sitting there talking over terms, which were much better than I was getting at Hibs, the phone rang. It was Jock. He told me to come back to the club right away to see him. I went back and he sat me down in the office and told me that an offer had come in from Celtic. Would I be interested in going there instead? Of course, you couldn't turn away from an offer like that. And that's what I decided to do. But it's what he then said to me that really shocked me and showed just how low the relationship had become: "If I discover that you have been 'tapped' I'll go all the way to see that you and the other club are punished for it." To this day I can't understand why he would have said such a thing, except that quite simply he didn't like me at the time. That was that. It couldn't have ended on a more sour note.' Simpson went on to say: 'Talking to supporters about my days with Jock, many of them brought up the subject of how shrewd it was to get me to Celtic before he went there, as if it had been part of a clever plan. Nothing could be further from the truth. I just have a quiet smile to myself when that theory surfaces.'

There was no sweet sorrow in the parting, but the dismissal of Simpson was an indication of a stern taskmaster who brooked no dissent nor tolerated anybody straying from his dictat. And the subject that riled Stein more than any was money. Anybody else's money. The Hibs players got to understand that eventually, but it was Willie Hamilton who decided to beard the lion in his den after hearing that the players were to be given a £50 bonus after a notable victory. The money hadn't been forthcoming for a couple of weeks, so the players, as a wind-up, kept on about how they needed a strong spokesman to take up their case. One morning Hamilton fell for the bait. 'Leave it to me,' he said. 'I'll sort it out with the boss.' Hibs forward Peter Cormack takes up the story. 'We let Willie climb up the stairs and when we heard him knocking on the door of the manager's office we crept up the stairs high enough so we could hear what went on. We heard Willie say to Jock, "Boss, are we no' supposed to get a £50 bonus for that game we won?" Now Jock must have been sitting back reading the racing news in the paper because all we heard then was a voice bawling, "If you're not down these effing stairs before I put down this effing paper I'll kick your arse right out of Easter Road!" We all dived back and got into the dressing-room before Willie. He just walked in with a smile and said, "There you are, lads, I've sorted it all out." You could have heard us laughing across in Fife.'

At about this time Bertie Peacock, in Northern Ireland, phoned Stein's home to speak to him but he was off somewhere watching football. He talked to his wife Jean and asked her how he was getting on. 'He's walking the floor at nights,' she starkly replied, giving more than a hint that although he was on a crest his obsession with the game was taking some toll on him physically even then. And this was at a time when he was at his most inventive and brimming with ideas, one of which seemed too far-fetched at the time, though he actually persuaded the club to fork out £12,000 – a tidy sum in those days, to say the least – to entice Real Madrid to come to Easter Road for a friendly. It was an audacious move which displayed Stein as showman and imaginative publiciser of football. It redirected media attention from the west and their preoccupation with the Old Firm, for nothing aggravated him more at any juncture of his life than being under-appreciated and largely ignored. The new season in the league had not started well for Hibs because they had lost to Hearts in the opening game, but their powers of recovery were evident, for while in the recent past such a start would have been a preface to a collapse, now they started to put some wins together. Then, on 7 October 1964, Real came to town.

The Spanish club had lost some of their power but none of their allure. The name still registered with the public like Pullman or Rolls-Royce. Some 32,000 turned up. The reality was that they were made to look like the star attraction upstaged by a pre-concert warm-up act. For although it was Ferenc Puskas and Francisco Gento in particular most people came to see, soon their eyes were being redirected to Willie Hamilton, who was carving open the Spaniards' defence and dictating the game in such a way that the match turned out to be one of his finest hours.

He was not alone though. Stein, almost akin to what he had done with teenager Alec Edwards in the famous Valencia match nearly two years earlier, fielded seventeen-year-old Peter Cormack, at the start of what turned out to be a splendid career, and warned his players not to sit back and admire these famous names around them but to work hard when Real had the ball. The crowd, which was not quite large enough to cover Real's guarantee, was not short-changed. The slight financial loss was to be a huge prestigious gain. The new teenager Cormack inspired thoughts of stardom by scoring with his first decent shot at goal in the twentieth minute. And when Zoco sent a neatly flighted free-kick by Pat Quinn behind his own goalkeeper for the second and final Hibs goal, Real became uncharacteristically desperate. Stein's side had claimed a notable scalp and added lustre to his reputation.

It was in the late autumn of that year that Wolves expressed an interest in him. Stan Cullis had been sacked brutally that September when the club was at the bottom of the First Division with only five points from eight matches. Insensitively, Wolves had sent him a letter with his name as manager scored out, demanding the return of his office keys. Andy Beattie, the former Scotland manager, was appointed caretaker coach, but the relegation threat still lingered. Hence their serious interest in Stein. By now Stein knew he had to make a move that hopefully would prevent him going south. He told me that he decided to play the Wolves card and let Celtic know what was on offer by contacting Bob Kelly, ostensibly to seek advice on the temptation being offered by Wolves. More was on his mind though. He, of course, made it clear that Wolves was an attractive option, but it was also clearly an overture. And it was then that the Celtic chairman responded in the way Stein felt he might: Kelly asked to meet him in the North British Hotel in Glasgow.

In a quiet hotel lounge in Dumfries many years later, when he was Scotland's manager, Stein spoke to me about those meetings with Celtic. We had been discussing his short period as manager of Leeds United when he was clearly intent on getting the Scotland job. The conversation was really about the importance of remaining focused and patient when he had some objective in mind; how to 'play the field' would be another way of putting it. I had been pointing out to him the scheming that went on in the background at that time at Leeds, and to which I will refer later. Suddenly he began to talk about his meetings with Bob Kelly as if they were examples of how well he kept his cool during proceedings which at first seemed to him surprisingly murky.

My recollection is that he described this with a certain ruefulness which suggested an initial disappointment at what was unfolding. He was very specific in what he said, as if I might have disbelieved what he was recounting. For they did not offer him the job on a plate. It came in three distinct parts. The first proposal by Kelly was that Stein be assistant manager to Sean Fallon. Even then, all those years later, he told me that as if he wanted any listener to share what clearly was his own incredulity at the time. He politely rejected such a notion. Here was a man who had exorcised the debilitating spirit of provincialism from one club and spectacularly revived the flagging fortunes of another and won trophies with both. Fallon was a popular and likeable figure but with no serious managerial experience. The offer could not be taken seriously. It suggests that the scepticism of the large Celtic support, which would not have trusted the board to put a pantomime horse together with any degree of success, was well founded. To be at the rear end of such a horse would really have been an indignity for Stein. He emphasised to me, though, that he was determined to hang on in there because he wanted the job badly. Nevertheless, he did underline to Kelly that he was interested in the Wolves offer. So they came back to him, but the second-phase offer was eminently rejectable as well. This time they suggested he become joint manager with Fallon. The rejection was swift. No three-legged race for a man who was the supreme individualist. Stein hardened his comments about his interest in Wolves, but at the same time he gave me the impression that he had known he was winning. Perhaps the gambler's instinct in him was guiding him.

So here were Kelly and the board, floundering around, trying to come to terms with what would be an historic breakthrough and finding it difficult to come out from behind their traditional mind-set. Stein made it clear to me that he had known what was going on in their minds although he obviously felt he did not need to specify to me exactly what that was. Others have, though. Billy McNeill put it bluntly: 'Let's not beat about the bush. They were reluctant to give him full control because he was a Protestant.' Even to this day it seems odd, given their much-trumpeted claim to be revolted by the idea of sectarianism. But Stein stood his ground and it was Kelly who blinked first. They were seeing the light. The chairman then made his epochal decision, unleashing a force that would completely change Scottish football. He offered Stein the post in full.

Stein's resolute stand in sticking to his demands when there was a possibility that he would put himself out of the reckoning in fact spurred the chairman into ditching his reluctance. But before any formal signing took place, the man still in charge of Hibs was in full Celtic spate and was about to make as influential a signing for them as the club had ever made, but by proxy. The man at the centre of it was Bertie Auld. 'It was a Friday night,' Auld recalled. 'Birmingham City were to play West Ham in the cup the following day. I got a phone call from a man called Dougie Hepburn. He just asked me if I would like to go back to Celtic Park. I said I would, of course, but I asked him who had told him to make the call. He hesitated a bit and then said Jock Stein. But I couldn't understand that because Jock was manager of Hibs and going well, as everybody knew. But I remember Dougie, who was a close friend of Jock, just saying, "Just you wait. Do you want to go back?" I was intrigued and, to be honest, excited.' Bertie played in the 4–2 defeat of Birmingham at West Ham the following day, 9 January 1965. Five days later he signed for Celtic, and the following Saturday he made his second debut for the club while Stein, who had engineered everything, was still plying his trade for Hibs.

It has to be recalled that Celtic that month had been beaten again in the Old Firm Ne'erday game and then had drawn with Clyde at Celtic Park in front of a rapidly dwindling crowd of 13,500. The chairman and the board of directors understood the rot had to be stopped, hence the ultimate acceptance of Stein. And without blinking, without any murmur of it publicly, the Hibs manager had already put into operation his plan for the future of Celtic by re-signing Auld, a man Bob Kelly had been glad to be rid of. It was an act of independence, for before they shook hands on it Stein made it clear he would be in control, absolute control, of all team matters. This might have been accepted at the time but, as I will reflect later, it did not mean that Kelly would give up the habits of a lifetime overnight, even though Stein was to write the following in his first article for the Celtic official match programme on 13 March 1965: 'I must make this point quite clear. I did not become Celtic's manager until after the directors and myself had come to an amicable agreement as to my position. I have been handed the reins of management and I alone have to do the driving. For the playing side, team picking, tactics, coaching and scouting I have full responsibility. I have been given great scope. The Board agreed that Celtic have to march with the times and I have been guaranteed expression of my ideas of what Celtic have to do to win the major honours of the game and at the same time to entertain the supporters and the public.' That seemed clear enough. But in fact the chairman was not to disengage himself altogether from team selection.

Hibs tried desperately to keep Stein. Chairman Willie Harrower even went to the family home to speak to Jean to persuade her to get Stein to change his mind, but she told Harrower that was impossible. She had known all along what he wanted and he had now achieved it. Peter Cormack admits that the players did not take it well. 'I was absolutely gutted,' he said. 'He was my father figure, my hero, and here he was just walking out on us. We were devastated. It finished us, you know. We had a great team and I think we could have won the double. But him leaving destroyed us. I have to admit that although nobody ranted and raved about it at the time, as I recall, we thought he had let us down badly. It was as if he had only been with us overnight. He went down in our estimation a wee bit. Of course, through time you don't feel as strongly, but at the time there was some bitterness in the dressing-room.'

The announcement on 31 January 1965 that Stein would leave his post and join Celtic at the end of the season, or before if a suitable replacement could be found, stunned not only Hibernian players and support. Had it been accompanied by a special appearance of Halley's comet along the firmament it could not have caused as great a stir throughout the land. Stein was not overjoyed that virtually every journal in the land heralded the fact that he would be the first Protestant manager of the club. But being a man of the world, and by now knowing the press inside out, it is not something that would really have surprised him. He tried to stress that it was simply a footballing matter but the media would have none of it as they firstly proclaimed it then hailed Bob Kelly for his decision, little realising he had tried to get Stein on a lesser ticket in the first place. The chairman, in a cute way, tried to play down the religious element by claiming that one out of four Celtic managers was Protestant, when in another sense there had only ever been three managers before Stein in the club's history. But the fact that Kelly had agonised over the decision for so long demonstrated that Stein's religion did weigh on him as a factor, although to his eventual credit not terminally.

Kelly also stated, 'He left Celtic because like everyone else he had to learn his trade, but there was always the understanding that he would return.' From all the evidence surrounding his original departure from Celtic Park there is nothing to justify even remotely this assertion that his return was part of a grand strategy. Indeed, the Stein family strongly refute it. Stein had unambiguously told his wife when he left Parkhead that it was tacitly understood he could rise no further within the club and that Sean Fallon would be the next manager. What he had achieved was to turn Celtic's thinking upside down by dint of his own remarkable achievements.

Stein left Hibs in robust health, near the top of the league, in the first week of March, once a deal had been concluded to bring Bob Shankly, a very close friend who was to be in the terrible car crash with him, from Dundee to Easter Road. Stein's last task as Hibs' manager was to guide the team to a 2–1 Scottish Cup victory over Rangers – the third time Hibs had beaten them in 1964/65 and Rangers' first defeat in the competition in 22 matches – in front of a crowd of 47,363 to put Hibs into the semi-final. It was his 50th game with the club. He entered Celtic Park to start his new career on 9 March. His relationship with Hibs had been no more than a dalliance – a brilliant one for all that, but no more. Now he was to get what he had wanted all along. Hibs tried to make light of it but they were shocked. They were not to win the cup and were beaten in the semi-final by Dunfermline, who then had to face Celtic and Stein. The league slipped away as well. But he had transformed them, made them proud again, put them up as contenders. Still, Stein himself admitted later, 'Leaving Hibs at that time was probably my most embarrassing experience in football.'

On the evening of that 31 January announcement, Ronnie Simpson, now with Celtic, turned on his television and heard the news. He turned to his wife, his memory of the conflict with Stein still fresh in the mind, and said with a sinking feeling, 'Pack the bags, dear, I think we'll be on our way out again.' Never has a lady's refusal to jump to her husband's command paid such handsome dividends.

CHAPTER TEN
THE RETURN

From the high vantage point of the press-box of the old Celtic Park of 1965 you could see for miles. The scene was not one of grandeur. It was the east end of an industrial city whose tenements clustered around the ground like a visible reminder of the club's roots and its association with the working class, the disadvantaged and the exiled, many of whom had settled there, well within earshot of the crowds who turned up faithfully at Parkhead at that time despite a period that could be described as the club's ice age. On the north side of the ground, always visible and sometimes even considered a counter attraction by the cynics who were pulverising Celtic for their current performances, was Janefield Cemetery. The disjointed, irregular tombstones there could look, in the dim light of winter, more like a spectral audience quite unmoved by the passions emanating from that special shed on the other side of the street from the graveyard called, affectionately, 'The Jungle'.

Even on a bright day the cemetery seemed to have some conjunction with the events on the field, as it was beginning to dawn on their more discerning supporters by the end of 1964 that the club was showing signs of the setting in of rigor mortis. Hugh Taylor, one of Scotland's most respected journalists at the time, wrote in the *Daily Record* of Monday, 18 January 1965, 'Like the Parkhead fans I'm tired of hearing about Celtic's potential, Celtic's bad luck, Celtic's missed chances … All right, I agree bouncy Celtic, non-stop Celtic, fiery Celtic can be an exciting, even an exhilarating team. But to me they're Bing singing "Please", a wall-of-death showground rider, a flip in a Tiger Moth – a pleasant and often exciting echo of the past.' And he concluded, 'I have come to the conclusion that one of the main reasons for Celtic's decline since they last won a major honour – in 1957 – is not so much the lack of the right players as their stubborn refusal to march with the times and incorporate ideas from abroad.'

Billy McNeill, who would assuredly have left the club had it carried on with its old ways, heard the news of Stein's appointment in his car radio and felt genuinely surprised. 'I thought nothing was going to change, so when I heard that I got a tremendous lift. To be honest, everything was a joke at Parkhead. We did nothing that you could describe as proper planning or preparation. We just went out and played. We didn't know any different. We thought all clubs did what we did, but that wasn't the case. Since I had known Jock when he was a youth coach I knew right away that times would be different.'

There was nothing, in truth, dramatic about his first day in charge. He gathered the players together and talked to them briefly and calmly about how he expected them to work hard for the club, as he would himself. They had mentally battened down the hatches, expecting a gale to blow through. Instead, the words were calm and measured. He did not indulge in any dramatics, which might have been tempting considering he was about as close to enacting the rescue of a ship heading for the rocks as you could get on dry land. Neither did he lay out any detailed plans, there and then; he was simply intent on making his presence felt. On that first day, as the players were shuffling out of the dressing-room at the end of his address to them, he shouted at Ronnie Simpson and asked him to stay behind for a moment. When they were on their own he told him to forget anything that had happened between them in the past and that they would be starting out anew with each other. Simpson, however, was never wholly convinced that they were about to become bosom pals. 'I don't think he ever got over the Hibs relationship. It wasn't that I felt that we would have a hard time with each other. It's just that I felt that we never quite got on together, whatever I would do on the park. I did feel uneasy about the future.'

In his first match in charge of the club, on 10 March 1965, just 24 hours after taking over, Celtic had to travel to Airdrie for an awkward league game, but his players responded to this honeymoon period, as many do under new management, and saw the Lanarkshire side off easily, 6–0, Bertie Auld scoring five including two penalties. But it was clear, both in the way Celtic were playing and in the response of the crowd, that something much deeper was being held in reserve for the Scottish Cup, since the league was beyond them. They lost their next game three days later to St Johnstone at Parkhead by a single goal in front of only 18,000. In the next game at home they lost again, agonisingly for Stein 4–2 to Hibernian, watched by only 19,000. His former Edinburgh players took special pleasure out of that. Then Celtic were destroyed 6–2 by Falkirk at Brockville, and in the last home game in front of only 11,500 Partick beat them 2–1. The league was a hardship that had to be borne bravely; in the meantime, the Scottish Cup was the goal. And it was that which clearly wakened the Celtic community.

Celtic's surge in the competition could be largely attributed to the announcement of Stein's inevitable arrival. Between 6 February and 6 March they had disposed of St Mirren, Queen's Park and Kilmarnock, and having had the way paved for him, on 27 March Stein returned to Hampden Park. Their opponents in the cup semi-final, Motherwell, were blessed with some of the most outstanding footballers of the day. Bert McCann, Joe McBride and Willie Hunter could play classy football, especially the latter, whose slight frame only made him look more evasive and inventive on the ball. Stein prepared for that match in a way few had experienced before.

The changes had already gripped the imagination of the players, especially when one day Stein appeared like a stern headmaster in front of them, shifting markers on a magnetic board to talk about tactics. Celtic defender John Clark felt as if he was going back to school. 'We never had tactic talks of any kind before,' he said. 'But now here he was illustrating moves on a board, breaking a game down, showing you what you had to do over a certain area and at the same time analysing the opposition, showing us what they would do. But the interesting thing was that he hardly ever repeated himself. You had to watch and listen very closely to what he was saying and take it in. He explained, quite simply, that if you made mistakes and committed errors in a game and went against instructions it showed you weren't interested or that you weren't thinking enough about your game and that you were no use to him. I know that sounds a bit brutal, but you had to listen carefully, follow his instructions, or else you could be in for a tough time with him.'

Knowing that he had untapped talent which, if properly organised and exploited, could produce a significantly better side than Celtic was, Stein put the early emphasis on developing an *esprit de corps*. His tracksuited presence was as much of a shock to the players as it had been at Easter Road, but they relished his presence in the middle of the training ground, cajoling, encouraging, swearing, bantering and making sure that a new intimacy was being developed between manager and player that would permeate their whole existence. They probably did not realise at the time just how ubiquitous his influence would be on their lifestyles, but they devoured his new approach like novitiates of a new calling.

One of the reasons the players warmed to him so quickly is that several had known him in his days as the reserve coach. He had helped develop most of them in their infancy with the club. But almost as if it was part of his natural inclination to scheme things out in advance, it only took him a couple of days to let the players know that times had changed and that the McGrory days were emphatically over. In that very first week of his return the players received their wage slips for that period and felt they had been short-changed. They had confidently expected their bonuses for the two most recent Scottish Cup wins against Queen's Park and Kilmarnock, but what they were reading was only one bonus payment. They were angry and asked Billy McNeill as captain to make representations. He did. Shortly after he returned to the dressing-room after delivering the request the door was abruptly kicked open and in Stein charged. 'You've got what you deserved!' he barked. 'You were expected to beat Queen's Park. You weren't expected to beat Kilmarnock. That's what you're due. One bonus!'

It wasn't just a case of an abrupt end to what might laughingly have been called a brief negotiation, it was more a highly significant drawing of a line between the previous Stein, with whom many of them had in the past shared a bag of greasy chips on the way back from training, and the new figure who now stood dramatically in their midst as the commander-in-chief who could swoop threateningly among them. That day he initiated a dramatic habit they were to witness often: the door being kicked open. If it did not sink in then and there with some of them, it certainly was not much longer before they all realised Stein would play the bonus system as if like an angler casting his fly invitingly over teeming waters. But if it brought them up short at the time, it did not depress them, as testified by the manner in which they approached the Scottish Cup semi-final.

It took two games to dispose of Motherwell, though. In the first game Celtic came from behind twice to put the game into a replay. It was mooted believably then that pre-Stein Celtic might have folded and lost the day. In the second game, as if they had simply been doing a recce for a demolition job in the first one, they trampled all over Motherwell and won 3–0. A final against the side that had made his managerial name beckoned.

Billy McNeill recalled the mood that was created for Stein's unique reunion with Dunfermline, who had beaten Hibernian in their semi-final. 'He tried to relax us. We didn't go into it as if the end of the world was nigh. Although not having won anything for so long you would have imagined that's how we might have felt. No, he took us to a hotel in Largs – not the traditional base of Seamill – and the whole time we were there over a couple of days it was as if we were on holiday. I just remember it as a fun time. The weather was great and that added to it. And that's when the solo schools started. We became great card players throughout all the time we were under Jock. It just made us relax. They were really competitive card games, but I think it was a good bonding exercise. Anyway, he made the training so enjoyable. I think he knew the whole club was in depression and that he had to make us see a challenge differently. Of course he analysed the opposition, but he was really trying to make us forget just how much this meant to everybody. We went to Hampden feeling good within ourselves.'

Some 108,800 fitted neatly into the stadium on 24 April. Stein's team for his first Celtic final was John Fallon, Ian Young, Tommy Gemmell, Bobby Murdoch, Billy McNeill, John Clark, Stevie Chalmers, Charlie Gallagher, John Hughes, Bobby Lennox and Bertie Auld; seven of these men were to play in Lisbon two years later. Celtic, with a strong wind at their backs, soon began to pummel the Fifers' defence and just beyond the half-hour they equalised Melrose's opener for Dunfermline with what Jack Harkness of the *Sunday Post* described as 'probably the strangest goal ever scored at Hampden'. It occurred when a fierce shot by Charlie Gallagher from 30 yards struck the Dunfermline crossbar and soared straight up heavenwards. Almost in agonising slow-motion it plummeted earthwards again, and waiting for it was one Bertie Auld. Auld, with his black mop of hair, his deceptively casual walk, his incisive bursts, his testing of referees' nerve and degree of tolerance, his jaunty acceptance of popularity and his apparent disregard for the moral certitude of chairman Kelly, was one of the most distinctive players Stein ever fielded. He stepped forward at that moment and among taller players bravely planted his head on the descending ball. It entered the net to a raucous eruption from the Celtic support.

The sense of relief they felt came to a shuddering halt just a minute from half-time when a goal came that bore traces of the Dunfermline self-confidence induced by Stein when he had been at East End Park. Melrose took a free-kick twenty yards out and touched it sideways to John McLaughlin who smote it directly into the net with a swerving shot that Fallon in goal could not touch. Celtic were behind again. Bobby Lennox did not feel wholly despondent, though. 'It was a quiet dressing-room at half-time,' he recalled. 'I think he realised that he had only had us for a couple of months or so and that if he lost his temper or bawled and shouted it might have tensed us up too much. I know you might think all managers get beefed into teams when they slip up, but sometimes it just doesn't work, and that day

Jock was more the big friendly bear. Another time, another occasion, he might have savaged us.'

Auld reacted the way Stein thought he might. Six minutes after the interval he slipped a ball to Lennox on the left, took the return pass and skimmed the ball beyond the grasp of Jim Herriot in goal. Twice behind, twice recovered, even the neutral observer was now expecting something of a special climax. Up in the press-box they felt in their bones that something special was happening in the frenetic Hampden atmosphere. They waited, and it came. Celtic's captain, Billy McNeill, a Bellshill boy who had played for the same Blantyre Vics club as Stein before him, had an assurance and stature that had suggested leadership to the beholder even when he was a teenager. Tall and handsome, with a bold, straight-backed, imperious stride, his commanding presence was topped up by a classic heading ability which time after time was to rev up the Stein juggernaut. Up he ran nine minutes from time to take up position in the penalty area. Gallagher's corner-kick swung outwards and tempted Herriot from goal like a fish to the hook. McNeill, taking advantage of the slight hesitation of the Pars defence which assumed it was a keeper's ball, rose majestically and with the absolute certainty of success rammed the ball into the net off his forehead.

There was no way back for Dunfermline. Hampden resounded to a jubilation that continued up to and well beyond the final whistle. Jack Harkness, writing in the *Sunday Post*, captured the fervour and significance. 'No matter how close you scan that same history book, you won't find a greater Celtic story than their winning of this tremendous final. To a whole generation who have wondered what their fathers and their grandfathers meant when they raved about "traditional Celtic spirit", this game supplied the answer. And surely it was worth waiting for. Yes, even 11 long years.'

We can see clearly now that this was no ordinary final. It demonstrated that the collusion between Stein's modernism and Celtic's historical self-belief, which had admittedly lapsed into self-delusion, could yet have a dynamic effect on Scottish football. Nobody assessing that final, even at the time, had any doubts that something special had happened before their very eyes. And however relaxed Stein's approach had been to the final it is clear he regarded the winning of the cup as absolutely crucial to kick-starting a new era. Had they failed, the Celtic story might have been entirely changed. As he himself was to say many years later, 'It wouldn't have gone as well for Celtic had they not won this game.'

Their celebrations were held in the Central Hotel in Glasgow, and before they entered the building Stein handed the cup to Jimmy Gribben to lead the way in. Perhaps the Celtic support, watching this, failed to grasp either the significance of that special display of affection and gratitude or even the identity of the largely anonymous man responsible for breathing new life into Stein fourteen years earlier.

Although he was a non-drinker, Stein could nevertheless be the life and soul of a party when he was in the mood. He liked to have friends around him with whom to joke and chatter, to let off steam, and he'd stay up all night if he could, for too often sleep was a trial and tribulation for him. He would also delight in gently chastising others for their drinking or show mock horror at their excesses – of which there were many – as others joined him to party during his long sequence of triumphs. They would also repair occasionally from Hampden just over the hill to the Marie Stuart Hotel, owned by a fervent Celtic supporter and solid personal friend of Stein, Jack Flynn. There they would enjoy, above all, the sing-song.

Give him an invitation to exercise the vocal cords and present him with a mike and Stein would be transported, although as an individualist by nature he would have detested karaoke as much as robotic football. He liked to croon as if he was an untapped talent striving to rise from the miners' welfare soirée level of Burnbank. He was a working-man's club singer with all the gallusness that entailed. But the singing would erupt without much prompting, no matter where he was, and sometimes while waiting for an interview at Celtic Park you heard him before you saw him as some ballad came wafting from the dressing-room after a post-training shower. According to his friends, his favourite song at club celebrations was 'Auld Scots Mother Mine', a Victorian music-hall ditty that can either have you weak at the knees with emotion or send you screaming from the room, depending on how well it is performed. He normally got pass marks.

It is an abiding memory of mine to have been outside on the lawn of a hotel in Rotorua, New Zealand, in 1982, surrounded on all sides by geysers emitting their sulphuric smells, waiting for Jock Stein to come to a function. Beside me were some Maori 'entertainment warriors' limbering up and practising for their haka, which they were to put on as part of a greeting for us and other football officials. From Stein's bedroom window suddenly floated the throaty tones of 'My Way'. The Maoris stopped what they were doing and listened. He went through the whole song as if he was performing solo at the miner's welfare. When silence fell, a polite applause broke out among the decoratively clad performers. I was never sure whether it was mock appreciation or genuine acknowledgement of a plucky talent. For that reason I didn't have the nerve to tell him, when eventually he appeared, that he had just halted Maori culture in full spate. Let us just say he was better at Sinatra than at Harry Lauder.

That cup victory night in April 1965 would have seen his larynx well exercised, whether from the depths of lachrymose Scottish sentiment or by the sophistication of a hit-parade ballad. Stein had now grabbed the microphone in celebration, spotlight directly on him, and his singing would have a great significance for the huge Celtic audience around the land, already screaming for an encore.

CHAPTER ELEVEN
THE GREAT DIVIDE

It was a Parkhead duet, though, that was touching the high notes. It was two men singing in apparent unison that fascinated the country – chairman and manager. For the winning of the cup was also put down to the sagacity of Bob Kelly, who had opened the door for new ways to be established and had given a dynamic young manager his head. The Kelly–Stein relationship was to turn out to be as potent as any other before or since in British football. There was nothing subtle in how Stein interpreted the chairman's role. He wanted Kelly to give him the nod to whatever he wanted. It was as simple as that. Almost always that happened. There had been an early indication of clinging to habit when Kelly had questioned Stein on his choice of Bobby Murdoch as a midfield player for the final against Dunfermline, for in the chairman's opinion Murdoch was much better as a forward. But Stein decided not to make some grand issue of this and deftly side-stepped a major confrontation by simply advising the chairman that all would work out to plan. And of course it did. That did not bring interference to an end, as we shall see, but it was not uppermost in the manager's mind. He was looking to take impetus from his first success and convert Celtic from being recognised as a good, spirited cup side into a force which would replace Rangers as the dominant team in Scottish football by winning league championships. He made that clear to his assistant Sean Fallon almost from the outset. 'It was Rangers he was after,' Fallon confirmed. 'It was all very well us winning a cup here and there. We had to take the league. That was the top priority. We hadn't done so for twelve years and he would talk about how we had to have more steel in our play and that we had to stand up to the physical power of Rangers better. But any game against them was to be like life or death. My God, it was so different.'

But if, after the pleasant way he had prepared for the Scottish Cup final, the players had felt that Stein had inched his way into the club with catlike tread and possessed only a cuddly image, they were to see another side four days after their cup victory when they went to play Dunfermline in a league game and were trounced 5–1. He had made certain changes to the side, but they were tinkerings. There was nothing wholesale about it. The players thought that as it was the last league game of the season it would matter little. But, as Bobby Lennox pointed out, they were in for a rude awakening. 'In all my time in football with Jock or with anybody else I have never experienced the pasting he gave us that day. The walls of the stadium must have been shaking. I certainly was. He called us all the names of the day and even though I tried to bow the head to sort of keep out of the way you could see the shock in all the faces around me. He just kept blasting us, and he seemed to get bigger as he did it. I could see the big frame swinging his arms and cursing and swearing. It was terrifying. He went through everybody, one by one. Nobody was missed out. Can you imagine him looming over you, bawling? Then I made a big mistake. He took a breath and I thought he had finished. I stood up and went to walk towards the showers. "Hey, you! Sit on your arse! I'm no' finished yet!" And that just started another tirade. We were like jelly. I don't care what anybody says, while we deserved a roasting I think the big man had the perfect excuse that day to show us what he was made of. Rub this giant the wrong way and you would be demolished. That was the bottom line. We discovered that day that Jock Stein ruled by fear.'

Ronnie Simpson, still slightly apprehensive about how his relationship with the manager would develop, had reservations about Stein's idiosyncrasies. 'At training you had to do what he said. The one thing he hated was anybody trying anything that he hadn't thought out in advance. If anybody tried some tricky thing with the ball, maybe a dummy or flicking it through somebody's legs, or anything unusual, he would shout out, "Hey, you! You're no' good enough to do things like that. Just you keep it simple. Keep it simple."' He created a barrier between his relationship with players and his family life, which was now based on the south side of Glasgow, but in truth, while he was devoted to them, his preoccupation with his job meant he lived another life constantly in parallel with that. He was fortunate to have a wife, son and daughter who realised they were living with a man whose addiction to the game was something they could not compete with. He would virtually open up Celtic Park first thing in the morning, so impatient was he to see the night through and get back to the tracksuit. Many a person phoning just after eight o'clock in the morning, on perhaps some trivial matter, would find themselves dealing with Stein at the other end of the line. His relaxation habits had not altered from his Burnbank days, though. He had loved and was skilled at bowls from his day as a youth in the mines and turned his hand to it whenever he could. More importantly, he had not lost his taste for a punt on the horses and he and Fallon would travel to Ayr races regularly where some weighty bets would be placed, the size of which would stagger his assistant. The winning or losing certainly did not affect his clear-headed approach to his job and the sound of hooves on the turf certainly allowed him to let off steam and undoubtedly relieved him of some tension. Certainly, from time to time, it lightened his wallet as well as his mood.

Now that he was getting more publicity because of his position with Celtic, he liked to be seen at all kinds of football matches, not just to scout but to show that he was constantly on top of his task. He was renowned for his sudden calls on people to travel with him in his car to go and watch games. Sean Fallon was virtually his constant companion, but he would also pull in friends from outside the club, like Tony Queen and Tony McGuinness, for he not only liked them as company but also seemed not to mind frightening the living daylights out of them with what can only politely be called his mercurial driving skills. When you saw a large Mercedes swerving into a car park practically on two wheels, the door didn't need to open for you to know it was Jock Stein behind the wheel. Liverpool one night, Aberdeen the next, back to Manchester the following night, then over to Edinburgh, all to watch matches. That would not be an untypical week for him; he clocked up thousands of miles, particularly on that stretch of road which crossed the border to the south and on which his career took a tragic turn. It was during these journeys that Stein would speak to people about the game and reveal his encyclopaedic knowledge of the current football scene. On one of those journeys, Tony Queen heard him analyse the Rangers team as if he were their manager. 'I just sat there as the Big Barra headed south, my heart in my mouth at the speed he was driving, and he went right through the Rangers team, player by player – what they did, what they couldn't do, their strengths and weaknesses, how they had scored the goals in their last few games. He couldn't have been at any of these games but he seemed to know everything that was going on. He had eyes in the back of his head, he had spies, he had gossipers, he just drew on everybody. I honestly think in that first few years at Celtic Park he knew Rangers better than they knew themselves.'

A toughening-up process was now going on at Celtic Park which even the most reluctant player, with all his reservations about Stein's style and method and the stern imposing of his personality on others, would accept eagerly if it brought success. And there was one match coming up only three months into the new season that would perhaps be the most telling proving-ground for the early build-up of the Stein armament to rid the club of its soft underbelly. But before then he had to look hard at how he could get the best out of what he had available to him. In the close season he made his sole major signing by acquiring Joe McBride from Motherwell for £22,000, whom he greatly admired for his toughness and his killer instinct around the goalmouth. He had plagued Celtic with his goals in the semi-final of the Scottish Cup, and as the player was a Celtic man at heart Stein felt he would be of great benefit. So he proved: he scored 43 goals in 1965/66.

Life did not run smoothly, though. In the first Old Firm game of the season at Ibrox on 18 September 1965 they lost 2–1. The game itself was something of a re-run of many previous encounters, with Celtic having much of the play but being repulsed, especially in the later stages, by a steady Rangers defence in which Ritchie in goal and McKinnon at centre-half were outstanding. Jim Forrest at centre-forward, who as one of the fastest players in the Scottish game normally gave Billy McNeill a torrid time, scored the first goal after only seven minutes. John Hughes equalised from the penalty spot in the eighteenth minute, but just two minutes later Rangers were awarded a penalty from which George McLean scored the winning goal. The fact that it seemed as if nothing had much changed in the footballing world, that Rangers still seemed to be Celtic's nemesis, cloaked the fact that Celtic in that match had shown much more muscle and resilience and with a little luck might have won the game, as McNeill had been injured and they had had to rearrange their side. The warning signs were there for Rangers. But in fact, outwith the Celtic community itself and some discerning journalists, few noticed. The *Glasgow Herald*'s reporter significantly noted of that game, 'The cheer which erupted from the terracing at Rangers' end of Ibrox Stadium was as much one of relief as of joy, for in the last ten minutes of the game it was touch and go whether Rangers would be able to hold on to their narrow lead.' The fact that Celtic then ran up sixteen goals in their next three league games might also have confirmed the sceptical view that indeed not much had changed, since they seemed to play their swashbuckling football successfully at will, as they always had, except when it mattered against their great rivals.

Stein knew that the quickest revenge he could seek would be in the League Cup final, if he could steer the club to Hampden for that in October. But they stumbled their way through the competition. They were beaten in two group matches in the first week, 1–2 away to Dundee United and, more surprisingly, 0–2 at home to Dundee. They then slaughtered Raith Rovers in the two quarter-final games, scoring twelve goals to their one, which set up a semi-final against his former club Hibernian, which they won 4–0 in a replay after scoring in the last second of the first game to equalise. This set up Stein's first major cup final against the great rivals. To this day the game is mulled over by punters on both sides of the great divide as one of the most controversial.

The *Glasgow Herald* chose to headline its main report of the 23 October final 'League Cup Final an Orgy of Crudeness'. Not pulling any punches, the correspondent, Raymond Jacobs, wrote, 'The physical aspect of the match must take precedence over any other because that is what the match was all about. There was only a passing nod to the most elementary skills of the game, and that came largely from Rangers. Power, stamina and scarcely containable vigour rode roughshod over any consideration of disciplined and thoughtful football. Some of the tackles were intimidating. Man went for man. Tripping, kicking, hacking and jersey-pulling were rife. How can Scottish football raise its hands piously in horror against the same gambits of continental players when the two leading teams in the country indulge in the orgy of crudeness which made this so unpalatable a spectacle?' Jacobs, of course, was not alone in assessing the match as brutal.

So what lay behind it? Stein did. He had taken over a team most of whose players in recent times had just seemed to roll over on their backs and surrender when Rangers so much as frowned at them. He was painfully aware of that and he was determined it was not going to happen this time. He knew, too, that there were many around ready to debunk what they saw as a developing myth that he was almost invincible when it came to taking part in a final and winning a trophy he was after for the first time as a manager. The media went into a feeding frenzy over such issues in the days before the final. As the tribal drums began to beat around the land, Billy McNeill understood that there was no way players on either side could be insulated from this. 'That was one of the worst finals I have ever played in,' he said. 'It was so tense it was frightening. Both sides were so scared of losing. You don't like to lose to Rangers at the best of times, but on this occasion, Jock's first major Old Firm final, Rangers wanting to slap him down so early in his career, his newfound reputation on the line, all that got through to the players. We couldn't avoid it. So while the Dunfermline Scottish Cup final preparation was idyllic, this was the exact opposite.'

Celtic retired to their traditional base of Seamill for a three-day preparation. It was intense and largely humourless compared to their Largs preparation for the Scottish Cup final. The players tiptoed around a tense and tetchy manager who looked as if he could explode at the slightest interruption of his well-laid-out plans. He prowled around the hotel like a captive lion ready to bolt at the opening of the cage. This was different, as the players could see. McNeill was watching a man embarking on a mission. 'I've had a good laugh at all those people who were taken in by Jock when he used to say, po-faced, that a game against Rangers was just another game, that all you got was the winning of points or a cup, as you would against any other club. That is a load of bloody nonsense. A game against them was the game. It was the be-all and the end-all. Outside of winning the European Cup, beating them was the greatest thing in his life. He lived for it. It meant the world to him.'

Thus McNeill identified that inner drive which propelled Stein throughout his professional life as a manager. The core of it was his attitude to Rangers. It is my view that it supplied a basic drive to everything he did in football. It was that element of his roots that he converted into a crusade to weaken Rangers and humiliate them whenever he could. Harsh though it may be to those who wish to paint a more benign picture, from my own observations it struck me that you could barely avoid using the word 'hate' when it came to making a judgement on how Jock Stein regarded Rangers. I often heard him talking about that club with undisguised distaste. McNeill, though, didn't go quite that far. 'I wouldn't quite describe it that way,' he said. 'I think what he wanted to do was to prove to the Celtic support that although he had been seen as a Rangers supporter in his youth and that his family were all on that side, he could go out there and put all that behind him. And he wanted to show the Rangers supporters, who kept on about what he had been in his early years, that all that was dead and buried. That's what had him keyed up for these games.' I think McNeill is accurate enough in this analysis, but perhaps more than diplomatic in his conclusion. One of the Lisbon Lions who was yet to figure in Stein's plans, Jim Craig, was sharper in his view. 'He detested Rangers,' he said. 'Hatred is not an inappropriate word. And you know, I don't think he would have been as obsessed about beating them had he been brought up as a kid on the Celtic side. It was because he had crossed over that made him so intense about that. There's no doubt in my mind that he was particularly ruthless when it came to taking them on.'

He was to demonstrate that in this pivotal match. It is the attitude and spirit Stein engendered in the build-up which set a light to this final. As a Celtic director was to say aggressively about the new Celtic Stein was commanding, 'We will meet fire with fire.' No wonder, then, that the late Alec Cameron, then of the *Scottish Daily Mail*, was prompted to say to me, 'We should have gone to that match wearing tin-helmets.'

The crowd of 107,600 that day seemed to be in particularly fine fettle for bouts of rancorous tauntings. The Queen and the Pope's reputations were never enhanced on these occasions, if you were to listen to the competing serenades of one side of Hampden Park against the other. It was as if Burns' lines '. . . a child might understand / The De'il had business on his hand' could have applied then as it did to a quivering Tam O'Shanter. For something special seemed afoot. And the evidence for that was clear shortly after the referee started the match. No matter which player you talk to about that game, they all talk with clarity about 'The Tackle' as if they had witnessed an assassination. It came only a minute into the game, on Rangers' left touchline. 'Ian Young clattered Willie Johnston,' McNeill recalled. 'He went down as if he wasn't going to get back up again. He got booked for it and so did Johnston, for retaliation, but the Rangers winger wasn't the same for the rest of the game. Big Jock had identified Johnston as a main threat to us and he told Young that his first tackle had to really matter. And he told him in no uncertain manner. Ian just went out and walloped him.'

Stein had wound up his players to take on Rangers physically, and at least one of them was willing to push the instructions to the limit, as Young instantly did. Bertie Auld, who was never a Good Samaritan on the park but essentially conveyed to the others the ideal spirit of engagement the team needed, also knew that before the game his boss was setting a specific agenda. 'Jock changed our approach dramatically simply by giving us licence to mix it. He always said of the first fifty-fifty ball, "Win it!" In other words, do what it takes to get that ball. He never said specifically to go out and kick people, but to give 100 per cent to the team, just as guys like John Greig were doing on the other side.' But when it came to Johnston, as John Fallon recalled, backing up McNeill's recollection, he might have been more specific. 'I recall Jock telling Ian Young, "Sort Johnston out first chance you get." Now that doesn't mean he told him to go out and foul the man and put him out of the game, but it does mean Ian was to show him who was boss from the start. Funny thing is, he gave Ian stick for that tackle afterwards and said he was stupid to do what he did to get himself booked so early. But his philosophy, even from the early days, about being sent off for something was quite simple: "If we're going to be reduced to ten men then make sure they're going to end up the same way." He never encouraged us to go out of our way looking for trouble. But what he meant was that if you were going to be sent off then it had to be for something that would put your opponent out of the game as well.'

The Young tackle might have been brutal and blatantly unscrupulous in its intent, but it sent out a message that Stein's side were not going to be messed about. As a warm-up act for the battle to come it followed in the good old Scottish tradition of pre-battle showdowns as set by Bruce when he flattened De Bohun before the hostilities commenced on Bannockburn field. Mayhem did not immediately follow, but in the next twenty minutes Rangers centre-half Ronnie McKinnon, Murdoch and Jimmy Johnstone were all booked for clashes that might have produced red cards had they existed in those days. It was going the way Stein thought it might, for Rangers were unsettled by this new, aggressive side; even the normally well-composed striker Jim Forrest, who was the bane of Celtic, had missed two early snips as a result of the sheer increase in tension.

The outcome hinged on two penalties awarded to Celtic. The first was an acute embarrassment for one player. In the eighteenth minute, Ronnie McKinnon, who had been having an excellent season for Rangers, inexplicably lifted a hand above his head and slapped at a ball coming from a John Clark free-kick, just inside the penalty area. His stunned side watched as John Hughes tucked away the penalty. Nobody could have budgeted for that freakish incident, but on the other hand, if a side has lost its accustomed equilibrium, as Rangers apparently had, then anything can happen under pressure. Celtic's second penalty, ten minutes later, is still contested to this day. Provan, finding Celtic's Jimmy Johnstone tricky and evasive, tracked him into the box and tackled him from behind. The winger went down, and despite the Rangers protestations that it had been a fair tackle, referee Hugh Phillips awarded a spot-kick from which Hughes scored again. This caused fury among the Rangers players, but instead of keeping their cool thereafter they began to lose their shape and relied too much on the individual heroics of the captain, John Greig, to pull them together. Yet they could do little against a Celtic side which allowed them a lot of possession but, playing to instructions, held their line, with John Clark outstanding in the sweeping role. Rangers did notch a goal, but it was scored by Celtic's Ian Young when he deflected a Henderson cross past Ronnie Simpson six minutes from the end. It was too late for them. Stein had won the cup he had personally coveted more than any other because he had taken it from Rangers. This victory was deeply personal to him, as his players clearly witnessed: his greeting of them in the dressing-room afterwards was of an order of jubilation they hadn't experienced before.

When Celtic paraded with the cup after the presentation, a few thousand Rangers supporters invaded the field from their end and looked as if they would attack the players. This scandalous intrusion was simply a precursor to years of Old Firm controversies through which Stein would steer his players and supporters with a resolution no Celtic manager before had mustered. He was also riled by press reports that the second penalty was 'soft', or not one at all. Raymond Jacobs in the *Glasgow Herald*, in trying to make sense of Rangers' anger at the referee's decision, pointed out, 'when Celtic were given their second penalty award, the congratulations bestowed upon one another by McBride and Johnstone were not only provocative but implied the referee had been cleverly deceived'. That sort of interpretation, accurate or not, enraged Stein, as did many other comments about that game. And so began his long love/hate relationship with the media.

As a player with the club he had quickly become imbued by the same sense of commitment that a boy brought up from the cradle as a Celtic supporter would display. Now, as a manager, he was adding to it his own personal conviction, which was that of the apostate suddenly seeing the world from the other side of the barricades. In that respect he developed a zealotry which sometimes exceeded the bounds of common sense. He was becoming a walking seismometer of perceived media bias, some of it real, a lot imagined.

He had still been at the club as reserve coach when Celtic had famously beaten Rangers 7–1 in the 1957 Scottish League Cup final. He knew all about the fact that it was a game which, in an age of increasing technological advancement in broadcasting, ought to have been treated with sacrilegious care for posterity. But it never was. When told that the second-half destruction of Rangers had mysteriously disappeared and could not be transmitted, Celtic were firstly bemused then enraged. The game had been covered by the BBC; it had been made in the old-fashioned telerecording manner in which a camera in front of a television screen filmed the action off the tube. But at half-time the technician in London in charge of the operation went for a cup of tea, turning the camera off and placing a dust cover over the lens; when he came back and turned on the camera again, he forgot to take off the dust cover. The consequence was that the famous second-half rout of Rangers was never recorded and never aired on public television. A dolt, not a bigot, did that, but Celtic understandably treated the matter as if it were a crime. It seemed to be the absolute proof of anti-Celtic bias.

All this happened long before Stein took over the managerial powers, but in his wry way he picked up that gauntlet in later years. I would approach him sometimes at the tunnel mouth for an interview after one of his many triumphs. He would contrive an air of innocence and then, with that knowing smile playing on his lips and displaying gentle scorn, he would ask, 'Did you remember to take the dust cover off this time?'

As for that disputed penalty against Rangers, taken up by the press with accustomed vigour, there was a postscript. The arguments spilt over into the new week and showed no signs of abating. A week after the now infamous game, while travelling to Italy with Walter McCrae of Kilmarnock in his temporary capacity as Scotland manager to see Italy play against Poland – a period we will return to in a later chapter – they had some time on their hands to spend in Rome. It was All Saints' Day and they decided to follow the crowds towards the Vatican. John Mackenzie, in an April 1970 *Scottish Daily Express* piece, recounted the story: 'Tens of thousands of people gathered in St Peter's Square as we went sight-seeing in the sun. We stopped to share in this occasion as the Pope blessed the huge gathering from a window in his Vatican apartment. He spoke, of course, in Latin. Walter McCrae, with his wry sense of humour, turned to Jock and said, "Right, boss. You're the Celtic man. Tell us what he's saying." Jock listened intently for a moment or two and then, without the trace of a smile, he answered, "He's telling them it *was* a penalty!"' Then he turned, laughing, and walked on towards an international task that was beyond such papal endorsement.

CHAPTER TWELVE
SCOTLAND EXPECTS

The principal commissar of Scottish football, the man who had consented to Stein's spying mission to Italy in the autumn of 1965, was Willie Allan, the secretary of the Scottish Football Association. Deep inside the man there might possibly have lurked a secret lover of football. If that was so then he was certainly a master of disguise, for he always seemed a passionless apparatchik who only knew a Denis Law from a Jim Baxter because of their differing dates of registration with the association. He made a curious contrast with the men around him who chose the managers of Scotland's national side. To see him shuffle after players with some finicky reminder of a little-known regulation, or standing with barely disguised distaste within the proximity of some members of the International Selection Committee as they raucously propped up a bar somewhere, would remind you of a cross between Uriah Heep and Grumpy from the Seven Dwarfs. Together, Allan and his selectors were interferers. Allan was the time and motion man. The selectors were anonymous assassins. Any manager was vulnerable to them. You would have thought a relationship with such a group would have appealed to Stein as much as a sing-song at the Kinning Park Rangers Supporters Club. But when the SFA dismissed Ian McColl from his post as Scotland manager in the spring of 1965, after a period of management which certainly was not disastrous and approached the recently installed Celtic boss to take over temporarily for the two forthcoming World Cup qualifying matches in Finland and Poland, Stein accepted.

This is an intriguing part of his career. It went past in a flash compared to all that was to follow, but it still fascinates. You could say that the patriotic streak in him found the appeal by the SFA to come to their rescue quite irresistible. I am sure there was something in that. But we have to recall he had had experience of how Scotland had prepared, as if by Mack Sennett, for the World Cup in Switzerland in 1954, and he knew all the stories taken back to him by the Celtic players involved in the fiasco. Despite the withering comments he had already made to people about the SFA and the manner in which they acted, the offer of the post, even temporarily, appealed to his ego. And why shouldn't it have? He was being extolled as the most exciting managerial prospect in the game. He had taken clubs from outside Glasgow to cup wins and notable victories over European opponents. He had jolted Celtic into a Scottish Cup win within weeks of returning to the club. So he was flattered by this offer, as a recognition of his phenomenal progress, as indeed was Kelly, the chairman of his club, who could bask in some reflected glory that the man of his choice was now universally respected and lauded. And perhaps Stein was confident that he could beat the system and achieve more than anybody else before him. So this was not just a case of a man taking on a new managerial commitment, but also a system just as hackneyed as the one he was transforming at Celtic Park. I believe it is that which he found so tempting.

Much, therefore, was expected of him now that the media realised he had the audacity to try anything. His first public statement was modest, though, and exuded sympathy for his predecessor. 'I just hope I get better breaks than the man before me,' he told the *Scottish Daily Express* on 14 May. The SFA had reunited him with Walter McCrae of Kilmarnock as his trainer, the man who had accompanied him to Italy to visit Herrera. They got on well together. McCrae's military bearing and shoot-from-the-shoulder style suited Stein. Standing shoulder to shoulder, it would have taken the phlegmatic indifference of a Sumo wrestler to take that pair on.

They travelled to Poland for their first match, on 23 May. His first meeting with his selectors lasted only a couple of minutes, during which time he announced the team he had selected for the first game then cheerily left them to mull over the startling implication of their sudden redundancies. He had not been able to pick the squad initially, but nobody was going to become involved in the actual team selection. Scotland achieved a creditable 1–1 draw and followed it up four days later with a 2–1 win in Helsinki. It was not a scintillating performance there, but all round expectations were building hugely after an unbeaten tour. The Glasgow *Evening Times* reported on 28 May, 'To say the officials in the party and the players were delighted with the work of the new manager is an understatement. Everyone agreed that his drive, enthusiasm and sense of humour have transformed Scotland.' On the last night of the trip, even though some of the players had initially felt resentful at Stein forbidding them to stay up late one night to watch the return Cassius Clay–Sonny Liston fight, they crowded into his room for one of his beloved sing-songs into the 'wee sma' hours'.

But when he took the side to Belfast on 2 October and saw the Irish win the Home Championship match 3–2 with a last-minute goal by Willie Irvine, his reputation was slightly dented. Eleven days later it took an unprecedented bruising. For then came one of Hampden's major historical anti-climaxes, in the return World Cup match with Poland, even though the crowd of 107,580 created a British record for a floodlit match. With Willie Johnston making his debut on the left wing and producing a performance that had the press raving about discovering a new Alan Morton (an Ibrox winger of legendary renown), it started well but finished disastrously. Denis Law partnered the Rangers winger that night. 'Of all the games I've played in around the world for club or country this one was the biggest disappointment of all time,' he said. 'I'm still trying to work out how the Poles could score two goals against us in the last five minutes and win the game. We had control of it for long periods. Maybe if there is an explanation, we relaxed too much. But the dressing-room afterwards was like a morgue. We had blown it, and we couldn't understand why.'

Stein had dropped the revered Jim Baxter and also his own Celtic player John Hughes, and before the game had made the stark comment, 'We have chosen players who can be relied on.' They failed. Scotland took the lead through McNeill after fourteen minutes' play, but the Poles scored twice late in the game to silence the large crowd, and 'Stein's Stunners' took on a whole new meaning. The press waded in with comments about Stein to which he was entirely unaccustomed. In later years he took great delight in beating Willie Waddell when that man became Rangers manager. No doubt this was in no small measure due to Stein lodging in his memory the following words Waddell wrote about that match when he was a prominent football writer for the *Scottish Daily Express*: 'Why was Willie Johnston, the young wonder man of the evening, completely ignored in the second half? Why was Billy McNeill allowed to wander and scurry about the field trying to pin a centre-forward [Liberda] who played mostly in midfield, thus leaving the vulnerable part of defence wide open? ... Two facts lost us the game – the wandering of McNeill and the starvation diet of Johnston.' This was a blunt challenge to Stein's tactics, and such a thing at that time, given the man's reputation for covering every eventuality and his open intimidation of many press men, was almost an act of daring *lèse-majesté*. But if Stein perceived such criticism simply as evidence of bias from a former Ranger, he would have found even less comfort in the impeccably fair Raymond Jacobs' *Glasgow Herald* comment that the visitors had given 'A simple, yet deadly demonstration of what modern football is all about. In the process they revealed that Scotland haven't yet reached 11-plus standard.' For Stein, a man who had convinced people that he was an innovator and a modern thinker, that was a brutal indictment, and knowing what he was like under criticism he would have been enraged.

To a certain extent he struck back at all that by returning to his Celtic duties, ten days later bullishly winning the League Cup in that towsy final against Rangers. Perhaps some of the adrenalin that day came from wishing to hit back at the press. But he still had his commitment to Scotland, and the Italian side that had just demolished Poland 6–1 in Rome was now heading for Hampden and a match fixed for 9 November. Expectations had now become less hysterical on the back of two successive defeats for the national side.

The Italians needed only a draw at Hampden to make them favourites to qualify for the World Cup, with the remaining game against Scotland to be played in Italy. With Baxter made captain, Billy Bremner man-marking Gianni Rivera and John Greig stomping around defence, elegance on the Scottish side, to be truthful, was at a minimum. But the defensive set-up worked. Greig made two marvellous goal-line clearances in the game then produced one of the great goals of his career when, with only two minutes to go and the game scoreless, he took a pass from Baxter and saw space opening up on the right. As he had been instructed to do, he made tracks for goal and from 25 yards out drove a low shot into the net to win the game.

Raymond Jacobs of the *Glasgow Herald* struck a cautionary note after the brouhaha had settled, for the big crowd at Hampden had greeted the tail-end victory as if the World Cup itself had been won. 'Before the blood rushes to one's head,' he wrote, 'it is sobering to recall the pattern of the 88 minutes which went before the goal. There were very few of them in which Scotland looked capable of penetrating a superbly organised Italian defence.' Few took heed of that. The sap was rising again in the football community. Big Jock had pulled it off once more. Optimism soared disproportionately. All they had to do now was go to Naples in early December and beat Italy again! Or at least achieve a draw to reach a play-off.

Walter McGowan, the former world champion boxer who hailed from Stein's home neighbourhood of Burnbank, once assessed taking on the Italians on their own patch this way: 'For a boxer to get a draw in Italy you have to knock your opponent out.' The inference was that Italians had ways of getting results that, put mildly, might not pass close scrutiny. So even with the strongest possible side going there, the odds were stacked against Stein. But he was to find out that this particular job made him feel like a bankrupt facing foreclosure, for his assets began to disappear one by one. Players called off, particularly the Anglo-Scots, and most notoriously Jim Baxter, who undoubtedly had been injured in a game against Wales two weeks before the Italian trip but who on the day of the game turned out for Sunderland against Dukla Prague in a friendly, thus giving rise to suspicions about the validity of all the withdrawals. Denis Law and Billy Stevenson joined Baxter on the injured list along with goalkeeper Bill Brown and Billy McNeill. Willie Henderson certainly travelled but was ruled out through injury, and they had to draft in Burnley goalkeeper Adam Blacklaw, who had played only once before for Scotland three years previously. These are the players who could not play that day: Crerand, Stevenson, Mackay, Baxter, Law, St John, Henderson, Gilzean, Willie Johnston – as fine a crop as any to provide a rich harvest, even within the frenzied air of Naples. Without them, Stein was as exposed as he ever was to be. He was already planning his exit strategy in some of his pre-match remarks, telling people that the system made it impossible for him to do the job properly. Of course he ought to have known what he was letting himself in for. He had even told his players during a training session watched by the Italian media to go about their business in a hang-dog way to give everybody the impression that their spirits were low and defeat was inevitable. It smacked of desperation. So did the manner in which they emerged from the tunnel on match day.

Few in the stadium or in the massive audience watching on television, on a day when the transmission almost brought the Scottish nation to a halt, will ever forget the sight of Liverpool's towering defender Ron Yeats trotting up for the kick-off as if he were to be a striker, and as soon as the game had started trotting immediately back into defence. You might have likened that to a Tommy Cooper trick, calculated deliberately to distract from a comical calamity about to happen elsewhere on stage. The Italians in fact turned the Scottish goalmouth into a besieged Monte Cassino for most of the match and broke through when Pascutti scored on 38 minutes. Then Facchetti, the tall, attacking full-back whom Stein greatly admired, added a second in the 74th as the Scottish players increasingly gave the impression that they wanted it all to end as quickly as possible. Mora added the *coup de grâce* five minutes from the end.

It is hard to ignore the depleted nature of the side, but the emphasis on defence was a failure nevertheless. Surprisingly, given Stein's nature, the effort was not adventurous enough. He had gutted and filleted his own beliefs by applying wholly negative tactics. Only once after that game was there to be discussion about a defensive ploy it was generally believed he had decided to adopt. That was in Prague in 1967 with Celtic, about which hangs a considerable tale, as we shall see. Stein simply hated to be associated with this performance even though he had plenty of excuses to offer. He had had enough, and was widely reported to have said, 'I wouldn't take that job again for £10,000 a year!' That, of course, was a sizeable amount in those days.

Free from that ultimate embarrassment which had brought him a more critical press than he had ever been used to before, Stein now directed his incredible energy towards attempting to win the league title above all else. An important watershed of sorts came on Monday, 3 January 1966. The Old Firm had matched each other almost perfectly in the first half of the league race, although Rangers did have an advantage in winning the first league game narrowly at Ibrox. It contained the clear indications of a re-emerging Celtic, who by the time of the traditional New Year encounter had drawn level with Rangers at the top but with a game in hand. On as cold a day as would have fitted Bud Neill's portrait of 'Glesca' suffering ('Winter's came, wee Josis nos is skintit, / Winter's diabolic, intit!'), Celtic, a goal down after only one and a half minutes, proceeded to thrash Rangers 5–1 with a sure-footed performance which, apart from anything else, sprung from Stein's decision to inspect the pitch beforehand and get his players to change their footwear appropriately. As Rangers slithered, Celtic strode to victory on the back of Stevie Chalmers scoring his only hat-trick against the great rivals.

However, that did not mean the beginning of an unbeaten sequence. Celtic were still a developing side with raw edges and they were to suffer significant defeats in the coming weeks. Aberdeen and Hearts took full points from them before January was out. It is the latter game at Tynecastle that contained the episode which, it is claimed, firmly settled Stein's relationship with his chairman. It had been assumed that Stein was solely in charge of team matters and that Bob Kelly now knew his place on that score. That, in fact, wasn't the case. As we know, Sean Fallon has already pointed out that Stein had the capacity to handle situations without confrontations, that he could neatly manoeuvre himself into having the upper hand with chairmen. According to Jim Craig, Kelly was indeed interfering, if not greatly influencing events. This particular Tynecastle team selection was the result of the direct intervention of the chairman, echoing the compliant McGrory era.

The whole episode centred on an incident involving Craig which took place in the European Cup Winners' Cup third-round second-leg tie against Dynamo Kiev in Tbilisi on 26 January. Celtic had beaten the Ukrainians 3–0 in the first leg and had travelled south to Georgia to play because Kiev was in the grip of a severe winter. It was a horrendous round trip. There were so many delays and so much rerouting coming back that Stein joked to the players that the dolls they had bought for their kids back home would be useless as the children would all be grown up by the time they arrived. But this trip had a huge effect on Stein's position within Celtic Park, as Craig explains. 'Unwittingly I was the catalyst which freed Jock from the yoke of the chairman. I got ordered off in that game in Tbilisi. The winger I was marking punched me after I had mistimed a tackle and I chased after him and gave him a mouthful. The referee sent the Kiev player off and then, to my utter surprise, turned to me and sent me off as well. I hadn't touched him. Jock saw me in the hotel after the game and came up and said, "You'll have to apologise to the chairman." "For what?" I asked him. "For being sent off," he told me. I couldn't believe it. I had been punched and all I did was mouth off at the man and was sent off. I felt strongly about it. An apology was not needed nor justified in my opinion, so I didn't give it.

'What happened next, though, was the horrendous journey back to Glasgow which didn't exactly settle the nerves and maybe aggravated the tension about that incident. We had played in Georgia because Kiev was in the midst of winter and their pitch was unplayable. But we were delayed there for two hours before we set off after the game, and then when we landed in Moscow for some reason we were kept waiting on the plane for five hours, without being allowed to get off. We then flew to Stockholm and stayed the night there. But the following day they discovered that there was something wrong with the plane after they had tried to take off. The chairman refused to have them try it again in the same plane, so they had to send for another one. It was just building up into one almighty mess. We got back late on Friday night and Jock took us straight to Celtic Park where we had a training session, would you believe, at eleven o'clock at night.

'The game was at Tynecastle the following day, and I discovered only about half an hour before the game, in the dressing-room, that I was dropped. Not a single word of explanation had been given me. Not even just told. My name simply wasn't read out. I came across [senior director] Desmond White who was in the stand who wondered why I was not playing. I told him I thought it was my lack of apology to the chairman. Desmond was incensed. It was years later that Jock himself told me, as he drove me down to Seamill one day, that at a board meeting at Celtic Park called specially for later that day Desmond had made his views known to the board that there had to be no interference in team selection by anybody in future, not even by the chairman. He asked Jock outright at this meeting if he would have picked me if it had been left up to him, and Jock answered, "Yes." That did it. Jock said that White actually confronted the chairman about that. What was the use of placing faith in a manager and then forcing him to compromise his ideas? Jock told me that was the turning point for him. According to him, it was from then on he really did have a free rein.'

White apparently riding to the rescue on this occasion is one of the oddest of the recollections about Stein, for the two men ended up disliking each other intensely. But whatever interpretation can be put on the White intervention, there is little doubt that the dividend Celtic reaped in the next year was down principally to the influence of only one man.

CHAPTER THIRTEEN
'THE CHASE IS OVER'

On 26 February 1966, a month after returning from their trip to Georgia, Celtic fielded a team that comprised eight of the men who were to go on and win the European Cup fifteen months later. They lost 1–0 on the small pitch at Stirling Albion. The team they were playing had the capacity to be tenacious opponents at home for anybody at that time, so the result, while it caused some surprise, was not entirely sensational. However, it was part of a sequence that had now seen them lose three away games in a row and had allowed Rangers to creep to the top of the league, two points in front. Equally significant, it was their last defeat in the league that season. For there was no evidence to suggest a lessening of Stein's dynamic self-confidence. He was now the most stimulating man on the Scottish footballing scene.

At the other end of the city, Scot Symon, the Rangers manager, was a hermit by comparison. At Ibrox, statements were made as if devised automatically by a Xerox machine. Stein, by contrast, aimed shafts of wit and insights towards the media pack which could send them away brimming with fertile copy, or conversely could make them feel as if they had just been caught in a tornado. Either way it was a vibrant experience. In those terms, Parkhead was a jacuzzi, Ibrox a cold-water footbath. Stein recognised the value of interaction and effectively was establishing the ritual of the press conference for the first time. You could sense, when a phone call came into a newspaper or broadcasting office, men mentally jumping to attention when they knew who was on the other end of the line. Often he would not announce himself, merely rush into the point he wanted to make on the assumption that you knew who it was you were talking to. He was skilled in the art of the pre-emptive strike. A BBC producer who worked with me tried to avoid his calls over a period for he knew Stein was going to be critical of some coverage of one of the games. It went on for weeks. One late afternoon his secretary told him a call had come in from the producer's uncle, Charlie, who wanted him on family business. He took the call. It was Stein on the other end of the line. How he had found out the name of the man's uncle never became clear, but that subterfuge rendered the man an almost shivering wreck by the end of the heavily one-sided conversation. That Stein could be witheringly dismissive of both players and media when it suited him added to his reputation of a man you ignored at your peril. But he was also unpredictable by nature, and even the most experienced of them found it difficult to read what was truly on his mind at any given time.

The volatility of his nature was to be fully exposed in the coming months, for although the grind towards winning the league title was still the top priority, it was cup games which produced the unexpected flash-points. After Kiev came Liverpool, in the spring, in the semi-final of the Cup Winners' Cup, and an assignation with Bill Shankly. There was indeed a kind of brotherly love between the two men, although true to the nature of siblings they would hate to lose to each other. Stein had got to know the man better through his wanderings in English football, and since Liverpool and Manchester were within a few hours' reach of Stein in his Mercedes there were frequent nocturnal dashes from Glasgow to see games there and just to have a blether. They did not need an interpreter. Their banter was natural and instinctive, although Shankly had the capacity to come up with verbal gems that seemed to some as unspontaneous as Neil Armstrong's scripted 'One small step for man' address to the moon and humanity. Stein could be brilliantly witty too, perhaps even more so than Shankly, despite the Liverpool man's renowned repertoire. It is just that he seemed to keep his sharper moments for more private occasions and did not seek the same status of self-publicist which Shankly easily adopted. Both were former miners. Both had experienced the same gush of release and freedom as they breathed the fresh air on surfacing from a pit. The instinctive gratitude for simple survival conjoined them. Both could be disarmingly pleasant then brutally frank in a matter of seconds, depending on who they were with. Both were willing to take on anything thrown at them. Neither would have strongly disputed the famous Green Bay Packers coach Vince Lombardi's dictum, 'Winning isn't everything. It's the only thing.'

Shankly was Stein's senior by nine years, and sometimes when you heard Stein talk about the great Liverpool man you felt he was talking about an elderly brother whom he envied for his gift of the gab but who was never to be taken wholly seriously. At a dinner in Glasgow in 1974, when Shankly was the guest of honour and Stein sat two places away from him at the top table, the former Glenbuck Cherrypickers player could not resist a dig at the Celtic manager. Apart from regaling us with stories about his career, he turned to the matter of a testimonial friendly game Celtic had played against Liverpool at Anfield weeks before, which Celtic had won 4–1. 'It was a friendly,' he said, 'so we put out a team of wine-waiters to play in it. And what did you do, John? You put out your strongest team. Wine-waiters against them. What chance did we have?' Stein's shoulders heaved in merriment, knowing that Shankly was deadly serious about that and hated losing. But the two games the clubs played against each other in that 1966 tournament were far from innocuous friendlies, and the latter of the two stretched the good-natured relationship between the two managers to the limit.

Some 76,446 turned up at Celtic Park for the first match, which Celtic largely dominated. After the home side had missed at least four gilt-edged chances, Bobby Lennox scored the only goal of the game to give Celtic a slender edge. Then came the fracas of Anfield. For this second leg Stein would have moved heaven and earth to achieve the right result, for the final of the tournament was to be played at Hampden Park and he felt that Celtic could not be beaten by anybody left in the tournament, playing in front of their own huge support there. Surviving Anfield would in a sense be the winning of the tournament itself. The game in fact ended with a controversy that embitters those Celtic players who took part in the match even now. Bobby Lennox was at the heart of it. 'To this day I know we were robbed,' he said. 'I know players will say that kind of thing about controversial incidents but nothing will change my mind about that. We had played them well by keeping the ball in midfield, defending as far from the goal as possible. I was always ready to make runs on the break and we thought we could sneak one if they kept pressing forward. Tommy Smith scored for them with a low shot that seemed to skid on the surface and then they got the second five minutes later when Strong headed in a cross. There wasn't much of the game left after that as I recall. I think it was only a minute or so to go. It was then I thought we had done it. Bobby Murdoch swept over a ball which was knocked down behind the defenders by Joe McBride. I had pace, as you know, and I was off my mark to get it, which I did, and put it behind the keeper. I had scored lots of goals like that, and as I turned away I thought there was no way back for Liverpool, being so late in the game, and we had got the away goal. I couldn't believe the flag went up for offside. You can imagine the Big Man's reaction. In the tunnel after that I thought Jock was going to explode. There was a lot of shouting and bawling going on and I thought somebody might end up in big trouble. But there was nothing we could do about it, not even with Jock snarling at everybody.'

Shorn of the possibility of a European final at Hampden, Stein was understandably enraged. A manager sometimes has to decant all that suppurating frustration from within and he did it in a way that startled one of his great admirers, the renowned journalist Allan Herron, then with the *Sunday Mail*. 'I thought Celtic had been robbed myself from what I could see,' he recalled. 'And as duty calls I had to go down to the dressing-room area for quotes and it was there I saw Bill Shankly. Now, I was friendly with the Shanks. I had known him for years and had many a great chat with him. So I put my hand out to him and we shook and I congratulated him and wished him well for the final. Jock wasn't there. But somebody seeing this must have rushed off to let Jock know. For the next I knew there was Jock advancing on me with a look of thunder on his face. He put out his hand to me, as if to shake it, and when I put out mine he withdrew his quickly and then shouted at me, "You're nothing but an effing traitor. What were you doing shaking his hand for? Don't you ever come back to Celtic Park again!" And then he stormed off. Now, the great thing about Jock is he never harboured grudges all that long, for of course I was back at Celtic Park and even travelled in the team bus coming back with the European Cup to the hotel in Lisbon. But he couldn't control his temper at times. He had to let rip at somebody that night.'

Letting rip at the media was something he would have preferred to do than fall out with his friend Shankly. Herron was learning that night, as others did watching this, that the wounded bear in Stein was an awesome sight. But the manager was also aware that there was no time for lasting negative recrimination. What he now wanted to do was convert the strong feeling of injustice that was almost dementing his players into something powerful and positive, for four days later they were to face Rangers in the Scottish Cup final.

On 23 April Celtic and Rangers, then joint top of the league, drew a massive 126,599 into the old stadium. It turned out to be a dour tale of two teams inflicted by that Old Firm curse, the fear of defeat. There was no scoring in the game, and apart from a Billy McNeill header which slammed against the crossbar and Simpson diving at the feet of John Greig near the end, nobody looked like making a mark. But even though the draw seemed fair enough, hardly any neutral gave Rangers a chance in the replay on the following Wednesday, for Celtic still gave the impression of a side on the up and up, Rangers only holding the tidal wave at bay temporarily. Indeed, a veritable tsunami came at Rangers that Wednesday as Celtic launched a long series of furious attacks on the Ibrox defence. But the game is not principally remembered for that.

The name famously associated with it is nowhere to be seen in the Celtic lexicon. It belonged to a man from Denmark, Kai Johansen. His winning goal for Rangers, scored with twenty minutes to go, purloined a cup when his side looked as if it might be overrun. It also prompted the deterioration of the relationship between Stein and one of his most significant players, John Hughes. Hughes, whose direct opponent was the Dane, had had the upper hand against him in previous games. The Celtic left-winger was big and strong, Johansen was slight but quick on his feet. That night one should have cancelled out the other, especially when it came to crucial marking. But any picture of that ball nestling in the net, with Simpson helpless, shows Johansen turning away in triumph and his marker John Hughes yards away, looking on as a sort of helpless but at the same time guilty bystander. Stein did not need a picture for proof of guilt. He read the situation immediately. After the match he turned his fury on Hughes. Unfairly, according to the winger himself.

'We had gone to Seamill for the build-up to the game,' Hughes explained. 'It was tiring because we had had all the games leading up to the final and then we had to go into a replay. It was during training that I felt my hamstring going. It didn't go with a bang, but there was something there tightening up and I knew I wasn't going to be fully fit. So I told Jock. But you know what he was like. At that time he was desperate for me to play in the game, for he knew I had done well against Johansen. He knew I could use my power against him. So he just refused to accept that it was going to be very risky to play me. He kept saying, "You'll be all right, you'll make it." Now I curse myself for not standing up to him and saying outright that I was sure the hamstring would hold me back. But he was a difficult man to stand up to. I suppose it was because of the fear of him. That's it in a nutshell. You could say he persuaded me to play, but in fact he actually made it impossible to say "No!"

'So just before half-time Bobby Murdoch sent a pass down the left and I started to chase after it. It was then I felt the muscle pulling up on me. It wasn't disastrous, but I had to slow down. I knew I was right on the edge of breaking down. I told them at half-time about it but all I got was Jock asking Steelie [Jim Steele, Celtic's much-loved physio] to give it a rub down. I should have given up there and then and said so. I couldn't bring myself to say it. I supposed I was just scared about his reaction. Then came the goal. Johansen started off on his run and I moved and felt the muscle pull. I couldn't track him. I couldn't get near him. He ran on to score. It might have been a great finish but honestly I cost Celtic the cup.

'Jock went for me after the game. He tore into me. He wasn't the only one who had a go at me. I took dog's abuse, even from some of my colleagues, and especially in the press. If only I had spoken up the right way at Seamill that goal might never have happened, for they should have had somebody else playing instead of me. But if you put the fear of death into players for speaking up on things, as he did then, that is what can happen.'

This notion, that Stein's control could be counter-productive, soured the relationship between the two men, which was to reach a sad conclusion several years hence. Stein knew, though, even in the darkest moments of that defeat, that he had a better side than Rangers. Certainly there was that problem of lack of consistency which had plagued the club before he had arrived, but that was gradually being smoothed out and the urge to redeem themselves was paramount among the players. Without any great need for Stein's motivational powers, three days after that loss Celtic went to the Tail of the Bank and beat Morton 2–0, which meant they were within touching distance of their first league title in twelve years, with only a couple of league games remaining, at home to Dunfermline and away to Motherwell. Rangers' surge for the finishing line had come to a shuddering halt in the month of March when they sustained two defeats and two draws. Alex Ferguson, now Sir Alex, tried his best to help his favourite club by scoring the first for Dunfermline at Parkhead in the second-last game of the season, but the lead lasted only five minutes before Lennox equalised, and within fifteen minutes of the start of the second half Johnstone scored the winner. This in effect meant that if Celtic avoided being beaten 0–4 by Motherwell they would be champions.

That might have seemed an incredibly remote possibility, yet Celtic, over the previous twelve years, had become masters of the anti-climax and had built up their support so often into a frenzy of anticipation only to let them down that even their fondest admirers could not quell their apprehension. But Stein didn't want to win his first championship in such a cack-handed manner as by goal average, as was the system in those days. He wanted an outright win, even though the following telegram arrived at Parkhead the morning after the

Dunfermline match: 'The chase is over. This proves that the Old Firm are not infirm. Congratulations on winning the Scottish League. Best of luck in Europe next year.' It was signed by Rangers vice-chairman John F. Wilson. However, Bertie Auld remembers that Motherwell's Fir Park looked as if it would collapse under the weight of the 20,000 who had shoe-horned themselves into the relatively small ground. 'Twenty thousand? That was the official attendance. When we ran out on to the park that huge big terracing on the right-hand side began to sway and roll with everybody looking as if they would fall on to the pitch. We could see people climbing up trees outside the ground to try and get a view. They were standing on the wall at the back of the terracings. They were on each other's shoulders. It was an amazing sight.'

But not an amazing game. It was a dour battle, and it wasn't until the last minute of the last game on the last day of the season that Celtic scored the goal which effectively started one of the most illustrious sequences of league title victories in the history of the game, anywhere in the world. Lennox scored it, Craig made it. 'I joked with Bobby about the goal,' Craig recalled. 'I told him my pass to him was so perfect that all he needed to do was to knock it in with his shins. But it made a perfect ending. We just relaxed and celebrated.'

A scrambled goal, as it was, in the final seconds did nothing to diminish the overall achievement of a man who had turned a dysfunctional family into a model of fraternal cooperation. Recognition of that was universal. On 11 May, four days after the title win, Stein was named Scotland's Manager of the Year. Six days later he was awarded British Manager of the Year. He had convinced his players that they belonged to the greatest club in the world and that what they had to do was perform with style, in keeping with that grandeur. Bertie Auld recalled how Stein would express that to him. 'He would come up and say to you, "You're here to entertain. There's a big crowd out there who have been working hard all week and paid a lot just to come and see you playing. Some of them have been down the mines all week. This is their only relaxation. They want to come and be entertained. You have the ability to do that, so get out and give them a right good time out there." He made you feel as if you were not playing for him, but for them. He loved the supporters. He never disguised that. And he got his players to do most of the thanking for him.'

After such a hectic season you might have thought the last thing the players wanted was a close-season tour, to Bermuda and North America, where football's attempts to consolidate a foothold on the commercial slopes of the sporting Himalayas were, and still are, feeble. But the club was perfectly aware that there was a large constituency of Celtic support in certain areas in the States, especially around Kearney in New Jersey, and that in any case supporters would travel to see the other games around the continent, vast though it is. Eleven games in all were to be played, stretching from coast to coast, the two substantial opponents Tottenham Hotspur and Bayern Munich among a medley of local ethnic sides. It was during that tour that Stein and his players bonded in a way which far exceeded in significance any kudos gained from winning games in close season.

On that influential trip, Stein was both manager and social convenor in a relaxed manner that ignited new respect for him. He was the life and soul of the party. The development of relationships between players and himself took a sociological turn on their first stop of the tour, in Hamilton, Bermuda. One Sunday morning the Catholic players, who comprised the bulk of the squad, went conscientiously to Mass. A few minutes after they had departed, Ronnie Simpson received a visit from Stein. 'Ronnie,' he asked, 'can you find us a Church of Scotland?' Simpson recalls it as the oddest request his massive boss ever made of him. The keeper went to a local phone directory and to his amazement discovered that there were several kirks on the island. Once he had reported back, Stein ordered the few Protestants in the side to join him in taxis and head for the church service. Whether he felt an urge to reveal an old and proud identity, or whether he considered that leaving Protestants to loll around the pool as others were demonstrating devotion was a sign of dissipation which did their tradition no good, or whether it was part of a desire to keep the momentum of discipline throughout the side and not have it unbalanced, even on a Sunday morning, one cannot tell. But end up in church they did, belting out hymns in a local gospelling style and ending up with Stein having tea with the minister and chatting about football. Point made, they went back to the togetherness and the exercise of unity, which made the church-going seem less relevant to Stein.

They then went on to play and defeat Spurs in Toronto to become the first Scottish side to win in that favourite tour spot since 1945. Stein might have been up to his foxiness in that game when, after the Bobby Lennox goal had given them victory, Eddie Baily, the Spurs coach, criticised him for transgressing an agreement about substitutes. Stein, po-faced, pleaded ignorance and claimed two of his players had been genuinely injured. The

Spurs coach was learning the hard way that a summer game in Toronto was being played with deadly seriousness by a man who quite simply hated to lose, at any time, anywhere. This was certainly underscored in the match against Bayern Munich in San Francisco when, as Celtic were competing hard to maintain their unbeaten tour record, the right-back marking Steve Chalmers turned round after being tackled and punched the Celtic player in the jaw. Chalmers chased the man behind the goal and some of the spectators rushed on to the field. As Chalmers grabbed the player and fell on him a Celtic supporter from the crowd tried to pull Chalmers away, not to stop the incident but to punch the German as well. If Stein and others had not rushed round to bring the incident to an end, the little dark-haired German who had caused it all might not have survived to go on and make his name, not as a defender but as one of the most prolific goalscorers of all time in the Bundesliga – Gerd Müller.

In between the games Stein encouraged socialising at various venues and mixing with the North American supporters, who imparted to the players the global dimension of the club's following, a ploy he thought would add to their appreciation of the importance of wearing the jersey. The entire entourage went to the races at Aqueduct Park in New York, where a trophy was renamed after the club; the Celtic Plate is still in competition to this day. Stein and Bob Kelly, in their favourite alternative environment, close to course railings and within hailing distance of a paddock, bet lavishly on the races.

There was no doubting the success of the trip. Eleven games were played, eight won and three drawn, reminding onlookers that this was not a holiday jaunt but a process of acclimatisation, not to the American environment but to the headier heights of the football about to come their way. As Stein wrote himself in the *Celtic View* at the time, 'The experience of playing so often against concentrated defence was valuable. I am certain we shall run into more and more of it in European football. And this is to be deplored.'

He was to tell me much later that he felt, at that time, a new mood of confidence develop within the club. The players were gelling naturally. The sloppiness of inconsistency was being squeezed out of their system. They were beginning to brim with self-confidence. All that, even then, had him eager to get his teeth into the new season. And when they returned, the famous 'Jungle' at Celtic Park had been revamped. That shed-like delicatessen of wit, invective, insolence, rebuke, devotion and undying loyalty was converted into a modern enclosure. On its new roof there was one league championship flag flying. Not even Stein could have anticipated that that flag up the pole would become a hardy annual.

CHAPTER FOURTEEN
COMETH THE HOUR

Many portentous words were written and spoken about Jock Stein and his 'new' Celtic after their return from the States in the summer of 1966 as the previews of the new season were churned out. I choose a simple statement made by Bertie Auld's father on the evening of Saturday, 17 September to his son as the harbinger for the most spectacular and successful season of all for Stein: 'Bertie, son, if you're going to play like that I'm going to have to leave the house an hour earlier for the games!'

There is nothing cryptic about that when placed in context. He was referring to the first Old Firm game of the 1966/67 season which had been played earlier that day. Auld senior had taken his place inside Parkhead only five minutes after kick-off, but he had already missed two goals for Celtic. The first was scored by his son, in the first minute; the second was from Bobby Murdoch three minutes later. And that was the scoring finished for the day. The deed had been done. Missing goals by your favourite team in an Old Firm game after having paid to get in, even if you savour success eventually, is like protected sex: better than nothing, but not quite like the real thing. Auld senior had been short-changed by a side revealing a new, aggressive impatience.

Stein had prefaced everything they were about to embark on in the subsequent months with the quite bald prediction, 'I think we could win everything in front of us. I think this could be a season to remember.' This is not something dreamt up by players in retrospect; he actually said that several times to his players during pre-season training. I have already noted that he felt something growing from within his players at that time that was inspiring them to do things instinctively, bolstered by a unity that was unprecedented at Celtic Park. Their self-awareness could once have been described as an inferiority complex, particularly in the shadow of Rangers. Now their self-esteem was rocketing. The 'new' Celtic had been unleashed by a man who was redefining the role of the manager in the dug-out, and who seemed to be umbilically tied to what was happening on the field. This was so to such an extent that you found your eye being inexorably pulled towards the bulky, neatly suited figure gesticulating on the sideline. That had never happened before in my experience. We were starting to feel that you could not accept the validity of a game Celtic were involved in without a statement of some kind or other from Stein, which brought a particular focus to a match. Before, during and after a game Stein's fingerprints were plastered all over the event. The conventional managerial figure held a respected but principally background role; Stein was streaking past that model like a Schumacher overtaking a horseless carriage. First he had popularised the tracksuit. Now he was establishing the cult of the manager.

On the one hand the press loved this. They dined out on him. On the other, some of them felt, in later years, that perhaps they had been party to elevating the role of the manager to an almost godly plane. But it was certainly Stein in Scotland who led them all down that road. He also displayed to everybody his hard-working devotion to the cause, which by another definition could be called an outright obsession to be on top of his job. He was virtually first into Celtic Park every morning. Only the cleaners beat him to it, and occasionally they were also-rans to him as well. Even if he had left Celtic Park late in the afternoon to travel to see a game at Manchester or Liverpool or Leeds and returned in the early hours of the morning – and that happened frequently – he would still be prowling the corridors and dressing-room of the stadium when some of his players were turning over for the third time in bed after hearing the alarm clock. Basic to the reason for his dawn patrol was that he was a continual fugitive from normal sleeping hours. He just couldn't put in the hours of sleep his large frame really required. Abroad in a hotel, you would note him being the last to bed, bar a hardy few of us in the media who imbibed while he did not. Then he would be up in the morning, before everybody else, for breakfast, or be lumbering around to see if he could catch an unsuspecting journalist or broadcaster sneaking off to a room after an all-nighter as others were heading for their croissants. This jousting with sleep and being ahead of everybody at the start of the day informed his demands for proper time-keeping by his players. He once dropped Joe McBride from a Celtic team at Firhill, even though he was there an hour in advance, simply because he had not turned up when told to.

Contrast that with his habit of joining the players after a game in the large dressing-room bath and starting the community singing, or encouraging a sing-a-long on the team bus wherever they were travelling, to great or small stadiums, and you see how he was determined to maintain the balance between the strict, fearsome martinet and being one of the lads. Although nobody was left in any doubt that he could display an unexpectedly soft-hearted and commiserative side to his nature, as I will show, if anybody tried to take advantage of him in any way they would see that other ruthless aspect to his character which could and did leave some of them mentally scarred.

No slacking was to be allowed within the ranks of the media either. Eventually he established a ritual for the Monday daily newspapers of having a press conference every Sunday morning. Starting the week with Stein became a journalistic constitutional without which you would suffer a decided vitamin deficiency. These occasions produced some of the most significant stories and back-page controversies the game had ever seen. He loved holding court this way. He loved gossip, either making it himself or listening to it. But the deadline was eleven a.m. The press would assemble in the foyer, and as the minute hand reached the witching hour he would send Neilly Mochan or Bob Rooney, his trainers, to shut the outside door. Nobody, famous or otherwise within the trade, would get in after that. Sometimes editors of newspapers would phone in, demanding that their man gain entry. Stein's stock response was, 'If they were interested in what I had to say they would get here in time. The door stays shut.' Short of camping out all night on the pavement, the lesson of the shut-door was not lost on those who suffered. For you would not dare miss what this man had to say, especially as Celtic looked more and more like generating most of the news that mattered. And they did so that season in the most spectacular way.

And, of course, set in the background of Celtic's robust, unbeaten juggernaut sweep from the opening day in August, when they beat Hearts at Tynecastle, until New Year's Eve 1966, when they eventually lost for the first time that season 3–2 to Dundee United at Tannadice, was the grinding, punishing commitment to the European Cup. In this period Stein's personality blossomed, his influence grew, his publicity burgeoned and eventually an intimation of his immortality was voiced by one Bill Shankly one late afternoon in Lisbon. An early hint of the way Celtic would go about their business came when they trounced a strong Manchester United team including Charlton, Law, Crerand and Best 4–1 in a pre-season friendly at Celtic Park, and overran Rangers 4–0 in a Glasgow Cup game at Ibrox. Not too many people paid much notice to these results, outside of the Celtic community itself, and even then not even in their wildest imaginings – and romanticising is not rare in Old Firm circles – could the Celtic support have had an inkling as to what was to emerge from this.

There were of course occasional glitches, and Dundee United merited almost a place of honour by beating this rampant club twice in the season, home and away in the league. But the domestic competition had to be interlocked with European football, which did not appear to take its toll in a greatly debilitating way. By the end of 1966, after their first defeat at United's hands at Tannadice, Celtic were leading the league by two points, which was something of a luxury for them considering what the club had become accustomed to before Stein's arrival – hanging on to the coat-tails of their great rivals. There was also an increasing feeling among onlookers that Stein had added an unquenchable desire not to be beaten under any circumstances, exemplified by an astonishing game at Dunfermline on 19 November when the team were three times behind, and at one stage 2–4 down, before recovering to win 5–4 after Joe McBride scored a late penalty.

Despite the plenitude of goals, three weeks later, to the surprise of many, Stein went into the transfer market and signed Willie Wallace from Hearts. 'What did he see in that player?' was the almost universal refrain. That was not a slur on Wallace, who had proved at Hearts that he was an extremely useful striker. It was just again, as I recall, the focus switching to the man who signed him. What was he up to? He already had two prolific strikers in Chalmers and McBride. But any action of his now was spiced by speculation and canny analysis in the media, which, of course, amused him greatly. Did he see something in Wallace that others didn't? On the other hand, it had been whispered that he had heard of Rangers' interest in that player and had acted accordingly. Whether that was so or not, it was remarkable that a quite mundane operation of the switching of clubs contained so much curiosity. If we are to believe that Stein was then uncannily aware that McBride was about to suffer knee pains and would shortly land up on the surgeon's table for an operation, we would be attributing to him powers normally associated with Nostradamus. Still, over two weeks later, on Christmas Eve, Joe McBride sadly played his last game of the season for Celtic, breaking down with a serious knee injury.

The simple reason for the transfer was that Stein wanted more firepower to hand. Indeed, the first time he played Chalmers, McBride and Wallace together, on 17 December, they ran riot and scored five goals in a 6–2 victory against Partick Thistle, Wallace and Chalmers getting a couple each and

McBride one. Chalmers admits that there was a new incentive to being a Celtic player, and that was fighting for a place in the side; prior to that many had taken their selection for granted. That was to be the recurring theme of the next few seasons. Celtic Park used to become as hushed as a crowded church before kick-off as the team was about to be announced, and sometimes that contained more intrigue than watching the game itself, as Celtic rolled over most of their opponents with ease, regardless of what tinkering Stein applied to the selection. He was only operating with about fourteen players who were outright candidates for a place in the team. But he would make most of his changes up front, where he would occasionally drop Johnstone, Hughes, McBride or Chalmers, although seldom Lennox, who nevertheless knew there was no such thing as a certainty for team selection. 'It didn't matter whether we got the points at Ibrox to win the league title and walked off the park,' Lennox said, 'there was no way of being absolutely sure you would be picked for the European final coming up in the next game. We could win 5–0 against somebody but that didn't mean you would be playing the following week. He kept us all on edge.'

The players were also seeing two sides of him when it came to preparation for games. For the ordinary league game he mostly walked in, announced the team, and that was that. Not the way it was done in the bad old days, though. Everything had already been worked out in advance. And as Stein had all his teams playing virtually the same way, from the youths right through to the senior side, there was an easy slotting-in of players from one level to the other if required. I would listen in later years to Louis van Gaal of Ajax telling me about the 'system' of that club which applied to every team of his, and was instantly reminded of how Stein, with perhaps less of the philosophical slant that the Dutchman put on his beliefs, had reshaped Parkhead on the basis of uniformity of approach. So many of the league games required little in the way of a systematic team talk. But for Europe it was different. Out would come the magnetic tactics board and in would go his input and his breakdown of the opposition. The players would listen transfixed, most of the time. It took a bold man to make a case against any of his ideas.

But in their first venture into Europe that season, against the Swiss side Zurich, a surprising discussion took place between manager and players which would perhaps throw light on the analysis of a much more significant game later that season and which has been shrouded in myth. For before the return game with Zurich in Switzerland virtually everybody in the squad disagreed with his assessment of how the Swiss would play. On 28 September at Parkhead Celtic had beaten them 2–0 with two late goals by Gemmell and McBride after a bruising game in which the Swiss did little other than defend and throw their weight about. When it came to the tactics board for the return leg, Stein insisted Zurich would play exactly the same way with their obvious 'sweeper' system. The players, at first, would not believe a team could play at home in such a manner and some of them were actually bold enough to disagree with Stein in the open. But he convinced them in his inimitably emphatic style that he was right. So much so that Gemmell sought out a bookie and, discovering that Celtic were 7–2 against for the win, couldn't get to his wallet quickly enough. He obviously went on to play with relish, for he scored two in the return, one from the penalty spot, and Chalmers with another gave the side an impressive 3–0 victory. So Stein's prescience, on that occasion, went a long way to convincing the players that their boss at the magnetic board was part tactician, part soothsayer. This was a massive step in increasing the self-assurance that lay at the root of their play.

Nobody raised a voice in doubt about the way he set out the next game in Nantes on 30 November. After going behind on sixteen minutes to a goal by Magny, they swamped the French with a thrusting display of attacking football that was theirs almost by nature now, and won 3–1. The second leg was no formality, but Johnstone was at his impish best and laid on goals for Chalmers and Lennox after having opened the scoring himself. Celtic were through to the quarter-finals with a second successive 3–1 victory.

Then came Vojvodina on 1 March 1967. Stevie Chalmers was suddenly aware of a different level of football. 'I think the Yugoslavs were the best team we played in the whole tournament,' he said, 'and that includes Inter in the final. Out there it was very hard. They really pressurised us, and I think it did us good to have that kind of opposition. For although the boss had read them well, as usual, and told us all about them, this time it was a real contest. Before that we seemed to be able to command the game, but this time they were all over us at times.' Such was the pressure put on the Celtic defence at times that Gemmell, attempting a back-pass to Simpson, fluffed his kick and Stanic, Vojvodina's outside-left, nipped in to score the only goal of the game. His error inadvertently led to, debatably, the most nerve-racking but dramatic ending to a game that Parkhead has ever seen. For a week after the Slavs' 1–0 victory they came to a stadium packed with 69,734 people for an emotional experience for spectators, players and management alike, which gave them an insight into how sturdy the nervous system in the human body is. As Tony Queen, the bookmaker, said to me later, 'It almost wrung the soul out of me that night.'

What it might have done to Stein, in a cumulative way, is really not in dispute, for he told me again on one of our trips that he really did wonder if all the preparation, all the self-confidence he had instilled in his players, was going to explode in his face, because they had run up against a technically skilled side. He did feel that it wasn't going to work out the way he had thought and he suffered perhaps the greatest tension since he had arrived at the club.

That night must have taken a heavy toll on him. From my commentary position, above the spectators in the new enclosure which still went by the name of 'The Jungle', I could look directly across the field into the Celtic dug-out. I recall him, above all, looking down at his wristwatch, holding it up to the floodlights as if he wasn't getting a proper sight of it, and doing it with growing frequency as the game came near its conclusion. In the 58th minute Chalmers had scored the goal that levelled the tie on aggregate when the giant keeper Pantelic fumbled a cross and the striker leapt on his chance to score. What then followed were repeated but perhaps too predictable charges at the Slav goal which were repulsed competently. With only a couple of minutes remaining Stein had given up hope. He had turned to Sean Fallon beside him and said simply, 'It looks like bloody Rotterdam!' That was where the third game was to be played if it ended in an aggregate draw. Salvation was on hand, though. Gallagher took a corner on the right and McNeill, storming through a gap in the Vojvodina defence, headed in the winner to mass exultation which reverberated in my eardrums well after the game was over. After such a tumultuous ending, anything was now possible.

But there was an army team to face next, and it produced one of the oddest games Stein's team ever played. Dukla Prague came from that pseudo-amateur culture behind the Iron Curtain in Czechoslovakia, and since they had in their side one of Europe's most famous midfield players ever, Josef Masopust, they would have to be treated with caution and respect. In the first game at Celtic Park on 12 April a couple of goals by Willie Wallace in the second half, to add to the one scored by Johnstone in the first minute, secured a bridgehead for the second leg, for the Czechs managed only one in reply.

The return game in Prague, of course, is distinguished for its historic outcome and has always been held up to be a collector's item in the Stein record-book. For this was supposedly the only occasion with Celtic when he deserted his positive principles and resorted to a defensive strategy, which affronted even his own purist sensibilities. Even Kelly the chairman, delighted with the outcome, still felt like disowning the manner in which the tactics had been laid down. That is all pure myth though. Of course it was a game noted for Celtic's stirring defensive performance. They were pummelled for almost the entire 90 minutes. But it had nothing to do with strategy. As Bobby Lennox said to me, 'If the Big Man set out a defensive pattern for us, then I must have missed the team talk. Not a word was passed on to us that we had to play a cautious game. Jimmy Johnstone and I had to go deep just to get the ball. We weren't told to lie deep.' Billy McNeill, who had perhaps his finest game for the club that day, confirmed to me years later that there was no pre-planning for defence. 'We were just played off the park by a very good team who just couldn't break us down. We couldn't get out of the stranglehold. It's that simple. We were told to go out and play our natural game.' Stevie Chalmers appeared to have a solitary role up front as part of a strategy, but, he said, 'That's nonsense. Not a word was passed on to me like that. We just couldn't keep the ball long enough. And once you're like that it is difficult to get back into a game. There was no defensive plan laid out for us.'

There is no reason to doubt their analyses of a game that ended goalless after some admittedly brilliant defending. So what was Stein trying to achieve when, after the euphoria of greeting an historic win which took them to a European final, he said on the record, 'I'll never resort to tactics like these again – never'?

Here we have to understand two things. Firstly, that Stein was a proud man, proud of his own achievements and the manner in which they were delivered by his men, who rightly had been lauded for their instinct to attack. He did not want that reputation dented by admitting that his side had clearly been outplayed. Secondly, the media rushed to judgement on the basis of a wonderful achievement and, according to Jim Craig's interpretation, may have sown the seed of an imaginary analysis in Stein's mind. 'The first remarks he made to the press immediately after the game, I believe, were misinterpreted,' said Craig, 'and when he saw the angle the press were coming from he let it ride, then encouraged it. They gave him an explanation and he accepted it.' He knew the press inside out and would not have needed to see John Ford's *The Man Who Shot Liberty Valance* to understand what the newspaper man meant when he said in that film, 'When the legend becomes fact, print the legend.' In this case they certainly did. Outplayed for virtually the whole game Celtic might have been, but triumph they certainly had. They were now the first British team to reach the European Cup final.

All that put Stein in the right frame of mind for the run-in to the championship, for even with all these commitments the Celtic players will tell you they felt no undue pressure and actually preferred playing all those matches since it meant they didn't need to train as much. The race boiled down to the final Old Firm game of the league season at Ibrox. Celtic needed only one point to secure another title and leave the European Cup as the only other trophy to be won that season. They had already lifted the Glasgow Cup and they had gone on to beat Aberdeen comfortably 2–0 in the Scottish Cup final, four days after the return from Prague. At Ibrox there was to be a deeply involved spectator though. Helenio Herrera, the Inter Milan coach, flew in by private jet to cast his eye over his Lisbon opponents.

It was 6 May, nineteen days before the Lisbon final. Rain fell insolently on Ibrox that day. I watched Herrera walk down Edmiston Drive to the entrance at the ground, surrounded by photographers and looking no more significant than a small, dark-haired, raincoated, inoffensive gasman come to check the meter in the stadium. Inside he had a grandstand view of Govan weather at its worst. He must have immediately pondered the basic difficulties Celtic would face in moving from the environment of the mud-track to the crisp lawn of the Estadio Nacional in Lisbon, even with a few weeks' interval. For the Ibrox pitch succumbed both to the weeping greyness of the day and the charging, sliding, frantically-paced commitment of both sides. Still, the churning of the pitch was but nothing compared to the churning of stomachs within the ranks of both sets of supporters as the game hung in the balance throughout. Celtic, meanwhile, had thrown off the Dukla 'shroud' that was now mythically attached to that game and were set for a traditional joust. They might have had good cause to shut up shop for their record of seven defeats and one draw in their previous eight league visits to the stadium could have encouraged extreme caution, but Stein would have none of that because he knew his players were better moving forward than in retreat. So they engaged Rangers in an out-and-out attacking game which, taken up as a challenge by the home side, made us forget the dreary elements. High up in the press box and commentary area I had a view of one of the best Old Firm games in history.

The first factor which made it so was that neither side seemed to succumb to the dreaded 'fear-of-losing' syndrome which can suck the imagination out of these fixtures. The physical nature of it was uncompromising, but measured and honest. And the swinging of fortunes from one side to the other meant that the surrounding triumphalism and gloating which naturally takes place on the terracings was rationed out in equal proportions, as illustrated by Rangers' first goal by Jardine on 40 minutes being followed by a Johnstone equaliser for Celtic just 60 seconds later. Stein had forgotten the note-taking Herrera; the Argentinian was absent from his mind during that game. There was to be no camouflaging of the talents of his team, no disguising of methods, no slackening of effort, no hiding of true personality from the spy. Attempting to beat Rangers again cleared the mind of all distractions, such as thinking about winning the European Cup. 'What you see is what you are going to get' might have been Stein's implicit warning to Herrera in that match.

The Argentine would certainly have spelt in capitals in his notebook the name Jimmy Johnstone. The wee winger, whose red locks stood out like a flame in a murky cave on that grey day until the rain flattened them on to his skull, danced as if to a toe-tapping fiddler whenever he had the ball at his feet and his twisting, squirming runs tormented the Rangers defence. His first goal had been a scrambled effort; his second, which put Celtic into the lead with just over a quarter of an hour remaining, has left people wondering to this day if it were the best he ever scored. He was supplied the ball from a throw-in by Chalmers, aimed for the Rangers penalty area; he veered diagonally left, defenders trailing after him, then smote a ferocious shot into the roof of the net with his left foot. After such a touch of greatness like that, which in effect settled the issue, Rangers' equaliser by Roger Hynd, Bill Shankly's nephew, seemed but a forlorn gesture, an anti-climax of little meaning, for Celtic did not look like conceding another, as the pitch had now taken its full toll and weary legs on either side made another penetration by anybody well nigh impossible. It ended 2–2. It was Celtic's second title in a row, their twenty-second in all.

Stein's delight was tempered by having to leave the stadium almost immediately to take a flight to Italy to see his opponents in their game against Juventus. It had been no surprise to him that an offer by Herrera to give him a lift in his private jet had mysteriously been withdrawn. Stein had kept his original flight booking, and after an exhausting journey he arrived in Turin.

The following day he was greeted, in a typical back-slapping manner, by Herrera himself who told him arrangements had been made for a car to take him to the stadium and that a ticket would be left for him. The transport never arrived, the ticket never materialised. Stein told journalists not to make too much of this, although it appeared that Herrera was treating him with some contempt. He went to the game with some journalists and had to cadge a press-ticket to get into the stadium. Again he warned the journalists that to make a fuss about this would play into Herrera's hands. He simply told John Mackenzie of the *Scottish Daily Express*, 'My time will come.' Snubbing Stein was like asking a Burnbank man for a fight. The 'jaiket' was definitely about to 'come aff'.

Inter were beaten 1–0 and the Juventus supporters waited outside the stadium after the game to howl abuse at them. On the return journey Stein was experienced enough to conclude that Inter had played that match with the serious intent of a side eager to win the Serie A title for the third year in a row. Just as it had been with his side at Ibrox the day before, nothing had been masked. But he did pick up something that lodged in his mind when he thought of the fresh legs he would take to Lisbon: it was the Juve supporters taunting the Inter team bus with the chant 'Vecchia Inter!' Stein barely needed a translation, for he could hardly have failed to recognise a basic characteristic of this Italian side that would influence even his thinking. The Juve fans had been shouting, 'Old Inter!'

CHAPTER FIFTEEN
GLORY

S o the miner from Burnbank, who had taken daily risks underground and displayed touches of benevolence to the rats down there, was now a surface-worker in a stadium in Lisbon where one slip could mean a different sort of catastrophe. It was 25 May 1967. He could see Herrera out of the side of his eye. They sat only yards apart on their benches in the unremitting sun, which scalded the 45,000 spectators within the Estadio Nacional, but in terms of football philosophy Herrera and Stein were as distant from each other as Earth is from the outer constellations.

The little Argentine guru, whose almost effete penchant for designer-wear contrasted with his Genghis Khan approach to discipline, had also been the midwife for the *catenaccio* system of defence which had emerged gradually from the gruelling Italian league. To defend was to win. To have that extra player sweeping at the back was the sign not of timidity and fear of losing but of supremacy, especially if you could find players to function properly. Herrera had. His side had won three out of the last four Serie A titles. He had lifted the European Cup in 1964, when Inter beat Real Madrid 2–1, and again in 1965, when they triumphed 1–0 against Benfica in their own San Siro stadium. Now, two years later, the fundamentals of style and method, almost cast in iron, remained. But as their own supporters were themselves wondering, had a slight rusting set in?

Stein preferred football on the front foot. In its simplest and best explanation he saw attack as the best form of defence. What he had in common with Herrera was that whatever system you chose to play, you had to have the players to suit. Stein had nine outfield players who could score goals. If you left out Simpson in goal and John Clark, who barely ever crossed the halfway line, all the others could and did score goals. This was 'total' football well before the Dutch laid claim to copyright on it. Stein was not up to creating phraseology to lodge in others' minds, but 'total' football is what it was, in an attacking sense. Perhaps the Dutch took it a stage further in terms of the interchangeability of players, but, looked at from the point of view of the opposition, when Celtic took the field teams were faced by threats from all angles. That is as good a definition of 'total' football as you can get.

Having won the battle of the benches through the efforts of his reserve keeper John Fallon, Stein and his staff saw Billy McNeill stride to the halfway line for the toss. Everybody was now edgy and desperate to get on with it. It is my view, and that of others who watched Stein closely over the weeks approaching the final, and especially in the last three days, that he did not believe Celtic were going to lose. It was not conveyed in any arrogant way. Quite the contrary: the confidence seemed to stem from his controlled tension and the perception that he was absolutely in control of the most minute detail of preparation. He also gave the impression in some of his banterings with the media, and in the unruffled manner with which he had quiet talks with individual players, that only some external and unexpected influence could alter the inevitability of it all.

That slight fear of the unexpected was to lead to an outburst at half-time that would rank very high indeed among Stein's series of volcanic outbursts against referees. For the game took a turn for the worse after only eight minutes, when Jim Craig tackled the Italian forward Cappellini, who came to earth inside the box in a way that was seen by Stein from the bench as belonging to the artificial death-throes of a singer in Italian Grand Opera. As the German referee Tschenscher pointed to the spot, Stein instinctively rose to his feet and gesticulated towards Herrera in disgust, as if to acknowledge that impropriety was the name of the game when it came to Italians influencing referees. Indeed, the tall German did look as if he was fond of a plate of pasta or two, and his adamant advance into the box indicating the offence obviously aroused in Stein, as we would see at half-time, an image of the Mussolini strut. But penalty it was. It was so technically a fudge – it could have gone either way – that it would have brought any protesting manager out of his bolt-hole, and it was greeted with disbelief by the Celtic players. Mazzola sent Simpson one way, the ball the other, into the net.

Watching from the television gantry beside Kenneth Wolstenholme, who adopted the 'us' and 'we' pronouns in a newfound affiliation with Celtic, we could not discern any slackening of the Celtic momentum after going one down. They probed and ran at the Italians as if the penalty incident had simply been a figment of their imagination. Jimmy Johnstone told me afterwards that he didn't think he had one of his better games in that match because he had been so closely marked by Burgnich. But it's what he represented to the nature of the game that mattered. He seemed to personify the unceasing urgency of his colleagues, who admitted they had feared losing an early goal to a team with a reputation for defensive technique equalled only by the Boulder Dam. Johnstone was looking tireless. The tide of the later stages of the game were hinted at when Auld hit the bar, and while Gemmell seemed to be relishing his deep running into their half, some of his shots at goal were proving that Sarti, the Inter goalkeeper, was having 'one of those days'; he thwarted one of the full-back's shots in particular that ought to have brought the equaliser.

Stein had recovered some of his composure after the penalty incident and was back to controlled, carefully rationed shouting from the bench. But that was the lull before the storm. For when the whistle sounded for the end of the half, with Celtic one down, the manager waited ominously on the touchline instead of following his players immediately to the tunnel. John Fallon, who in the first season of goalkeeping substitutes in the competition had of course watched the game from the bench close to Stein, witnessed his approach to the referee.

'As Tschenscher came walking across with the ball, Jock let rip. "You're a Nazi bastard!" he shouted at him. "A penalty kick? You were conned! Where are you gonnae get your villa?" He gave him dog's abuse. The referee looked stunned. I don't think anybody had ever talked to him like that before. You could tell he knew exactly what the boss was saying. He tried just to ignore him, but he was definitely shaken. I couldn't believe it myself. He just kept at it until we went into the tunnel.'

It has to be said that later that evening Stein was to be heard complimenting the referee on his control of the game. But the desired effect at half-time was to make sure that if there had been anything underhand going on, considering the reputations the Italians had amassed as manipulators of officials, then the German was under the scrutiny of a man who looked as if he would make a citizen's arrest if he felt there were any more dodgy decisions. And he wasn't finished there, because on entering the tunnel he became embroiled in a heated exchange with Herrera which must have had more to do with body language than anything else because of the language barrier. But bitterness was swapped unambiguously between the two, even though the Celtic manager had been an admirer of the Argentine when they had first met in Italy. Stein poured contempt on him. The respected magazine *France Football* reported that 'Jock Stein et Helenio Herrera faillerent en venir au mains', meaning they almost came to blows, and then went on to say that Stein had addressed the Inter coach 'avec beaucoup de véhémence', which is easily translatable. The magazine then claimed that Stein had accused Herrera of asking his defenders to execute 'le jeu trop irrégulier', which means 'playing dirty'. This was all in stark contrast to the initial impressions he had made of the man when he had gone to Inter's mountain retreat to study his methods and come back impressed by his totalitarian control of players. Now, Herrera must have regretted allowing Stein to come anywhere near the Alps.

But the man who appeared in the Celtic dressing-room at half-time was not the man who had just imposed a one-man blitzkreig on the German and Herrera. He was controlled and coherent, which suggests that what happened on the touchline and in the tunnel was a deliberate calculation. The players noted that he was showing no undue concern, but simply talked to them about not losing the impetus they had gained. The players did not need to be reminded of that, for they were still surprised that the Italians had really offered nothing much to worry about. They were beginning to realise that perhaps they had overestimated their potential. They were never going to be overawed by them, but they had thought the Inter players had some tricks in their possession that might catch them out. But these hadn't appeared and, as Stein himself noted, there were sure signs out there that the Italians were beginning to tire.

The Inter players had to be called on by the referee several times for the resumption of the game. Whether that indicated a ploy to have Celtic wait out in the broiling, sapping 85-degree heat, or whether it was basic arrogance or a team in need of a longer rest, we cannot be sure. But it didn't matter. Like many others in Lisbon that day I can remember that second half as a celebration of the positive properties of sport, of a triumph of the master of optimism over the peddler of the dark arts. The television-viewing public around Europe were watching what might have appeared to be an improvisational group of men told to go out and play their natural game against organised puppets. That would be an over-simplification. But in truth, anybody seeking complex tactical structures in the Inter side would have been hard put to do so, for as that half proceeded they looked as cool and sophisticated as a bunch of navvies trying to mend holes in a dyke. For at the time, and not with the benefit of hindsight, you could feel almost overpoweringly that Inter could not hold out, and so it proved.

They had just one redeeming feature on their debit sheet of wholly sterile play, their goalkeeper Sarti, who was presumed to be the weak link. Instead he made a series of bewildering saves, including one from a six-yard header by Murdoch, which he fielded behind his back with one hand in a manner of which Meadowlark Lemon of the Harlem Globetrotters would have been proud. The equaliser, when it came in the 62nd minute, was sweet justice. It also affected both Wolstenholme and me in the commentary position, and I am sure also neutrals throughout Europe who were wishing well the virtues of attacking football. Instead of the presumably banal words we used, our exclamation ought to have been, 'Thank God, justice prevails!' Inter had been winning no friends in looking as if they wanted to hijack the game by deciding not to play football, merely to spoil, guard, shuffle and look as if they were defending not just a goalmouth but a theory. They were about to get what they deserved.

Gemmell retains the goal he scored in his mind like a valuable original canvas jealously guarded in his own private gallery. It is painted thus: 'I was screaming for the ball. Screaming for it. I screamed three times for Jim Craig to square the ball to me. Then it came. If you watch the tape of the goal you will see something interesting. An Italian defender comes out to meet me. But then he stops about two yards from me and turns his back. If he had kept coming and kept facing me I would never have got that shot in and the whole history of the Lions would have been changed.' Hindsight and tape viewing can lead to undue modesty, for if it hadn't happened then, it would have later in the game.

Then came the moment that had almost been destined from the time the final whistle had blown in Prague. As a winner, its significance far exceeded its execution, but it has been pickled and jarred to be preserved for all time by those who witnessed it, and for those who didn't but have had it recounted to them. It came five minutes from the end. Chalmers cunningly invaded the penalty box as Murdoch struck at goal, and screwed the ball away from Sarti with the side of his foot into the net. Compared to Gemmell's strike it was quite mundane. The striker had scored many more spectacular goals before, but this is the one that elevated the occasion to a new level and perched the club on an historical shelf from which they could never be removed.

In the few remaining minutes thousands of Celtic supporters crushed down the marble terracings to press around the other side of the perimeter moat, ready for an invasion that would make the dry trench look an irrelevance. All this inspired Auld to take the ball 'walkies' to the corner and waste time. But in truth, the Italians were done. The legs were gone. Whether

Stein assumed that or not, he began to walk towards the tunnel before the final whistle sounded. He would not admit it, but it did look as if he couldn't bear sitting out those few minutes. When the whistle did sound he managed to get on to the field to hug Ronnie Simpson and Billy McNeill before the multitudes in green and white surged over the moat and took possession of the rest of the day in an outpouring of relief and joy which almost ventured into mass hysteria as they went after the players. It wasn't just homage they wanted to pay, but to take from the players' perspiring bodies any memento they could get. Nothing was sacred. Shirts, pants, boots, anything. But it was good-natured, and Stein had to come back on to the pitch to help clear it, as it looked as if the cup presentation would be impossible.

Ronnie Simpson thought he had a headstart, being at the goal near the tunnel, and rushed off quickly, then halted and raced back, for he had left his false teeth in the back of the net. So he was collared too. Sent by the BBC to get the first television interview with Stein, I landed among the crowd who by that stage were trying to touch their heroes, anoint them with their adulation. I saw Tommy Gemmell being almost ripped apart; the exhausted player's arms were being pulled in opposite directions by worshipping supporters. By then, Stein was in the middle of it all, grabbing supporters and throwing some aside like empty sacks to persuade them to leave the field so that the presentation of the cup could be made. Failing to get Stein because of the turmoil, I was asked by the Portuguese authorities to make an announcement to the Celtic supporters to clear the field, but they wouldn't have been driven off the field by the militia. They were enjoying themselves ecstatically, and who could blame them?

In the dressing-room, eventually, and a considerable time after the final whistle, Bobby Lennox, looking for the captain, asked, 'Where's Billy?' They had forgotten a cup had to be presented and the captain had been secreted around the stadium to the podium just in front of us in the commentary position, where with considerable poise and unbridled pride he lifted the cup high above his head. The other players never saw this emotionally vibrant moment.

Inside the dressing-room there was, of course, bedlam. By this time the press had invaded, to which obviously Stein now offered no resistance. Alan Herron of the *Sunday Mail* was one of the first there, and just behind him suddenly appeared Bill Shankly, who pushed out his hand and uttered the famous words, 'John, you're immortal now!' Stein, covered in perspiration, simply laughed. He did not look ecstatic; he looked more a relieved man. Bertie Auld said to me in reflection once, 'I got the impression that all Jock wanted to do then was to go away into a quiet corner and cry. He had done the job.' When Billy McNeill returned with the trophy they had been playing for and handed it round for the sipping of champagne, he presented it to Stein. The manager lifted it to his lips, then lowered it again without taking so much as a sip. 'No,' he said. 'Why should I?' He was as loyal to his teetotalism on that day as he had been to his ethic of attacking football.

The players received their medals eventually in a restaurant in the old town of Lisbon where they gathered for a banquet and where Billy McNeill handed them out one by one, without ceremony. As Bobby Lennox said, 'It was like he was handing out sweeties.' Not that the players cared then about what might have appeared to be an anti-climax. Stein sat at the top table, looking somewhat ill at ease, as if he were suffering withdrawal symptoms now that it was all over. As I have said, he could be the most central party animal when he was with close friends, but on the other hand he hated the formal occasions and small talk. And he was still on edge. There was a residue of tension still lingering within his large frame, and I made the mistake of approaching his players as they sat at a long table at the far end of the room. I had obviously crossed that invisible line the players kept talking about, which if crossed brought Stein down on you like a clap of thunder. For he came storming down the room, grabbed me by the arm and pulled me away from the table, as if I was trying to steal one of their medals.

So, as was evident from his refusal to sip the champagne, he had not metamorphosed into a different personality. He was exactly the same man who had arrived in that country two days earlier. Success had not instantly redefined him, but it had been pocketed away somewhere for some more deeply private reflection. And it was in that mood that Bertie Auld overheard him telling Bill Shankly in the bus, 'That team will never be beaten.' It was said with such a soft and sincere intensity that it took Auld aback. When he remarked to Stein that that was an almost impossible prediction to make even about the eleven players who had just reached the pinnacle of club football, the manager simply repeated it. 'That team will never be beaten,' he said. It wasn't until later that Auld realised precisely what Stein had meant by that. It became dramatically more evident only two weeks later in Madrid. In fact, many of the Lisbon Lions were affected by that statement as their memory of other matches with that precise Lisbon selection have been fogged by Stein's seminal declaration, which became part of the legend of that day. However, they did play together again, no fewer than eight times, and were beaten once, by Dynamo Kiev four months later. But he did try all he knew to make his statement stand the test of time.

The following morning, as he relaxed around the pool, Lord Gordon of Strathblane, then Jimmy Gordon, one of Scotland's leading broadcasters and journalists and the writer of the film *The Celtic Story*, sat down beside Stein for a chat. 'I really didn't know how to start the conversation,' Gordon recalled. 'What do you say after such a momentous day? I couldn't think of anything else other than "Well, it's been a marvellous season." He just paused for a moment and then replied, "Yes, but what about next season? What's going to happen then?" It was then I realised that even this great man, after a great feat, was no different from any other manager in the game. They all have to live with an underlying feeling of insecurity. He had reached a peak, but only one day later here he was thinking of how long he could stay there.'

Stein had no contract and never did sign one at Celtic Park. But not even the winning of Europe's greatest club trophy could give him a feeling of indemnity against the perils of his trade. And some of these were lying in wait.

CHAPTER SIXTEEN
DOWN ARGENTINE WAY

The return to Glasgow was climaxed by a tumultuous welcome at Celtic Park where the cup was duly paraded in front of an exultant, adoring crowd – minus, of course, many stragglers from the terracings of the Estadio Nacional who by various routes were still attempting to get back to the city. Normality was difficult to attain after such a victory. But although Stein was in evidence, not as a flamboyantly rejoicing figure but more as an elder figure allowing youngsters in the next room a party with a midnight curfew, he still couldn't throw off the nagging thought of how to follow that triumph.

In a practical sense there was the immediate challenge of Alfredo Di Stefano's testimonial match against Real Madrid in the Bernabeu Stadium, to be faced up to in the next two weeks. They had accepted that commitment even though some of the players would rather have gone off for the summer break. But Stein couldn't resist it. When he announced his team for this game, it began to dawn on Auld and others what Stein had implied by saying that his Lisbon side would never be beaten. For he did not select it for this next prestigious match. It was not the Lisbon Lions, as they were now called, who were to play in Madrid, for Stein made two changes: Simpson was replaced by John Fallon, Gemmell by O'Neill. Coming so soon after Lisbon, Stein feared that should they lose in Spain at least he could claim it was not the original Lisbon Lions. He was beginning to guard a reputation.

The Bernabeu game, friendly though it was, remains one of Celtic's most timely performances. The danger for them was an embarrassing anti-climax, so Stein prepared for it with the gravity of a man approaching another major final. He told Auld, for example, to make sure the great midfielder Amancio was kept subdued. Auld took that instruction to extremes, eventually feeling so provoked by the niggly player that he threw a punch at him. Both were sent off after a fracas that underlined the fact that this match was not being played in the Corinthian spirit. The game was won by a single goal scored by Bobby Lennox, who stunned the vast arena into silence with his lightning strike. It was confirmation that a new power had been established in Europe.

The Celtic party took special pleasure in the compliments they received as they came off the pitch. John Fallon, the goalkeeper, thought he personally had had an especially productive night. 'I had one of my best games ever in Madrid,' he said. 'It was just one of those nights where I was getting to everything. So at the end we were all delighted to become the first British team to win in the Bernabeu. I remember Bob Kelly standing there and all the handshakes that were going on. I was getting my fair share of them for my performance and was looking pleased with myself. Somebody came up to me and was saying that I had had a great game and I was just about to shake hands with this man when I felt a hand pulling my arm away just as our hands touched. It was Jock. He just barked at me, "You're bloody well paid to play like that!" That put a right damper on me. He seemed to think it was right to bring you down with a bang. He didn't like anybody to get carried away with himself. How could you read this man?'

This further suggested that Stein seemed to regard goalkeepers as a species lower down the evolutionary chain from others. He himself had once played for 40 minutes in goal for Albion Rovers in an emergency, an experience that obviously scarred him for life. In an article in the *Celtic View* of 21 January 2004, Stein was quoted as saying this in reference to the marvellous goalkeeping display of John Bonnar in the Coronation Cup final: 'Lots of people say we were lucky and that Bonnar saved us, but then that's what he was there for!' Stein's eruptions and capricious swings of mood came from a pressure that sought outlets virtually 24 hours a day. His enigmatic, unpredictable temperament was one of the most identifiable features of his personality and seemed to be crucial in exerting unquestioning power.

He had all of that put to the test when Celtic embarked on their attempt to win the World Club Championship five months after the European Cup win. The squad had to travel south of the equator for the first time in the club's history to take on Racing Club of Argentina, the South American title holders, after a first leg at Hampden Park on 18 October. Celtic, as exemplars of a healthy democratic system that had triumphed in fascist Portugal, might not have been fully aware of the political phenomenon that had surrounded them in the Lisbon spring, but they were about to discover that the legacy of a Peronista Argentina was a *pro patria* fanaticism many of us were to experience full blast in 1978, and which would make violent interplay between crowd and game almost inevitable.

That first match at Hampden, shortly after Celtic's exit at the hands of Dynamo Kiev at the first stage of their defence of the European Cup – a setback which had caused people to wonder whether Stein was losing his touch – would have been a warning even to less sensitive souls, as the Argentines indulged in niggly, spasmodically crude and wholly defensive football. They wished to stop Celtic playing any form of positive football, and almost succeeded. It was again McNeill scoring in his inimitable way, with his head from a Hughes corner-kick, that lent Celtic a slender lead to take with them to entirely new surrounds where they experienced the kind of hostility you might have thought was reserved only for an invading army. Through their entire stay in Buenos Aires they were under constant supervision by the police. In the shopping precincts, when out for a stroll or sitting around the hotel, and even in church when they went to services, the guns and batons surrounded them. Water cannons were used on some belligerent fans as their bus entered the stadium on the day of the game, just to give them a foretaste of what was to come, and then during the warm-up came the ultimate warning of how their journey might end disastrously: Ronnie Simpson was struck on the head by an iron bolt thrown from the crowd and was knocked unconscious. John Fallon had to strip for action only minutes before kick-off. Stein was enraged and worried, but there was nothing he could do about it. The game had to be played.

In the first few minutes of the match on 1 November, one of Racing Club's forwards systematically went around spitting in as many Celtic faces as he could find. At half-time Johnstone had to wash his hair to cleanse it of the mass of spittle that had accurately been dumped on him. That Celtic scored first through a penalty by Gemmell only incited the Argentines to greater mayhem. They kicked and hacked their way around, the Uruguayan referee looking as if he were complicit in all of it. On one occasion their goalkeeper ran all of 40 yards just to pat Johnstone on the head in commiseration when he was lying on the ground after having been felled; he also added a furtive kick to the little winger's ribs when the referee turned away. In the growing disorder, Racing Club scored twice through Raffo and Cardenas to set up a chapter in Celtic's history that would better have been side-stepped. For now the final had to go to a third game in Montevideo, across the other side of the River Plate.

It is easy enough in retrospect to say they should not have gone since there was scant chance of their receiving justice or charity: there was clear evidence of the inability of South American referees to corral the wilder Latin temperaments. But although chairman Bob Kelly simply did not want to take this third match on, he was in effect overruled by Stein. But, as Bobby Lennox revealed, the manager had the backing of the players. 'We felt we were a better team than them and they could be beaten,' he said. 'Maybe we were a bit naïve to think it would be a straightforward match. But we wanted to go because we felt that outside of Argentina we would do it. If we were allowed to play it was going to be all right. But it wasn't about football though. They made it a battle and we fell right into their trap. Maybe we were naïve about it all.' John Hughes believes that Stein's own ambitions fuelled his thinking. 'He wanted to do something that nobody had achieved before in Britain and get a world title. I believe he put that above every other factor. He wasn't going to give up that readily. Yes, the players wanted to go, but he should have read the danger signals and gone along with the chairman's thinking. It was a disaster for us and he should have seen it coming.'

Stein felt that not to go would mean a charge of cowardice could be levelled at the club. What ultimately occurred, however, had an almost total measure of inevitability about it, and it almost compels you to conclude that it was a tragic if understandable mistake on his part to proceed, for under severe provocation again the Celtic players could restrain themselves no longer and fought back. In that match in Montevideo on 5 November six players were ordered off, four from Celtic and two from Racing Club, and twice the police had to be called in to restore order on the field. From the kick-off the spitting started again, the ankle knocking resumed and the elbowing in the ribs on the wrong side of the referee recommenced until certain of the players could stand it no longer.

Gemmell decided on retribution against the untitled world champion of spitting, the winger Raffo. Nobody gives a more graphic description of the incident than Gemmell himself. 'They were all standing around watching someone getting treatment with about fifteen minutes to go and I saw this thug standing there with a great big grin on his face and I decided he wasn't going to get away with it. I did a tip-toe through the tulips and I hit him one almighty kick in the bollocks. I can still hear him screaming to this day. Down he went. Five of them started to chase me. Big Jock came running on, screaming at me, "What are you trying to do, for God's sake?"' This unacceptable incident was captured by the television cameras and beamed around the world. So also were other incidents involving Celtic players, who by now, being human, could stand the Argentine antics no

The lean and hungry-looking Stein, as Albion Rovers centre-half, in pursuit of his prey, and life-long friend, Airdrie's Jock Aitken at the old Broomfield Stadium in 1944 in front of 7,000. It was not his day as the local rivals won 3-2.

The Celtic captain at Ibrox in 1953. He had a snappy left foot and a sublime right knee. The origin of his powerful use of the right knee as a substitute for his weak right appendage is slightly misted in dispute.

Jimmy Gribben, the Celtic trainer on the left, assisting Celtic's Dick Beattie from the field in April 1956, offered greater historic aid to the club by whispering in the chairman's ear one day the name, ' Stein'.

From his earliest days he took to the mike like he took to a pair of football boots. The range of his repertoire of songs never ceased to amaze his friends.

May 1966. A holiday snap from Bermuda. John Hughes, Bertie Auld, Joe McBride, Neilly Mochan and the manager reflecting the more serious undertone of a North American tour which helped forge the triumphant team spirit of 1967.

The triumphant return to a packed Parkhead with the trophy on 26 May 1967 with Stein, amidst the adulation, lending more than a hint that he was thinking, 'What next?'

Deluged by congratulations Stein could afford a little relaxation after Lisbon by dallying with the European Cup and using it as the most valuable paperweight in the history of the game.

December 1967. Stein and Busby. The Celtic manager receives the BBC Team of the Year award from the other Lanarkshire man. It simply excites the question, 'Why did they eventually knight one, and not the other?'

Master of all he surveyed at the height of his power in the early 1970s. Almost like the laird walking his estate it suggests rightly that nothing happened at Celtic Park, from cutting the grass to designing a new stand, without his personal approval.

A rare public picture. With his wife Jean, welcoming his son George back from a trip playing for Celtic's Boys Club in the USA; Stein normally protected his family fiercely from the glare of publicity.

After December 1969, the Old Firm rivalry took on a personal gladiatorial duel between Willie Waddell, manager of Rangers on the left, and Stein. The Celtic manager did little to disguise that he liked winning these more than anything else.

No hiding place for bigotry. Stein about to leave the terracing at Stirling Albion's Annfield ground in August 1972 after launching himself into the crowd to scatter sectarian chanters.

Stein as the hands-on manager. He took unkindly to pitch invasions and in clearing Parkhead one day in April 1977 he did not wait for assistance. Seconds later the photographer got the message too.

*The last of Kenny. His final game at Dunfermline, on 10 August 1977.
Stein's deeply etched regret seems to symbolise the end of a golden era for the club.*

*Desmond White, Celtic chairman, and Billy MacNeill as new manager of the club
contrive an awkward handshake of acceptance in May 1978. In this tableau a humbled giant
could not avoid the chilling role of outcast.*

Ernie Walker, the secretary of the SFA, tickles then new Scotland manager Stein with his typical repartee just after his appointment on the 4 October 1978. Their bonding defied all cynical predictions of a clash of personalities.

Before the last game in Cardiff against Wales in 1985. The situation is obviously no picnic for Stein and his assistant Alex Ferguson. There is strain and uncertainty here. Rubbing shoulders with Stein though helped the other man further his career.

*Under
unprecedented
media criticism at
times in his role as
Scotland manager
in the early 1980s,
Stein's obvious
anxiety on the
Scotland bench
contrasts with the
coolness of Don
Howe and Bobby
Robson.*

*Cardiff. 10
September 1985.
Wales-Scotland.
The incident.*

*Friday 13
September 1985.
The sun shone
that day as it had
in Lisbon.*

longer. Bertie Auld was ordered off by the referee but refused to go. As Gemmell recalled, Auld was abrupt with him. 'He told the referee to eff off as he wasn't going to go, and Bertie did stay on the park. Now, if he had gone off the referee would have had to stop the game because there would not have been enough Celtic players on the park. And what did he start the game with after that Auld incident? A free-kick to Celtic. The whole thing was a farce.'

Cardenas of Racing Club won the world title for his team by scoring the only goal of this infamous match in the 55th minute. It is a statistic that stands out like the stark irrelevance of the text of the play Mr and Mrs Lincoln were watching the night John Wilkes Booth intervened. For an assassination of Celtic's character was now underway by those, particularly outside Scotland but not exclusively so, who had paid scant attention to the preliminaries before Montevideo and who in any case could not accept Celtic's achievements as anything other than fortuitous.

One such was Peter Lorenzo, an English journalist and broadcaster who was known to have given Celtic some savaging in his reports and who was upbraided by an equally famous Scottish journalist James Sanderson, or 'Solly' as he was generally known, in the airport lounge before flying home from Montevideo when there was a delay for two hours because of fog. In keeping with the mayhem of the preceding day, Solly, who would have entered a boxing ring as a bantamweight, decided to defend Celtic's honour against the heavyweight Lorenzo's bad-mouthing by delivering him a swift right hook to the jaw, which floored the Englishman. Although apologies were made for this misconduct, by other journalists, Solly had acted as many of his colleagues had felt like doing, though they opted to uphold that old adage that the pen is mightier than the sword. A more measured response was John Rafferty's, in the *The Observer* of 12 November: 'Their main condemnation is that they lost the championship of the world because they lost their heads, and that is the thought that they will have to live with, but in the circumstances to condemn them for this and to pillory them and to castigate them and to forget about their astonishing good behaviour of the past year is shameful.'

Bob Kelly had no option but to fine his players for their conduct, however much they had been provoked. Kelly did so by not paying the bonus money of £250 which was due to them after their 5–3 victory over Dundee in the League Cup final prior to their trip. That money was donated to charities of

Celtic's choosing. But Stein had already decided, even as he flew home with the criticism ringing in his ears, that like his basic football belief, which had brought him such success over the past year, the best form of defence of his players was to attack.

CHAPTER SEVENTEEN
DEFENDING THE FAITH

When he returned from South America Stein was 45 and in his prime as the major club manager of his era, having in May 1967 been awarded the British Manager of the Year title for the second successive time. He was in good health, apart from the usual limp, which could produce the occasional grimace when he put his foot down heavily. In his immediate post-Lisbon mood he was bristling with good humour and sharp in interview, sending off journalists and commentators with quick shafts of wit; you felt he was the master of all he surveyed. Although he was a large, bulky man, there was a roguishness about some of his ripostes during interview which suggested that you could take the lad out of Burnbank but not Burnbank out of the lad. He would spar with the media with a biting humour that seemed to echo some of the banter I was told he had been capable of as a young man, hanging around with his mates at the cross in his native village. Other notables in Scottish football of that period looked amateurish by comparison in their handling of issues in public with interviewers, and were rigidly formal and predictable. With Stein, you always felt he was ahead of you, thinking of how to rebut or to add something of the unexpected to knock you off balance. He could toy with you.

But when he returned from the other side of the equator that autumn we saw glimpses of a blacker, more mistrustful mood, especially directed towards the organisation I represented, the BBC. He had been deeply hurt and angered by some of the television coverage from South America, which highlighted Gemmell's kicking of the Argentine player and which in its incessant surfacing on the box was tending to convey the notion that Celtic had been principally at fault for the breakdown in discipline in that series of games. There was, of course, no alternative for any television company but to show scenes that highlighted misconduct. Gemmell's blatant and furtive attack was irresistible for any producer. I should admit that as we met to review this particular cameo of the Celtic full-back creeping surreptitiously around a group of players to swiftly kick the *agent provocateur*, our production team simply burst out laughing. In a sense it was almost like a scene from an early Charlie Chaplin movie, the little man wreaking unexpected revenge on a bully, for after all the full-back and others had had to endure extreme provocation. Stein, not surprisingly, did not see the funny side of it and concluded that his player and his club were being deliberately stitched up. He was especially sore about London's interpretation of events, as if it was not only Celtic who were being traduced but, by implication, Scotland as well. He went for the jugular.

In a radio interview – which he insisted on doing live because, as he said on the air, he could not trust the BBC to edit a recording properly – he lambasted the corporation for showing the Gemmell incident without putting it in the context of the brutality of the Argentines. All the exposure of that, though, had originated from BBC London's handling of the game and had nothing to do with the Scottish end of it. But we were all being tarred by the same brush. When he was in that frame of mind it was impossible to reason with him. A rant then developed into the sort of prejudice against the corporation that was to run for a good couple of years, until we had an intense shoot-out, he and I, in the Celtic boardroom which helped clear the air. Years later, of course, he was to become the BBC's most esteemed football analyst throughout the UK. And in December 1967 Celtic were awarded with the Team of the Year trophy in the BBC TV *Sportsview* presentations programme.

It is also true that Rangers did not have anybody to match Stein's stature, even though they had produced a new young manager in Davie White, a former Clyde player who always talked intelligently about football but lacked presence and credibility. The first opportunity to put this starkly obvious imbalance to the test was on 2 January 1968 at Celtic Park. The Celtic players noticed an even greater air of anticipation about their manager for this fixture. It was also only the second time that this traditional game had been moved away from 1 January. The players could sense that kick-off could not come quickly enough for their boss. Stein knew that a victory, and a handsome one at that, would seriously dent the new man's relationship with the Rangers support, which had begun to worry seriously about the future and doubted White's credentials. Now was the time to inflict heavy damage on that embryonic and fragile Ibrox bond.

But it did not quite work out that way, for the game hinged on a selection choice by Stein that brought about another embarrassing Celtic goalkeeping story. For John Fallon it brought pain, then retribution. 'I had been told that I was to play against Clyde at Shawfield in a match the day before the Rangers game,' he recalled, 'and when I sat there in the dressing-room waiting to get ready I saw my boots being taken away and Ronnie Simpson's put in my place. I said nothing. You didn't ask any questions. For some reason Jock had changed his mind. Ronnie played and went over on his ankle. After the match the big man said about Ronnie, "Don't worry, he'll be all right. He's at it. He'll play tomorrow." So I reported to Celtic Park for the Rangers game firmly believing that I would be sitting it out. I was in the table-tennis room just about ten minutes before the game started when the door was kicked open and in came Jock. He grabbed me and said, "You're playing." I couldn't believe it. I had stayed out late the night before, not thinking of a game, and I had had a big late breakfast. When I went into the dressing-room ,the referee Bobby Davidson was actually waiting for me to check my boots, for the rest were ready to go out. It was that late. I just wasn't geared up for it.

'And I suffered. I lost a goal to Willie Johnstone, which I should have saved, but John Clark had been in front of me and I didn't have a clear view and when you look at it again it wasn't as bad a blunder as it first appeared. We had been one up through Bertie Auld, then there was that equaliser by Johnston. Bobby Murdoch put us back in the lead. And then two minutes to go when the game looked well won by us, Johansen made a long run from deep in his own half, with our defence backing off him. I remember him saying afterwards that he didn't hit the ball right. That was correct. He sliced it. I was anticipating the high ball, but it swerved and went right under me into the net. It was a howler, I must admit. Rangers had got off the hook.

'After the game Jock didn't miss me. He looked at one stage as if he would strangle me. I've never felt so scared. I still recall that, and I honestly shiver at times when his name comes up, thinking he's going to come back to haunt me. The upshot was that I was effectively "sent to Coventry" for a year. I never kicked a ball in earnest in all that time.'

The game hung like a black cloud over that player's head for the remainder of 1967/68, for if Rangers had not dropped three points in their final three games, Fallon's mistakes might have cost the club the championship. Stein did realise that the blunder by Fallon had let his new young managerial challenger off the hook. There is no doubt in any player's mind that he wanted to embarrass White seriously that day. It was a memory, he was to tell me, that kept coming back to irritate him and he was after revenge. But this was nothing more than a slight dip in his upward march, and Celtic went on to win the title for the third consecutive year.

Stein knew that if White were to be of any value to Rangers the challenge would come in the following season, and indeed in their first encounter on 14 September of season 1968/69 at Celtic Park, Rangers won 4–2 and it began to look as if the Rangers board had made the right managerial decision. Stein frankly admitted that the result annoyed him but did not disturb him unduly, and subsequent events were to show how right that attitude was. And only three weeks after that he had to deal with a public insurrection that was to test his mettle in handling player relationships.

Sitting in the commentary position for the Celtic v. Dundee United game on 5 October, I watched Stein decide to make a substitution. He called off Jimmy Johnstone, who was having one of those dithering days that even the best of mercurial ball-players can have. But Johnstone was always a trier, and more often than not what he tried came off. That day it was not happening for him. As he left the field, to the astonishment of everybody present including myself, Johnstone took off his jersey and threw it in disgust into the dug-out where it just happened to strike Stein on the face. The little man then raced up the tunnel. It was difficult to believe what we were seeing. It was as near as you could get to a Pamplona street-runner baiting one of the bulls and then scarpering.

Now, there was abundant admiration and affection for Johnstone among the support, but I swear you were immediately conscious of the 46,000 crowd holding its breath collectively as they waited to see the response. It came in a nanosecond. Stein leapt from his seat and hirpled, with that distinct limp, faster than I had ever seen him travel in pursuit of his little red-haired winger. Both men disappeared from sight down the tunnel and you were left to wonder what sounds of woe would emerge from within. Would we see a river of blood running back down the tunnel on to the track? Johnstone takes up the narrative: 'As soon as I did it I thought, "My God, what have I done?" and I belted up the tunnel as fast as I could, but I knew he would be right behind me. My first notion was just to run straight out of the front door without changing and head down London Road and just disappear for ever. But I got into the dressing-room, slammed the door shut, then locked it. I was about to dive into where the big bath was and shut that door when I heard him kicking the door, then battering it with his fist. I knew then I was in deep shit. I stood behind the door ready to put my shoulder to it if needed, then I knew I had to say something. I shouted out, "I'll let you in if you promise not to hit me!" Then the battering suddenly stopped and there was a kind of silence, and, would you believe, he burst out laughing at what I had said. He just laughed, and I heard him walking away, for the game was still going on out there. He had calmed down when I saw him eventually and I was suspended for seven days for that. That was nothing, considering that if he had got his hands on me I might never have lived to have a suspension.' Celtic went on to win that game without Johnstone, although it is clear the manager valued this player so much that he was liable to turn the other cheek from time to time, even though it occasionally brought adverse publicity to the club.

Stein did enjoy publicity, if basically he had control of it. The media desperately sought ways of discovering what made this exceptional man tick, but he revealed very little of himself. He shielded his family fiercely. His wife Jean would go to all the games at Parkhead and sit in the directors' box but was aware of hardly anything that went on beneath her in the dressing-room. She was a perfect foil for Stein. He, brusque and charismatic in public, was counter-balanced by this delightfully calm woman who nevertheless exerted a huge influence on him. Her tastes were simple. She was dedicated to bringing up her son and daughter above all, and she laid great store by retaining long friendships with the wives of those men to whom Stein had become close during his rise to the top. They were working-class people who had attained new status, but they had not deserted their roots, nor could they. Jean never sought new horizons. And that was as big a factor on Stein's future than any other. A night at the bingo and the evenings of celebration and sing-songs after Celtic triumphs were the most exotic forms of her social life.

George, Jock's son, quiet, reflective and intelligent, was to enter one of Glasgow's most famous grant-aided schools, Glasgow High School, from which he emerged eventually with academic distinction. I can recall Stein talking to me about George from time to time, not in a boastful way, although he was distinctly proud of him. When I asked him once if he would have liked his lad to follow in his footsteps, he dismissed it with a look of amazement. 'He's getting on with the more serious things in life,' he told me. He was not the first father to have felt relieved that a son would not need to try to beat the path he himself had to follow. But coming from a man who was enjoying at that time great trappings of success within the game it sounded like self-admonishment; that occasionally he had to remind himself and others that football was just an adjunct to the more important necessities in life, not the other way round, as suggested by Shankly's dictum 'Football is not just a matter of life or death – it's much more important that that'. There are some who would have us believe that Stein was something of a romantic in his approach to football. Many of us saw enough of him in action to conclude the opposite: that he was as soberly practical about it as he had been with his work at the coal-face.

That 1968/69 season was to see Stein's hunger for success replenished by suggestions that the club had lost its image of invincibility, or, as expressed in its most extreme and crudest form, that the bubble had burst, or was about to. Far from bursting, it attained a flinty surface and even at times seemed to float like a free spirit during a season which saw his club win their fourth successive league title, five points ahead of Rangers despite being beaten by them twice in the league. In the League Cup final against Hibernian on 5 April 1969 they were six goals up before relaxing and conceding two goals for a final score of 6–2. It was one of the club's most outstanding attacking performances, with the Lisbon Lions forward line in place for that game. And the European Cup still drew some of the best performances from them, the most notable of which was a home game against Red Star Belgrade on 13 November 1968 which saw Stein at his wittiest and most cunning.

It all centred on the man foreigners around the world were now calling the 'Flying Flea', Jimmy Johnstone. On his game, the little red-haired winger was unequalled for the irrepressible mazy runs that dragged defenders around as if they had completely lost their sense of direction. But he detested getting into an aircraft. He had as big a fear of flying as any player I have ever met, but valiantly did not hold up the club to ransom over it, as Dennis Bergkamp has done with several of his managers. So, as Johnstone recalled, half-time came with the score at 1–1 in that game, and the portents for Celtic were not good. Stein acted, in the toilet. 'I was in having a pee when the big man came in and stood beside me. There was nobody else there, just the two of us. He just said quietly to me, "Wee man, if you go out there and change the game for us you won't need to fly to Belgrade for the next match." Now, I hated flying. I had been on our trip to America in 1966 and on one of the flights the plane almost fell out of the sky when it tried to land. It scared the hell out of me. So here he was giving me a way out of what was always bloody terrifying. Now remember, he just kept that suggestion between the pair of us. He didn't tell anybody else what he had offered me.

'Needless to say I was really geed up for it. I don't think I've ever tried harder in a game, and of course we thrashed them with four second-half goals, ripped them apart. I scored a goal only two minutes into that half, for I was really meaning business. In the last ten minutes I was back practically on my own goal-line kicking and heading the ball away when the score was 4–1, for I didn't want to concede another goal and make it narrower or the big man might have changed his mind. And Billy McNeill was screaming at me, "Get down the field, you wee bugger, get out of here, get back up front!" because he didn't know anything about the deal Jock had struck with me, and I was damned sure we weren't going to lose another goal. Well, I did get back up the field in a breakaway, and when I scored the fifth goal and started running back up the field I was screaming at the top of my voice, "I don't have to go! I don't have to go!" and they were all looking at me as if I had lost my marbles because they weren't in on this.'

Johnstone in fact had his finest hour that night. Not only did he run the Serbs ragged, he also scored a monumentally great goal nine minutes from time after a piercing run and a blistering shot. So, was the deal with Stein secure? There was a corollary. 'The following day, when it was known by everybody what had happened and it was even in the newspapers, he came up to me and said, "Look, the Red Star coach thinks it would be a great attraction if you played in Belgrade. He thinks the crowd would love to see you. I think he's right. You could turn it on there as well." Then he just walked away as if he had changed his mind about me flying. I ducked and dived for the next couple of weeks thinking the worst, but he was just having me on. He was making it up. He did like to take the mickey out of you. He was true to his word. I never saw Belgrade.'

They drew 1–1 in that city, and then a fine defensive performance in a snow blizzard in the San Siro against AC Milan in the first leg of their third-round game brought them a goalless draw. The return leg on 12 March, however, saw Celtic succumb to Italian football at its most frustratingly negative but at its ruthless best. Prati scored the only goal of the game after twelve minutes. It was the sort of early goal Celtic had been able to overcome in Lisbon, but this was an even more professionally organised outfit than Inter had been, and in Anquilletti and Schnellinger they had superb markers who blotted out Johnstone and Hughes, absorbing everything that was thrown at them. That result meant that Stein had endured two seasons of relative disappointment since Lisbon, and he was still dogged by another thought.

He still felt the hurt of that late equalising goal in the previous season's Ne'erday game through a goalkeeping blunder. He had been waiting much longer than he thought for revenge. Losing to Rangers twice in the league on top of that in the following season, 1968/69, even though Celtic went on to win the league, simply meant a build-up in frustration. It erupted creatively at Hampden Park at the end of that season. Winning the title was one thing, losing to Rangers twice in the process was unacceptable. It gave Stein a special reason to look forward to the Scottish Cup final against Rangers, for there was a feeling developing, and it was eagerly promoted by some of the media, that perhaps Davie White, after all, did have the measure of Stein. Such a suggestion simply brought out the best of his motivational skills.

There is not a manager I know who is not on edge in some way or other prior to a major final, and since Stein was still desperate to destroy White's credentials you could say there was an even greater sense of urgency and anticipation within him about this match. However, in terms of his general attitude, journalists had never known him to approach a significant match with such equanimity and absolute frankness. He exposed that side of his frame of mind to Alan Herron of the *Sunday Mail*. 'I couldn't believe how confident he was of winning that day,' Herron said. '"You watch us," he said to me, "we're going to win this game, without doubt. We can't fail to win it." He was so confident about how he had laid out his tactics that he was telling me, a journalist, openly and candidly about how inevitable a victory it was to be. It was staggering, for he knew that something like that could be cast up to him if it went wrong. But he just knew it wouldn't. He went on to tell me that he had worked everything out, having learnt his lessons from their two defeats against Rangers that season. And that's how it developed. He couldn't play Jimmy Johnstone because he was suspended, but he had Rangers thinking that George Connelly, the player he brought in, would play directly as Johnstone's substitute on the wing. Well, he did play on the right-hand side but tactically he was more the midfield creator, and wonderful to watch on his game. Rangers had no answer to that. They just looked bewildered.'

That final at Hampden on 26 April 1969 in front of a crowd of 132,870 was to prove a virtual walkover after Billy McNeill scored with a header in two minutes. Celtic overran their opponents with a sense of the importance of the occasion their opponents could not match. Rangers were ragged, and they suffered. Connelly laid on the second goal just before half-time, then scored another himself a minute later. At half-time it was 3–0, and I recollect looking to my left from the commentary position at some 40,000 pairs of eyes belonging to Rangers supporters which had glazed over in a display of mass stupefaction. Stein had done that to them. It was as if he had raised his hand calling for silence from that end.

The manner in which his team had come out like a swarm of killer bees was down to that air of superiority he had personally engendered and which he had accurately revealed to Herron. I cannot recall another final in which Stein had publicly impinged himself so dominantly on the outcome. Another goal by Chalmers, near the end, sealed the 4–0 victory, and Stein could not disguise his pleasure. He had observed his tactics working to perfection. A young man had come on to the stage and performed like a veteran, although it was only the first chapter of the ultimately sad history of George Connelly. And he must have been conscious of the fact that no Rangers manager could survive such a humiliation. It was their first Scottish Cup final defeat in 40 years. He had killed Davie White off. Six months later 'The Boy David', as he had been witheringly described in a *Scottish Daily Express* headline, was sacked. What Stein probably could not have anticipated at the time, even with the uncanny prescience which preceded this game, was that the man publicly blamed for Celtic's first goal, for not marking Billy McNeill properly, had just played his last game for the Ibrox first team as a result. Never in the history of football has such ignominy been a precursor to such distinction. For six days before White was sacked, Rangers transferred their errant striker to Falkirk for £20,000. He is now Sir Alex Ferguson.

The Celtic manager had looked for, and had now seen, positive transitional signs in his side that day which seemed to bode well for the future. But even with renewed confidence in his own ability to outwit opponents, to anticipate the shapes of games and to deploy with tactical shrewdness, he was about to enter a period that will be remembered principally for a colossal miscalculation.

CHAPTER EIGHTEEN
BITTER SWEET

At around eleven a.m. on the morning of 7 May 1970, Malpensa airport on the outskirts of Milan resembled that area of the Sistine Chapel in the Vatican which portrays Michelangelo's awesome *The Last Judgement*. Thousands of men, women and children stood, sat and lay in packed conclaves as, outside, incessant, torrential rain battered the airport and heightened the impression of a descent into hell. Crushed miserably together, huddling up against their own luggage like refugees, the supporters found the cramped, claustrophobic conditions a form of torture no one who had travelled there for a sporting occasion before had expected. The airport had lost control of itself: aircraft seemed neither to be arriving nor departing, and information was non-existent as to what was happening or how long people would have to wait until they departed for either Rotterdam or Glasgow. The agony suffered the night before in the San Siro stadium by the entire Celtic community was being re-run. It was as if a diabolical hand could not allow failure in a cup final to pass without a touch of purgatory. That's how it felt, standing or walking around there for hours (for you would have had to kill somebody to get a seat).

Leaning against a wall, Stein looked pale, drawn and, not surprisingly, tetchy. At one stage during the long wait he was observed having a blazing row with one of his directors, James Farrell, about something or other that could not be heard above the babble of noise but seemed to indicate a less than amicable relationship. No concession amid the chaos was to be allowed to anyone with rank either, for a knight of the realm was also having to tolerate the indignity of being part of the crushed herd. Bob Kelly was now Sir Robert, having been listed in the New Year's Honours of the previous year, 1969. Ashen-faced and with a distant, detached appearance, he was not a well man. He had not been helped by watching his club unexpectedly lose the European Cup final to Feyenoord. The knighthood had not changed his demeanour. He was still the Bob Kelly from Blantyre who had become accustomed to bearing misfortune through the years preceding Stein with a stoicism which had led his many critics to interpret that bearing as nothing other than unthinking obduracy. Bluntly put, Stein's triumphs had won him his knighthood, even though it had been delivered officially on the basis of his services to Scottish football through the presidency of the SFA. But now, while there was certainly pain in defeat, it was not like the bad old days. Life for Sir Robert with Stein was an adventure; before him, it had been a self-imposed drudgery. He now had an honour to cushion himself from the harsh memories of the past, but Sir Robert had certainly not expected this outcome. Neither had Stein, nor his players, nor the media, and certainly not the supporters. So what had gone wrong?

The manager had certainly remained in ebullient mood long after the 4–0 victory over Rangers in the April 1969 cup final. The performance offered such evidence of comprehensive supremacy in Scottish football that Stein realised Rangers would not take this lying down, and that something at Ibrox had to give. They continued to offer no real sign of loosening Stein's grip on them. They lost their first league match at Ibrox 1–0 on 20 September 1969 through a goal by recent Celtic signing Harry Hood, even though Celtic had played for 23 minutes with only ten men after Jim Craig had been sent off. They had knocked them out of the League Cup with a goal by Tommy Gemmell in their second-leg game, so Stein knew his great opponents would have to sort themselves out sooner rather than later. In an interview he had given at the beginning of that season to Arthur Montford, my counterpart at Scottish Television, Stein, in more reflective mood, calmly said, 'Rangers' time will come again.' I suppose this was a warning to his own supporters that his great rivals were simply too big a club to roll over and have their stomachs tickled from the east of the city.

Apart from anticipating that sort of future, he was trying to ease his club into a transition, which has led to persistent discussion even to this day as to how over-zealous he was in breaking up the Lisbon Lions, almost as a matter of inevitability. There is no member of that side I have spoken to who does not harbour some reservation – some with a deep grudge – about how Stein handled the generational change. Some would say that he was over-affected by having read too much into the way Inter had gone downhill, playing with the same men and the same system for too long. If that were the case then it would be an admission that the team Celtic had defeated in Portugal was then a seriously waning force. But that has never been greatly articulated, neither by Stein nor by any player, because they probably felt it would dilute their triumph to an extent. But the fact was that Inter were in decline at that time, and Stein knew it. The game still had to be won, of course, and was, in style. So the manager was right to take note of how important it was not to be mesmerised by past glories.

What is incontestable is that Celtic, as the 1960s turned into the 1970s, missed a glorious opportunity to bolster their squad because of the parsimony of the board. It angers Billy McNeill to this day. 'Jock wanted big money to go into the transfer market and compete with others to get real quality and supplement what we had,' he said. 'We could have gone on to greater things and definitely won another European Cup if the board had given him what he wanted. But they didn't. They were content to rest on their laurels. It was a major mistake by the directors of the club.'

Stein certainly had superb young players just begging to be given their chance at the start of that 1969/70 season. George Connelly, Lou Macari, Davie Hay and Jim Brogan were in stock, along with experienced but fresh transfer-signings Harry Hood and Tom Callaghan, for example. But it was his dealings with one of his most respected players from Lisbon that throws some light on the idiosyncratic way in which Stein sometimes handled matters, and which runs parallel both with the dropping of Jim Craig at Tynecastle in a previous season and to other such episodes in future years. There was a distinct pattern in how he dealt with sensitive matters. This emerged that season in the autumn, when he travelled with the official SFA party to watch the World Cup qualifying game in Hamburg against West Germany on 22 October. It was in his interest to travel because he had three of his players involved: Johnstone, McNeill and Gemmell.

Stein, as I observed on this trip myself, was in great form. He was much in demand to talk about football and he duly delivered. He would lie back on the sofas amid the wood-panelled splendour of the Reichshoff Hotel and hold court. He would poke fun at the SFA councillors quite openly, and had a field day after it was discovered that two of them had to be bailed out of a police station for refusing to pay a champagne bill in a Reeperbahn clip-joint. This gave him raw material for his stand-up comic act in the lounge, as he amused us with tales of the free-loaders. But underneath it all he had contempt for the blazerati who went on these trips. You could sense it would not take much to tilt him into a severer mood. But he was delaying that. Something had occurred in the game which was already bothering him and which would have a spill-over effect on the game he was returning to Glasgow to face up to: the Scottish League Cup final against St Johnstone at Hampden the following Saturday. For Tommy Gemmell had misbehaved.

'I was sent off for kicking Haller in the match,' Gemmell recalled. 'He had got away with murder during the game and I think they were annoyed that Jimmy Johnstone had scored inside a couple of minutes. The Swiss referee was losing control and, all right, I shouldn't have got involved the way I did, but these things happen. So off I went. I flew back with the SFA party and was close to Jock on the journey back but he didn't look in my direction and he could have come up to speak to me, but he never did. He was close to me during the training in the couple of days down at Seamill, when he could have said something. Not a word did he speak to me. I travelled to Hampden with the rest for the final. He still hadn't opened his mouth to me. Now, it was my habit to strip for any game as late as I could. You got players like Stevie Chalmers who'd have his boots and jersey on about an hour before kick-off and ready to go. But me, I couldn't do that. I used to go out and have a blether with pals and the likes, and then come in and get ready quickly about half an hour to twenty minutes before kick-off. I did the same that day. I came in prepared to put on my jersey and I saw that somebody else had it and was sitting where I should have been, getting ready to play. It was Davie Hay. I hadn't been picked. But not a word had been said to me. It came out of the blue. Now, frankly, I was staggered. I suppose I wouldn't have minded had he said something to me about it beforehand. It felled me. I was disappointed he hadn't told me. Not a word in advance.'

Bobby Lennox, like the rest of the players, was surprised by this. 'I will always remember how Big Tam took it,' he said. 'He was wearing a white coat. He just looked at where his place should have been in the dressing-room and it must have hit him there and then – he was axed. He just said, "Ah well, you win some, you lose some," and then just walked out.'

Gemmell got little sleep that night waiting to call Stein on the Sunday morning, which he did. 'Firstly I told him I had been let down and I deserved to be told about decisions affecting me. He said that my behaviour in Hamburg in the [Scotland] game was not compatible with the traditions of Celtic Football Club and that is why I had to be punished. I pointed out to him that to allow me right up to kick-off to think I was playing was cruel. And given what he had said about me being punished, to uphold the good name of Celtic, I asked him outright, "If we had been playing Rangers instead of St Johnstone would you have dropped me?" He didn't really answer that and I don't think we were ever the same again. I put in a request for a transfer and he granted it eventually.'

This incident was part of a behavioural pattern that affected several players throughout Stein's career. In his handling of selections like that he would appear to be utterly ruthless. He picked the team, and that was that. No explanations were required. You were in or you were out. You did not need your hand held in sympathy or a shoulder to cry on. This wasn't a crèche he was running. You had to be steeled to accept his method, but the players on the receiving end were sometimes bemused and often angered by it. Most did not query this particular technique – and, as we shall see, the Gemmell incident was not exceptional – because they were too scared to speak up. But it is hardly surprising that they sometimes harboured deep resentments about it. At the same time, when some players were in some kind of trouble, like Jimmy Johnstone, he would be the one to commune with them and help them out. Much of what he did to benefit players on the side, to help them domestically or to help get them out of a jam, he kept quiet about. So the contrast could not have been more stark.

In this particular case, Stein had reservations about Gemmell's lifestyle. There is perhaps just a tiny step that leads from a volatile relationship to a fractious one, as this now appeared to be. However, the incident did not prevent Celtic from beating St Johnstone in the final 1–0 with a goal by Auld after only two minutes. Gemmell came back into the side two weeks later as a regular, Stein wisely warming him up to play against Benfica in the European Cup. It paid off handsomely when the player opened the scoring with a blistering free-kick in the 3–0 victory at Celtic Park. Nor did it stop them edging in front of Rangers in the league by the end of 1969, by which time the Ibrox club, at last, had seen the light.

Although he privately wished Willie Waddell well in his new appointment as Rangers manager in December 1969, Stein did reserve some stinging comments for the media. There was a huge response in newspapers and broadcasting, as expected for a famous ex-Ranger like Waddell riding to the rescue of a club, as Stein himself had done with similar, if not greater, press interest. But as he had now started talking to BBC Scotland again he gave me an interview which was heavily larded with sarcasm. 'Are you all forgetting us now?' he asked facetiously before pointing out that if there was such interest in Rangers and the crowds were now expected to go back to them after dwindling catastrophically, then it surely had to do with 'factors other than football', as he put it. It was his way of saying that although his club was marching on successfully, the anti-Celtic/anti-Catholic forces would still coalesce around a Rangers team, come what may. It was said in that beaming, knowing way of his that required little interpretation. It was also stiffening his resolve to fight the old sectarian habits as hard as he could, because he knew Waddell would produce a tougher Rangers, as indicated by his first back-room signing, the 34-year-old Hearts coach Jock Wallace, who once, when asked to speak at a dinner, had replied that he didn't do much after-dinner speaking but instead proceeded to give the audience a rousing sectarian chorus of 'The Sash My Father Wore'.

Stein had a hunch, though, that it wasn't a Protestant tune of triumphalism the club needed, it was better players and tactics. They could sing like linties, but could they play? I believe that he felt he would still have the better of them. He could also claim the moral high ground. For a tacit, very secretive and circuitous approach had actually been made to him to leave Celtic and go to Ibrox, long before Waddell arrived. This was done through the promptings of director David Hope, who felt that an offer of the Rangers job would be irresistible to Stein, who essentially was 'one of us', in that Ibrox phrase picked up and dusted down later by Margaret Thatcher. Rangers denied all of this when people in the media started to whisper it about. There was no direct proof of 'an offer', but again, according to Stein in an aside to me once, a 'suggestion' had been quietly put in front of him.

The ferment generated by the newly emergent challenge resulted in a nasty Scottish Cup quarter-final between the Old Firm on 21 February 1970 which Celtic won 3–1 after Rangers had taken an early lead with a Craig own goal. Lennox, Hay and Johnstone put the game beyond any reasonable doubt though. But it was the wild manner in which the game was played, and the resultant crowd trouble and subsequent arrests which were made, that prompted the Glasgow magistrates to write to the SFA asking them to take some remedial action. Consequently, all 22 players and the two managers were asked to appear before the SFA to be lectured and warned about future conduct. They sat there dutifully, like penitents before an ecclesiastical court, humbly accepting the admonishments. Did it work? Let Jim Craig be the judge. 'The very next game I played against Rangers, the following happened. Before the match Jock came in with Sir Robert and asked us all to be quiet, that the chairman wanted to say something. He spoke in a dignified manner about how Celtic did not want its reputation besmirched, that the eyes of the world were upon us and that under no circumstances would he condone any bad behaviour by any Celtic player. He wanted us to be fair and that our good name was at stake. Then he turned and walked out. Jock kept the door open and peeked out to make sure the chairman had disappeared along the corridor and obviously out of earshot, then slammed the door shut, turned to us and said, "You can forget that effing crap. Get stuck in. Any fifty-fifty ball will be yours. Anybody drawing back will be answerable to me!" I suppose the same sort of thing would have been said in the Rangers dressing-room.'

Stein versus Waddell certainly whetted the appetite of the media. Stein saw it as a rising chorus, within newspapers especially, of those who wished to see Celtic put in their place and believed that Waddell was truly the man to do that. He used to tell me of that initial period after Waddell's return to Ibrox that he'd noticed a change in the manner in which some media people dealt with him, as if somehow all they had been doing previously was 'patronising' Celtic, as he put it. There is no doubt that having Waddell there on the other side of the city gave him pause for thought, and I think he went through a period during which he was ridiculously over-sensitive about how the press behaved.

That had no bearing, though, on the influence he was exerting on his players, who still left the strong impression they were capable of beating any side in Europe on their day. This had been evident when they disposed of Basle in the first round of the European Cup, when after a goalless draw in Switzerland they won comfortably 2–0 in the return leg, Harry Hood scoring his first European goal in only two minutes. This took them to a two-legged tie with Benfica in the next round. After an early and spectacular goal by Gemmell after two minutes in the first leg on 12 November 1969, in one of those whirlwind starts for which they were now becoming famous and which suggested that their build-up in the dressing-room was akin to the revving of a Grand Prix engine, they won 3–0 with apparent ease. But Benfica still had the great Eusebio playing for them, and he scored the first goal in the return leg two weeks later. Graca then scored a second, which led to an amazing finish. Two minutes over the allotted 90 minutes, Diamentino, a second-half substitute, scored a third, giving the Portuguese champions a 3–0 victory and sending the game into extra-time. As there was no more scoring, Billy McNeill was then presented with a situation which at the time must have seemed worse than being tied down to railway lines as an express train approached: he had to guess the outcome of the game on the toss of the coin. I am sure he would have preferred the current method of the dreaded penalty-kick shoot-out.

Now, Stein was a heavy gambler. On that basis you might think he would have wanted to be involved in the toss-up. But when he and the two captains, the referee, the linesmen and some pressmen all crowded into a small room for the ludicrous event, Billy asked Stein what he should call. Stein simply said, 'You're on your own.' The man who fluttered constantly on the horses simply wasn't prepared to have the destiny of the club hinge on his guess. The Dutch referee used a guilder for the ceremony. Firstly, they had to toss to see who would make the call. McNeill won that. Then came the deciding toss. McNeill had the shout. Up it went. It landed on the floor, rolled, hit the referee's foot then turned and lay still. Bodies bent down, peering to see what it revealed. McNeill punched the air. He had been right. Stein muffled his pleasure because of the tiny confines of the room and the unsatisfactory way Celtic had played in the match itself. Tony Queen, his friend, recalling that moment, said to me once, 'That just added to Jock's reputation. You just felt the Big Barra couldnae lose when it came to a real crunch.'

He wasn't the only one to start thinking there was something mystical about this big man. Winning a toss in a small dressing-room in a foreign country stoked the imaginations of those who build their Old Firm heroes around the notion that somebody 'up there' likes them. The intensification of the ingredients of myth, which were beginning to surround him, ought not to be ignored, for by the end of that season circumstances would evolve that perhaps would lead you to think Stein was beginning to allow himself to share some of that belief in his invincibility, and that it would be disastrous for him.

But there was no awareness of that halfway through the season, and the course seemed set fair when in the next European round they disposed of Fiorentina, reasonably comfortably, 3–1 on aggregate, while keeping well ahead of Rangers in the league. In fact, they seemed to be gathering momentum for another bountiful harvest, especially when the draw paired them in the semi-finals with Leeds United, the first leg to be played on April Fools' Day 1970 at Elland Road.

Celtic travelled by train to Leeds and reserved a special carriage for themselves. What they hadn't realised was that a famous Scottish comedian managed to get into their area. He happened to be Lex McLean, one of the most renowned Rangers supporters of that period, who wrote songs about the Ibrox club that echo to this day. However, from the moment the train left Glasgow until it got into Leeds, McLean, who was going to see the game himself, entered into the spirit of the occasion and entertained the squad with his ribald humour which left them in a buoyant, optimistic mood. Never before had a Rangers sympathiser done so much to prepare a Celtic team psychologically, to bolster morale, and probably never since. Stein later repaid this gesture by appearing on McLean's television show, playing straight man to a well-known 'blue-nose'comic.

Stein had great respect for Don Revie, the Leeds manager, as an original thinker in the game, but he did not think Celtic deserved the treatment they received both before and after the match. The English press annoyed him by writing off his team as 'no-hopers'. Revie did not help matters by being irritating. As both teams normally wore white stockings the visitors had to change, but as Celtic did not have an adequate replacement the Leeds manager offered them two alternatives that were to hand. The colours were blue or red. 'Aghast' was certainly not the word bandied about the Celtic dressing-room at that choice. A Celtic team with red or blue would have tested the loyalty of their support to the limit. What to do? Stein's humour soothed the savage breasts. He kept any anger about that confined to the dressing-room so that Leeds would not detect they had been upset. 'We'll wear the red stockings,' he said. 'Under their floodlights they'll show up more orange than red and our supporters will think we're wearing the colours of the Irish tricolour. That'll please them.' It did.

In fact, the supporters were in an optimistic mood after just 45 seconds, which is how long it took young George Connelly to open Celtic's account. From that point on Leeds, baffled by Johnstone's trickery in particular – he gave the great England international Terry Cooper the hiding of his life – were on the receiving end. Tommy Gemmell knew that was the major factor of the night. 'It was so pointed a "doing" wee Jimmy was giving them that we heard Norman Hunter, Leeds' infamous "hard man", shouting blatantly to Cooper to chop him down, and Cooper shouting back at him to come and try it himself if he wanted. He did. They swapped positions, and Jimmy just did the same to him and ran him ragged.' Bertie Auld had, though, been warned by Stein that it would be tough physically. 'The Big Man was right. They didn't really think we could play and when we started to move the ball around they got very rough. I had a tussle with a big centre called Jones who thought he could kick and get away with it. He didn't. I gave as good as I got. At half-time he came up to me and said, "Hunter's going to sort you out." Norman Hunter was a hard man for them. In my view he did more damage off the ball than on it. He just tried to terrify you. I think they were surprised at how we stood up to them. I think when you had the Big Man's presence about you, you fought your corner. They were worried at the end.'

That, in fact, is the first thing Stein said to his players on the evening of 15 April at Hampden Park when he came into the dressing-room prior to the second-leg match with his side 1–0 to the good. 'Revie's shitting himself,' he told them. 'I've never seen that man as nervous in all my life. He's as white as a sheet. If he's like that, what do you think his players are like? They are there for the taking, believe you me.'

This game has long been considered one of the most spectacular in Stein's career, and in essence was regarded as a cup final in its own right, for most people considered Celtic and Leeds to be the best teams left in the tournament. Much of that interpretation came with the benefit of hindsight, in light of what was to happen later in Milan, as dejected Celtic supporters tried to make sense of the major Italian anti-climax. But that night in front of a European Cup record crowd of 133,961, Stein inspired his side to heights that easily drew parallels with Lisbon. In the minds of most observers it was indeed a surrogate European final. Marvellous though the occasion was, the only man we might have assumed would not be taken in by such an illusion was Stein himself. But apparently he was.

Before the game started he singled out one of his players for a special word. John Hughes was taken aside and told, 'I know you were sick about missing the last final, but if you do well for me tonight and we reach the final, you'll definitely play.' Hughes was an inspired man that night, but paradoxically it was to lead to a moment in Milan that he always believes effectively ended his career at Celtic. So he looks back on the Leeds match with affection tinged with a final regret. 'I really did play well,' he recalled. 'Billy Bremner had scored a superb goal from about 35 yards to give Leeds the lead, not long into the game, but far from discouraging us I think it brought out the best in the side. We just ran it from then on. Of course the support was the loudest I had ever heard. I scored the equaliser about a couple of minutes into the second half with a header from Bertie Auld's cross, and then after Leeds had replaced their goalkeeper when Sprake got injured and Dave Harvey came on, Bobby Murdoch scored the winner with a tremendous shot. I think that night was the best of all the Celtic performances I took part in and the crowd just didn't want to leave the stadium. But you know, I think that's when it all started to go astray. For I think that night Jock Stein thought he had won the European Cup itself. If ever a man got it wrong from that moment on, it was him.'

It didn't seem like it at the time, especially when it became known that the other finalists were from Holland. The Scottish media, in unison, added to the notion that nothing could prevent another European triumph. Feyenoord? The first thing you had to do was discover how to pronounce the word, and then wonder how a team from a Dutch league which had been fully professional for only thirteen years could live with Celtic. We were all united in the gratuitous assumption of the superiority of the Scottish side.

Despite the obvious workload he and his players had had to bear, a strange mood seemed to descend on Stein from our viewpoint in the media. While preparing for the commentary on the final, I became aware, like others, of a slackening of discipline creeping in. The pre-Lisbon man of fanatical observation of detail, of a tensile eagerness to grasp the day by the throat and have done with it, had given way to a more relaxed man. That is not to say he would not lapse into a rebuke or use that sharp tongue to effect, but overall there was little evidence in the run-up to the fateful week of the final of the obsessive side of his nature. It would have been a misinterpretation to come to that conclusion purely as an outsider interviewing him occasionally, but the players were very conscious of it themselves. And in any case, it became more dramatically evident when we all assembled together – players, officials and media – in a hilltop hotel in Varese, a small Italian town near the lakes just north of Milan, to prepare for the final itself in the San Siro.

It was difficult to get Lisbon's preparations out of the mind's eye. By comparison, Stein's players looked as if they were settling in for a friendly against a village eleven. There was a carefree, casual ambience within the group which you felt at any moment would come to a dramatic end with Stein, swooping from a hidden corner of the hotel, re-imposing his stern dictatorship. But he never did. Players were carrying on negotiations about money and sponsorship deals helped by a journalist, Ian Peebles, who certainly had leanings towards Ibrox. That in itself, given Stein's sensitivity and full awareness of journalistic allegiances, was surprising. All this was being played out in front of and with the permission of the manager. Players and press mingled, chatted, joshed around, even surreptitiously had a drink or two together. We lapped it up. Ours not to reason why. The Big Man had it all planned out. Out of doors, let loose in the sun – which now was adjudged not to be the enemy it had been in Portugal three years earlier – the players enjoyed themselves in this more liberal environment.

The docility of Stein's approach would have been a total culture shock had he not come into the hotel the night before the game and found me sitting with Hugh McIlvanney, then with the *Observer*, in a crowded lounge. He decided to grill me about the Feyenoord team and how they would play. He put me through the hoop and found deficiencies in my assumptions about the Dutch side. This was the Stein we had come to know, the Lisbon man surfacing again, the man with a victim in his sights, a receptive audience of bystanders and, ultimately, the upper hand. Before he walked off to bed he said, 'You should be up all night thinking about this game. I'll kick every ball tonight. I'll go through it, over and over again. I can see everybody's face. I can see their build. I can see the way they run. You should be the same, thinking out all the possibilities.'

But his thinking, however much of it he did that night, was apparently distorted. He had been to see Feyenoord and had returned with reports which virtually handed the trophy to his players. The contrast with the reality of the quality of Feyenoord caused some players to wonder if had actually made the trip to see them at all. For the reports bore no relation to what they came up against. Of course he did see them play, in a domestic game in Holland, and sometimes their technical passing game in a smaller stadium could create a false impression of passionless, predictable football. To say the least, he was not overawed. He had started off by reminding his players that when Ajax had played in the European final in Madrid the year before and lost 4–1 to Milan, five of the Ajax players had virtually collapsed with nerves before the match. 'These Dutch players will be shitting themselves,' he assured them. In fact, not a single trace of nerves could be detected anywhere in their side throughout that long night. He told Bertie Auld in particular that Wim van Hanagem was 'a slower Jim Baxter with a right foot just for standing on'. But when they saw that same player nutmegging Bobby Lennox in the early stages of the game and waltzing past him with ease, they knew something might go seriously wrong. He also mentioned that the man who was to become Celtic's manager in 1997, Wim Jansen, could only play for about twenty minutes before disappearing and that he wouldn't be seen again. As Bertie Auld said, 'Jock was right enough about that. I never did see Jansen after that. He got faster as we seemed to get slower. He was just too good for me.' Feyenoord were, in Stein's overall assessment, a team without pace, without any great mental toughness and ultimately without hope. As Tommy Gemmell summarised it, 'I didn't agree with his team selection and neither did others. And as for his team talk, it was so downbeat that you would have thought we were going out to play Partick Thistle. The man Van Hanagem, who was supposed to be a one-footed weakness, was still running stronger than anybody in extra-time and pinging beautiful passes all over the field.'

One of the great strengths of Stein, as I have already highlighted, was his ability to read the opposition in advance with the accuracy of a geiger-counter sitting on top of a plutonium pellet. But here, this time, was not so much an analysis as a prescription for disaster. It bred indifference. Jimmy Johnstone, however, is quite adamant that the result had nothing to do with the manager or his underestimating of the opposition, and that it was all down to the players' attitude themselves. 'Nobody can say a word about Jock on this game. We just didn't play well. If we had played to our strengths we would have won that game. We were nothing like ourselves, it was as simple as that.' Essentially, Johnstone is claiming that the players let the manager down, not the other way round. Admirable though his loyalty might be in that respect, he seems to be in a minority of one. The consensus view of the squad was that Stein was so astonishingly wrong in his judgements that he must have been hoodwinked. The causal effect of that was enormous, principally because the players had the utmost faith in whatever he said about football. So they got off on the wrong foot as soon as they set their studs on the San Siro pitch on that wet, drab night.

Despite all that, Celtic only lost that match 2–1. All the players admit they played badly, but even so, the game was won by a goal near the end of extra-time. Gemmell had scored with a marvellous free-kick after 30 minutes. Israel equalised for Feyenoord seven minutes later, and then in the 116th minute Ove Kindvall, the Swede who had run Billy McNeill ragged throughout the game, lobbed in the winner. But early in extra time John Hughes, who had of course made the team as the result of a special promise by Stein, had been through on the keeper with the best chance of the game and squandered it. It would have won the cup, despite the brilliance of Feyenoord that preceded it. 'I honestly believe that my career effectively came to an end at that moment,' said Hughes. 'I was never really forgiven.' It might also have signified the beginning of the end of a glorious European chapter, and the heralding of a newer era.

When we returned to the hotel that night the lounge of the hotel was deserted except for Stein and Sean Fallon, sitting by themselves. We went straight up to commiserate. He was in fact quite relaxed, which would probably have astonished those, including close friends, who would admit that he was the worst loser in the world. But he didn't talk about the game. Clearly he didn't want to, having decanted everything to press and broadcasters at the stadium. He started to talk about the fact that the Dutch had seemed to have the bigger support, not just because of the ease of travel but because they were probably better off than the Celtic support. Without indulging in a précis of the Dutch economy, he seemed to have sussed that out. He told us to help ourselves to champagne from a case they had laid out in preparation for a celebration, then rose and went off to bed.

The following day, in that hellish scramble in Malpensa airport, which lasted from nine o'clock in the morning until five o'clock in the evening, I only had the briefest word with him, and that was when I asked him for the name of a young lad in the Celtic party who was helping out with loading the cases at the check-in desk and whom I couldn't recognise.

'Kenny Dalglish,' he told me. 'He'll be some player.'

If only his assessment of Feyenoord had been as accurate as the one he gave me of that young man's future then Celtic might have been travelling back to Glasgow with the European Cup.

CHAPTER NINETEEN
A TEST OF LOYALTY

The excess baggage, which might have been preoccupying Stein as he flew home from Milan in May 1970, was not in the aircraft's luggage-hold but sitting in seats around him. In his mind, certain players were now beginning to look surplus to requirements. After all, four weeks before the Milan final, on 11 April, they had been upstaged in the Scottish Cup final by a youthful Aberdeen side inspired by as irascible a manager and as shrewd a coach as ever sat in a dug-out, Eddie Turnbull, and lost 3–1. The result sent such a shockwave through the Celtic support that many overreacted and misbehaved. Police reported one hundred arrests before and after the game for breaches of the peace. The fact that Stein, so incandescent with rage at the refereeing by Mr R.H. 'Bobby' Davidson in that match, had voiced his opinions so loudly that the Hampden stand trembled as his voice echoed out of the dressing-room area towards the press area might in itself have been an indication that a feeling of injustice, however regrettable, lay at the root of the violence. Hugh Taylor was just one of the writers who sympathised with Stein's views when he wrote in the *Daily Record* on 13 April, 'The highly arguable decisions of the referee, however, were shattering for Celtic's morale and there is no doubt they had an effect on their play afterwards.'

The Stein anger stemmed from a ten-minute period during which Aberdeen were awarded a penalty, from which Harper scored, and Celtic had a 'goal' by Lennox disallowed and an appeal for a penalty kick turned down. Stein was eventually fined £10 for his remarks, which hardly bankrupted him and surely would not have had a subduing influence on him. He would pursue R.H. Davidson for the rest of his career, like the posse who kept on the trail of Butch Cassidy and the Sundance Kid, hoping for some blatant slip-up. Davidson thought exactly the reverse, that it was he who was doing the pursuing, ready to pounce. Between them it was a kind of *danse macabre*.

But if Stein felt the close season would bring a time of relaxation and stability, he was mistaken. An end-of-season trip to the States was in the offing after the European Cup final. For the players it promised relaxation and stimulation, for hadn't the tour to the other side of the Atlantic in the early summer of 1966 helped forge their Lisbon identity? It seemed the obvious health cure after the indignity of Milan and the acute sense of grievance over their defeat at the hands of Aberdeen. It turned out, though, to be as much of a health cure as sticking one's head in a gas oven, a trip that earned the wrong kind of headlines.

Harry Hood, who in the coming season was to be Celtic's top scorer with 33 goals, recalled the afternoon in Toronto when Stein disappeared before the end of a game. 'We were playing the Italian side Bari. Just before the kick-off their goalkeeper made a throat-cut sign to Bobby Lennox, and then the battle started. Now, we went into this game as a friendly, but after ten minutes it was self-preservation. Lou Macari, who was now getting games in the first team, was deliberately punched behind the referee's back. I was never a dirty player, but I went over the ball about twenty times in that first half as self-preservation. And so it went on. Now, Jock had his travel-bag in the dug-out because we knew he was heading for the airport to catch a flight back to Glasgow some time that afternoon. As punch-ups were starting all over the field and getting out of hand, Jock was getting angrier and angrier. So at half-time, he'd had enough. As soon as the whistle blew for half-time he threw his bag out of the way and dived into the Italian dug-out, which emptied pretty damn quickly except for their coach, who was pinned down by Jock. All I saw was the Big Man punching lumps out of him. Then he just got out, picked up his bag, and that was the last we saw of him on the trip. He left for the airport, the game was abandoned in the second half and we were lucky there had been no serious injuries.'

Stein's sudden exit had nothing to do with fleeing from his attempt to recreate the Allied assault on Monte Cassino during the war, but the Italians were left in no doubt that this man could in fact 'take his jaiket aff' when opposed by brute force and the men who condoned it. But he was gone. He would explain later that he had to see a specialist in Glasgow about recurring problems with his ankle, but there were also player problems. Jimmy Johnstone was unsettled, and it looked likely that he might leave the club, with Leeds definitely interested in a move. That was bothering Stein, apart from anything else. But with Manchester United also having played Celtic in the first match of the tour, certain murmurs were heard around the press rooms that he might have been tapped by United and it was that which hastened his return. But that was not so, although ten months later a tapping did occur.

The squad was now left in the care of assistant manager Sean Fallon, of whom the players were greatly fond as he was out of the old-school Jimmy McGrory mould, an affable man who was difficult to dislike. But without the commanding and perpetually threatening presence of Stein, some of the players acted as if they had just been released from solitary confinement. Certainly, had he gone to that hotbed of Celtic supporters in New Jersey, Kearney, a couple of the players would not have indulged in booze-fuelled pranks. As it was almost impossible to prevent these incidents from leaking out, Fallon decided to act. Bertie Auld and Tommy Gemmell, bosom pals and both feisty, independent characters, were sent home on the first available flight. The publicity was embarrassing, but it was Stein's departure that drew interest as much as the misconduct in the States. Players, particularly in the close season, can sometimes go off the rails, so what had happened was not scandalously exceptional.

I recall the suggestion that Stein, for some reason or another, was taking his eye off the ball. Those wishing to make mischief of his departure interpreted this as him in effect deserting his players. It is also worth recalling that whenever there was adverse publicity for his club – and that, of course, was infrequent – he used it to his advantage to stoke his players' resentment about it. 'He would start off sometimes in the dressing-room by saying that most people would want us to be beaten,' Harry Hood recalled. 'He would say all the papers were against us, so go out and stuff it up them. He used the anti-Celtic idea to fire us up. And of course it usually worked.'

Privately, though, Stein slaughtered Auld and Gemmell and both were fined, for if there was one situation he tried manfully to avoid it was leaving himself exposed to criticism for dereliction of duty, even down to when he habitually strove to get to Celtic Park in the mornings for training. In the mid-1970s I travelled around Scotland extensively with him. We had been booked to appear at public forums by a brewery firm. There was only one stipulation he laid down, and that was that wherever we went he had to be back at Celtic Park before anybody arrived for training in the morning. He was fanatical about that. On one occasion, when I was flying back with him in a six-seater plane from Elgin, fog meant we could not land in Glasgow and he got mightily upset when he realised we were being re-routed to Edinburgh and that he would not get to Parkhead until at least eleven a.m. He pushed the pilot to see what alternatives he could come up with because he needed to get back in time. When the pilot suggested the tiny landing strip at the new town of Cumbernauld and started to descend towards it, Stein showed he had not lost his sense of humour: he looked out of the window and, seeing the thick mist there, asked the pilot if he could sign-write in the sky to the people at the midget airport 'You must be effing joking'. The pilot took the hint and landed in Edinburgh, and an upset Stein was put in a fast car towards Glasgow, which he reached by midday. He simply hated the idea of the players feeling he was not obsessive about his job and that he might be loosening his grip on them.

Being aware of that sensitivity now makes me appreciate how exposed he must have felt being thousands of miles away while some of his players were misbehaving. But more importantly, the club was in transition, and the temporary upset concerning team discipline was less significant than engineering the changes. New names were appearing as virtual regulars: Lou Macari, Harry Hood, Jim Brogan, George Connelly, David Hay and, battering at the door for inclusion, Kenny Dalglish, maturing with every game in the lower ranks. Three years on from Lisbon, Stein was well stocked with emerging talent as he drove his club towards their sixth successive league title. The Waddell–Wallace nexus was not producing the dividend many had thought it would at Ibrox. And the manner by which Celtic generally disposed of Rangers during this period, give or take the occasional game when they did not, suggested a mastery of tactics that might have led you to think Stein had a plant inside the Ibrox dressing-room.

So much so that on 2 January 1971, eight points ahead of Rangers in the league but one point behind Aberdeen, the leaders, Stein boarded the bus for Ibrox for the traditional holiday game with little apprehension. It was bitterly cold, the atmosphere tinctured by a seeping Govan mist. But when he returned later that evening to Celtic Park he was not thinking of football or the result or the title race. He was in fact consumed by sorrow. Some fifteen seconds before the final whistle, Colin Stein (not even a distant relation) had scored an equaliser for Rangers to make the final score 1–1. Although greeted with appropriate delirium by the Rangers supporters, the late goal has long been identified as a potential trigger for a disaster. For the popular belief was that those leaving at the bottom of the staircase, on hearing that a goal had been scored, turned to go back up, and that one tide clashed with another coming down. In fact the official investigation showed that it had been caused by someone tripping at the top of the staircase; this produced a domino effect which led to a mauling and crushing that took the lives of 66 people. Stein did not know of this incident until word seeped into the Celtic bus, just as they were about to leave the stadium. He ordered the players to return by bus to Celtic Park but told them that under no account were they to go out on the town that night; they must stay at home with the door tightly shut. Then he and Neilly Mochan turned back into the stadium to lend any help they could. He saw the dead being lifted from the terracing at the traditional Rangers end and placed along the Ibrox pitch, where they lay in a simple, pathetic straight row. His experience was no different from the rest of us who witnessed this: disbelief merging with a feeling of nausea. Some idiot of a reporter asked Stein a question about the game itself as, eventually, he stepped out of the main entrance at Ibrox. He was sharply rebuked with a 'This is no time to talk about football.'

Although there was a sense in which everyone hoped that such a tragedy would erode the old enmities between the two sets of supporters, Stein never ascribed to that view. He was simply too street-wise to envisage a fraternal bond being forged over the sectarian demarcation line. Of course, in public he did everything sincerely to promote the various functions held to raise badly needed funds for the bereaved, including, notably, the charity game played between an Old Firm Select and a Scotland XI on 27 January, which the international side won 2–1. He gave his full blessing to that and encouraged his players to cooperate as much as possible in the joint eleven, managed on that special occasion by Willie Waddell. But instead of total harmony there was a dispute when Harry Hood, angered by insulting chants directed towards him by the Rangers supporters in the crowd that night, refused to come off the bench to play, walked back to the dressing-room, and left the stadium in disgust.

Stein's view remained that it was naïve to imagine the old hostilities would ever disappear. Indeed he long held the view, expressed several times to me, that the Old Firm fixture was a great 'safety valve'; that it allowed people to let off steam, however obscenely, however provocatively, so that the sworn terracing enemies could go back to work with one another on the Monday morning relieved of a lot of the bitterness. He even went so far as to say that if the fixture did not exist – and we should recall that from time to time major figures in Scottish society called for its banning, even during his reign at Parkhead – then certain forces in that nether region of sectarianism would turn to a Northern Ireland mode of expressing their hatreds. The sinister elements, as he saw it, were held in check by this footballing outlet. This was not a glib dismissal of the violence that occurred from time to time, but a persuasive arguments which he pursued with enthusiasm occasionally, if certainly laced with regret. But watching him sign autographs for men and women in Rangers colours outside Glasgow Cathedral after a memorial service for the victims of the disaster was to witness a man clearly embarrassed by this natural act. It was as if to do so was insensitive, given the nature of the occasion, but that not to do so would have been a gross insult to these people.

These supporters of Rangers would undoubtedly have been ecstatic at his discomfiture a few months earlier when on 24 October 1970 at Hampden Park, in front of a crowd of 106,320, a sixteen-year-old called Derek Johnstone scored the only goal of the game with a header in the 40th minute to take the Scottish League Cup to Ibrox against all expectations. That ended Rangers' 1,641 days in the wilderness since their last triumph in the 1966 Scottish Cup final. It was a reminder to Stein that although he knew he had better players in a more organised side, Rangers had their own strong motivations on these occasions and could prove formidable opponents. Indeed, it was that same young man who on 8 May 1971, with a deftly timed header after chasing a long punt downfield, scored an equaliser in the Scottish Cup final against Celtic in the dying minutes of the game. Lennox had scored just before half-time and it looked like a foregone conclusion until those final moments. The replay four days later was to be particularly characterised by one of those nights when Jimmy Johnstone produced such sublime moments of skill that among the viewing media there was simple wonderment in beholding this spectacle. But it was also notable, in a less heralded way, for the fielding of a player who was ultimately to have a tempestuous relationship with Stein: 21-year-old Lou Macari.

'I was on the bench for the first game,' Macari recalled. 'I can remember Jock was angry at the way the goal had been conceded in the last minute. We left Hampden and went straight to Seamill Hydro again where the manager was not in the best of moods and the training we undertook was heavy. I think he was annoyed that there might just have been an element of complacency creeping in. For there was no doubt he worked us hard, and by the time we got back to Hampden we knew that any slip-ups and we'd be in for it. Of course I didn't think I was playing, and since this was my first final and I was a surprise selection, people used to ask me how Jock had built me up for it. He didn't. I just sat there in the dressing-room as usual, thinking I would be on the bench again, but when he read out the team I was in it. And that was that. Nothing special was said to me. No instructions in depth. I knew what I had to do and I went out and did it. It was remarkable how well he had read Rangers to know I could disturb them with my speed.' Macari began to establish himself as a Celtic star when he opened the scoring after 24 minutes. Harry Hood got the second from a penalty two minutes later when Johnstone was pulled down. Rangers only scored when Jim Craig diverted in a shot from Derek Johnstone in the 58th minute. 'Remember, I only knew I was playing in that game about 50 minutes before kick-off,' Macari continued, before going on to make a significant personal point about that. 'That was Jock's way. You never knew, or hardly ever knew, that you were playing until as late as he could make it. Now, when I ended up in the law courts in my case against Celtic over my managerial style, it was said that part of the reason I wasn't managing properly was that players were never told they were in the team until the last minute. I was only following in the tradition of a great manager. Nothing more, nothing less.'

Stein's delight at Macari's selection coming up roses for both of them that day was evident when in the pitchside interview with me afterwards he took pleasure in saying, 'That was a good result for Rangers.'

'But it was you who won,' I replied, slightly nonplussed by his remark.

'Aye,' he said. 'But it could have been a lot worse for them.'

Game, set and match to the man who limped off again with a relaxed smile on his face, as if he still could not deal with the BBC without some little sting in the tail.

In fact, it was another two years before the relationship between Stein and the BBC changed dramatically. Just before a Scottish Cup tie replay against Aberdeen late in the following 1972/73 season, I was sitting in the entrance hall at Pittodrie when Stein swept past heading for the dressing-rooms. He snapped at me that he was going to place a ban on a commentating colleague of mine from ever working at Parkhead again. It was part of his method to leave you open-mouthed, speculating about what was on his mind. You knew, of course, that he wasn't joking. Unknown to anybody at the corporation I decided I would take my life into my hands and confront him. I wasn't feeling particularly brave about the prospect, but I felt it had to be done. I turned up unannounced at Celtic Park and asked to see him. We met in the boardroom just after the training session and his tracksuit, as usual, was spattered with mud. He seemed a bit surprised that I had turned up, but he immediately launched an attack on Peter Thomson, head of sports broadcasting at the BBC, and made it clear he thought the man could not be trusted to be impartial. This was a completely distorted picture, but that is what he thought, despite my saying that he was simply listening to hearsay and that Thomson wasn't so clever as to be able to deflect credit from Celtic when it was due.

The conversation then took a philosophical turn as he talked about the evils of our sectarian society.

'How many Catholics do the BBC employ?' he asked me bluntly.

I didn't know, but it was fair to reply honestly. 'I suspect, not many,' I said.

We then rambled our way through the iniquities people suffered because of one thing or another in religion.

'Kids should all go to the same schools,' he concluded, almost with a sigh, before making for the door. Football had not been discussed.

'And can our commentator come back?' I asked him.

'Aye, but don't send him near me,' he replied, and walked out, starting to sing at the top of his voice.

Here was an underling from the BBC making the first attempt to communicate with the leading manager of the day. I had done this without anybody's seal of approval and decided to go one further. On my return, I suggested that we should get Stein into the studio to analyse our next major live game. Thomson could not believe this, for he had now determined that Stein was the devil incarnate. But I knew it would be impossible to reject his services if he consented. To the surprise of everyone associated with the BBC, Stein did accept, and thus began a long association with the very organisation he had berated for so long. Whenever the Celtic manager came to the studios, usually at my instigation, to work as an analyst on games thereafter, Thomson usually absented himself. He was a bit like the Major Major character in *Catch 22*, whose policy of facing up to an issue was to pick a window and leave before the door opened on confrontation. However, on Thomson's retirement, Stein came to his presentation at Queen Margaret Drive and made a gracious speech, wishing him well for the future after all his devoted service to the corporation. It was so unexpected and expressed so genuinely that Thomson was almost in tears.

Back at the end of the 1970/71 season, the emotions within Celtic Park were somewhat mixed, even though they had bagged the double of cup and league. They had missed out on the treble because of their great rival's win in the League Cup, and in Europe they had reached the quarter-finals of the

European Cup only to be knocked out in March by Ajax 3–1 on aggregate. But this did nothing to diminish Stein's burgeoning reputation. He was nearing 50 years of age. His habitually stern features were being beamed throughout the land when anybody wanted a statement about any issue in European football. Journalists would come to pay a kind of homage from all parts of the world. He was an oracle-cum-agony aunt.

And the rumours were increasing about his future. In the previous season, as we have seen, his sudden departure from the USA trip and the publicity it received had revived stories about Manchester United's interest in him. However, on the Ides of March in 1971, a plot was being hatched to rob Celtic Park of its greatest asset. At the heart of it were a fellow ex-miner from Lanarkshire and a man from the Gorbals. At Old Trafford, Matt Busby had a conversation with Pat Crerand that was eventually to cause a division within the Stein family. For during it Busby admitted that it was time for him to think of retiring as manager as he was feeling his age. He asked Crerand for advice on whom he should pick as his successor. It was then that Pat Crerand used his friendship with Stein to try to change the man's career.

'I suggested to Matt that Stein would be the best man to replace him,' said Crerand. 'It wasn't as if he hadn't thought of him, but he had imagined that he would be on a solid contract. Of course, he never was. So I volunteered to feel Jock out about this. I went up to see the Ajax match at Hampden, where they won 1–0 but lost on aggregate. After it I travelled out to Jock's house. He hadn't arrived back. But in the house were Jean, Bob Shankly and Tony Queen and their wives. When he did come back I couldn't discuss the matter I really wanted to see him about because of the other folk being there. Eventually Jock told me to go upstairs as his kids wanted to see me. His son George was there on his own at first, and I thought it would be worthwhile letting the cat out of the bag to him, for I knew he loved United and adored Denis Law. So I put it to him: "How would you like your dad to go and join United as manager?" He was over the moon. I could see the excitement in his face. Then his sister Rae came in, and when I put it to her as well she was just as keen. But we were up there a little while and Jean came up to see what was going on so I decided to let her in on it. I put it directly to her that United wanted Jock. What a different reaction. I could see right away this wasn't on as far as she was concerned. "I love it here too much and I love Celtic. There's no way I am going to Manchester." So here we were upstairs talking about the Big Man's future and he knew nothing about it. His kids and his wife were the first to hear that Matt wanted him at Old Trafford. Now, I knew that if Jock really wanted this job he would go for it, despite what Jean thought. At least that's what I believed at the time. There was so much that would have been offered to him and his family down there.

'Of course, eventually I talked this over with Jock and I could see more than a spark of interest there. He travelled down to meet Matt and Louis Edwards, the United chairman, in his house at Alderley Edge where they laid out the terms and agreed another meeting which the two of them thought was a formality. When Jock came down with his son George to see a Fairs Cup game between Liverpool and Leeds, he met up again with the United pair and it is there the final talk took place. Matt always swore to me that at that meeting Jock Stein shook his hand and agreed the deal making him the next United manager. Matt went back thinking another Lanarkshire man was going to take over. He was delighted. But only 24 hours later a very angry Matt approached me and said, "Some pal you've got. You wouldn't believe it. Jock's turned it down. He's just phoned me. He's not coming." And I always remember he said, "I think that man has just used me to get more money out of Celtic." It wasn't often you saw Matt being bitter about something, but he was that day.'

But that is the Busby version. Stein's accountant Gerry Woolard would claim that Stein did not accept the job after discovering that Busby might yet be an influence in the background at the club. Stein found that unacceptable and turned the offer down flat, before returning to Glasgow. That seems nearer the mark, for neither had it anything to do with an attempt to extract a larger salary at Parkhead. In any case, screwing more money out of Celtic has traditionally been a task even beyond a crack unit of the SAS. Stein was never handsomely rewarded for his efforts and the United episode did little to change that. Neither was the man a money-grabber. Quite the contrary. The rejection of the offer had principally been down to a wife who loved her home environment and would not budge. All the intimidatory powers Stein could bring into powerful effect in the outside world would vanish within the four walls of his home. However, also coming into play was his love of the Celtic supporters whom he thought were the salt of the earth, and through that affection there was the constant thrum of duty and service to them still pounding in his mind. He was not going to sacrifice that with so much more still to do.

CHAPTER TWENTY
A TIME OF CHANGE

On 14 August 1971, a young man playing in his first Old Firm game for Celtic was given the task of scoring from the penalty spot twenty minutes from the end of the game at Ibrox. At the time Celtic were leading 1–0 and the match still hung in the balance. To score would put the game beyond dispute. Not only did the fledgling fail to exhibit any twitchiness in front of the gaze of 72,500 pairs of eyes, he also had the temerity to bend down, tighten and then re-tie a lace around his boot before standing erect to gaze sternly at the Rangers goalkeeper Peter McCloy. Watching it, as I did, was like seeing a slender youngster awaiting permission from the lollipop man to cross the road. He then stepped up and swept the ball into the net with a strength and panache that in one fell swoop bestowed on him the bearing of a fully fledged Celtic player. Kenny Dalglish had just scored the first of seven goals he was to rack up against Rangers in a manner which suggested ice ran in his veins. We probably did not realise it at the time, but this coolness was quintessential Kenny. There were many more to come from those feet in that sanguine manner.

In Dalglish, Stein had signed and developed a scourge of opposition defences and a tormentor and destroyer of Rangers in particular. Satisfaction might have derived also from the fact that his young player came from a Rangers family, and from the knowledge that the insignia of that club was prominent in the Dalglish home when Celtic turned up on his doorstep for his signature. It is interesting to note, as Stein told me, that a few months after arriving as manager Kelly took him aside and asked him why he had not signed any Protestant players thus far since the club wished to retain its image of being free from sectarian bias. This surprised Stein, for he had not given it much attention. He had only been receiving young players recommended to him by the current Celtic scouts and they were coming from Catholic schools. This jolted Stein into his now famous dictum that it would always be better for him to sign the Protestant rather than the Catholic lad, if they were of equal value, because it prevented Rangers from signing either of them, as they would not touch the Catholic. A double whammy, in other words. But that was never a studied and developed policy.

It was executed more in thought than in deed. It was merely a Stein reminder to the world at large of the blindfold Rangers wrapped around themselves. He went after players according to what they would do for him, not as a ploy to stem a supply to Rangers. So Dalglish and Macari became the most notable of a group of young players at the club nicknamed 'The Quality Street Gang'. They had fresh legs and a fresh outlook on life which also exhibited independence of mind, a factor that eventually would be looked upon less favourably by Stein. For he was now facing a breed of young men with a different outlook on life, who had learnt of the riches to be had in the south and who had become aware of the disgruntlement in the Celtic dressing-room, particularly over money.

But the changes that had engaged Stein's mind for months were solidly underway. On the last day of the previous league season, 1 May 1971, he had emotionally fielded the Lisbon Lions for the last time, minus a retired Ronnie Simpson, who nevertheless did take part in the pre-match warm-up shoot-in, and they swept to victory 6–1 over Clyde. That selection turned a dull end-of-season match into a money spinner as the turnstiles whirled in tune. Bertie Auld left the club five days later, on a free transfer to Hibs; John Clark went to Morton a month later where he was eventually joined by 34-year-old Stevie Chalmers; Tommy Gemmell moved on in December, just two months after John Hughes and Willie Wallace had departed for Crystal Palace; Jim Craig left for South Africa after the 1972 Scottish Cup final.

Since his entry to Celtic Park, these players had been at the core of Stein's success, and it has long been a bone of contention among his ex-players that he broke up the unit too soon. But four years on from Lisbon, it does not seem unreasonable to accept that what he did was logical. In that 14 August game which saw the emergence of Dalglish, only five Lisbon Lions were in the side. But the success of the youthfulness of the selection that day, and for the major part of the 1971/72 season, seems proof enough of the wisdom of Stein's belief in gradual transition. However, none of the Lions were particularly happy to leave the club and did so with feelings ranging from disappointment at the way the transactions were carried out to outright bitterness over the manner in which they were treated. Stein was not at his best when handling players' departures from the club. In virtually all cases there was a clumsiness involved that strongly suggested he preferred clinical splits and nothing more than that. He certainly had no time for the niceties and protocol of departures. If he shed tears at any time, it must have been in private. And if in the background to any change there was a long-term dispute with the manager, there was only ever going to be one winner.

The circumstances surrounding John Hughes' demise are perhaps the most interesting of all. It is a case study in its own right of how Stein, once he had established his view on a player, would barely budge from it. The context to the frayed and eventually destructive relationship he had with the manager was offered by Harry Hood. 'Jock knew how to handle the board at Celtic Park. I suppose he would have liked to tell them to their faces that they knew nothing about football and that that was his business, so piss off. But of course he never did that. They would all make suggestions of one kind or another to him at meetings and he would parry them cleverly. But we all knew that the board loved John Hughes. And I had heard that his name was being brought up from time to time at board meetings, when he wasn't playing, asking Jock for his reasons for that. He would patiently explain it away. But he didn't like this quizzing.'

The board's view would not have helped Hughes' career within Celtic Park, for only one man mattered and that one man had obvious reservations about Hughes. The big striker was one of the most colourful players in Scottish football and a prolific goalscorer. Off his game, though, he could look clumsy and awkward, and he was inconsistent, which Stein clearly could not come to terms with. As mentioned, Hughes has always believed his miss against Feyenoord was not career-enhancing. And the player felt that matters became too personal between them. 'There was a long spell towards the middle and end of the 1970/71 season when I just wasn't getting a game,' he said. 'I knew I had fallen out of favour. I couldn't even get a game with the reserves. I would turn up for a reserve match and I would discover I wasn't even playing in that, and I had to sit in the stand and suffer. You can imagine how that feels for someone who had given great service to the club. It was a bit undignified to say the least. I had asked for a transfer. Well, one night I reported to Celtic Park for a reserve game and lo and behold I wasn't picked again. I couldn't suffer it any longer. I just walked out to the car, jumped in it and went home. I didn't regard that as serious, as after all I wasn't playing. That, though, was reported back to Jock.

'A few days later I got a call from the club asking me to report for a game against Kilmarnock in the Frank Beattie testimonial down at Rugby Park. I was surprised by this for I knew I was right out of favour, but I was told to turn up for the team bus. This is one of Kenny Dalglish's early games for the club and he scored six goals. When we got into the dressing-room he read out the team and I wasn't in it; I wasn't even to strip at all. He turned to me in front of everybody and said, "And how are you going to get home from here? You don't have your car with you." He deliberately humiliated me. Here is a man who took me all the way down there knowing I wasn't playing, just to get back at me for not staying to see a reserve match. Now, we're talking about a man who had achieved great things, but here he was being unbelievably cheap and nasty. And I wasn't the only one who got that kind of treatment, I can assure you.

'Now, in fact, that made me all the more determined to stay at Celtic. I loved the club. I didn't want to leave. But he gave me no options. What had he against me? I think when I missed that chance against Feyenoord my career was effectively over at Celtic Park. I don't think he ever forgave me for that. For instance, when I played against St Johnstone that year [on 6 February 1971] I got a bad tackle which required twelve stitches in the front of my leg. He asked me if I was going out in the second half and I protested that if I got another knock it would burst open. So I didn't. We lost 3–2 and he blamed me directly for that. It was all adding up. So when Crystal Palace came in for me I was negotiating with them but still hoping I could stay at Parkhead. But then he walked in on me one day and said, "Sign, or else. You're leaving here. You've no choice." I understood afterwards that other clubs were in for me but that was never mentioned. I was only 27, but even so I had been at the club eleven years, and I think as well he just didn't want to give me a testimonial which I would have been coming up for. When I went to Crystal Palace I lasted about eighteen months, for apart from a serious injury I picked up, my heart wasn't in it. He effectively put me out of the game at the age of 28. I have to be honest and say I couldn't bring myself to go to his funeral.'

It would be exceptional for any manager to go through a generation of players without incurring a degree of bitterness from some of them, for hell hath no fury like a player told not to strip to play when he expects and feels he deserves a game, especially over a long period. It is in the nature of the managerial job to make decisions that will hurt people inevitably, and the Hughes aggravations stem from the fact that once out of favour with Stein it was clearly difficult to return to the fold. But at the centre of Hughes' rocky relationship is his accusation of Stein's insensitivity when dealing with certain people. The picture he draws is not just of the disciplinarian but of a vindictive man who, once the prey was identified, would not give up the hunt.

But while you cannot doubt the deep hurt felt by Hughes and the sincerity with which he has tried to portray that period, it does not give a complete picture Stein. He certainly was not wholly indifferent to personal feelings. Jim Craig, who was, of course, also to leave the club for South Africa in May 1972, lapsed into an icy relationship with Stein too. Craig was married to the daughter of James Farrell, a director of the club and a prominent Glasgow lawyer. Craig would claim that his marital connections did not influence Stein's views on him, but since the manager had little time for directors in general it probably did not enhance his stature in Stein's eyes either. But there came the time when, as Craig vividly recalled, the shutters came up. 'He fell out with me,' he said. 'He just snubbed me, didn't talk to me, didn't look in my direction. I was cut out of things. I may not have been at my best on the field at that particular period, but I think he might have felt I expressed views too often which he didn't approve of. In other words, I spoke up. And, to be absolutely truthful, Jock demanded a master-servant relationship. That's what you had to agree with or you didn't get on. However, sadly, during that time my wife had a miscarriage. When he found out about that Jock could not have been more solicitous towards her. He sent her flowers and kept phoning her up to find out how she was recovering and told her not to worry about anything in the future. I joked with her that Jock was talking to her more often than he was to me. But eventually he drove me up and down from Seamill to the training to see her when she was recuperating and you could not have talked to a more sensitive person over our sadness at that time. And when I left the club I did regret it, but it was inevitable.'

Shake the Stein kaleidoscope and you come up with different patterns. The mix of colours depends on whom you talk to. Out of the man's depths came different moods which seem to be beyond disentanglement. You feel, when considering the evidence offered by some players, that Stein was not one person, but several. You prospected for qualities in him never knowing what you were going to find.

Tommy Gemmell left the club in December 1971 – reluctantly, like the others – after coming through the peaks and troughs of a relationship. 'He was very good to me at times,' he said. 'I was fond of the shooting and fishing and I would ask him for a Monday morning off occasionally, and sure enough he would let me do that and I would bring him back a brace of pheasants, perhaps, as a thanks. He once looked at them and said, "What the hell do I do with these?" After I got them plucked for him he was more appreciative. I also went to the races with him – Ayr, Hamilton, Musselburgh – and we got on fine. So in many ways we could be friendly. But he also disapproved of certain things, and after being dropped from the League Cup final without a word of warning I discovered the other side. I put in a transfer request, more out of anger than anything else, for I loved being with Celtic. I was on holiday at that time and I was tapped by a certain club who went on to ask me if it was all right if they approached Jock, which I know they did. But when I phoned him up to ask innocently if anybody had come in for me, he denied it. Nothing doing, he told me, when I knew all the time he had been approached. Of course, since I had been tapped I couldn't say anything. I thought that meant he was going to encourage me to stay, but that wasn't the case. I could have given further service to the club if he had just shown me that he was keen. But I knew he wanted rid of me. Not just that, but he wanted him, not me, to decide where I went.'

Bertie Auld, effectively Stein's first real signing, admits that he did give Jock some tricky moments to deal with, but nevertheless he was highly thought of by the manager as the spicy ingredient in his side, even though he would be angered by the player's occasional off-field antics. Even so, his ending at the club looked cumbersome as well. 'I had a major fall-out with him. I was on the bench against Thistle in a cup-tie at Firhill in January 1969. It ended up a draw and I didn't play. For the replay in midweek he kept the same team but changed the substitutes and dropped me without me having kicked a ball. I was incensed. I strode into his office from the dressing-room after learning I wasn't playing and told him what I thought of him in no uncertain manner to be treated like that. I didn't even give him time to reply for I walked out, got a taxi and headed into the Vesuvio restaurant in Glasgow, which he frequented himself by the way. The situation was awkward after that. If he had only spoken to me about it in the four days in between it would have made a difference to my reaction. As a manager myself, of course, I fell out with players. But Jock stunned everybody I think with the suddenness of some of his decisions that just left you looking daft. You had to ask yourself: why wouldn't he just speak up about matters?'

Willie Wallace left for Crystal Palace at the same time as John Hughes and with no discussion offered about options. John Fallon left training one afternoon in February 1972 after learning from one of his colleagues that he might be on his way out of the club. He went back home later that day to find Stein sitting in his house, waiting to tell him he was being transferred to Motherwell, whether he liked it or not. Fallon refused to go. Stein persisted. There was a confrontation. Fallon insisted that he was badly underrated and that Celtic would suffer a goalkeeping weakness. To an extent he was right, for with respect to the others who followed, Stein never quite discovered a genuine goalkeeping champion. Fallon left Celtic Park for the last time that very week.

All these men who left the club around that period simply did not want to leave. They had all enjoyed great success. They were fêted by the Celtic support in ways that could not be matched anywhere. Anything else in life would be an anti-climax for them. I believe their views on Stein would therefore have been coloured by that salient fact. They were also discovering that if this man saw the need to change with the times, or to stimulate the Celtic community by introducing new talent, then he would do so in his own way. But certainly his handling of these transactions was maladroit at times and without the niceties of diplomacy, to say the least, on the evidence of what the players had to say. Harry Hood, however, believes that most of the players didn't know what management was all about. 'I played under six different managers,' he said, 'so I could make comparisons. Jock was head and shoulders above every one of them. I say that even though he was very hard on me sometimes. But the others in the club couldn't make these comparisons and they didn't know just how effective he actually was and why he had to be hard on them. He had different moods. But the whole effect was to make us play better.'

In *The Sun* on 24 January 1973, Lou Macari, after leaving the club himself on the back of what had been a long period of bitter dispute with his manager over money, said in an interview, 'He couldn't have really trusted players because he never treated us like anything other than children ... There were other reasons for my wanting away, most of them stemming from Jock's influence over all club affairs. He was an extremely keen disciplinarian.' Thirty years later, Macari, talking to me, was apologetic about what he had said then. 'I was a young, brash boy who didn't know any better. Now I do, having had managerial experience. Jock was right in the way he went about his business. His entire purpose was to get you to think football. What he did for me and others was to make us better players, and that is what he was paid to do. I was certainly much better off financially when I went to [Manchester]

United. But, looking back, I regret not being aware of how much of an education I got under him.'

And the indisputable fact is that Stein was still producing success. In 1971/72 Celtic, in the process of significant transition, created a Scottish record by winning the league title for the seventh consecutive time. They scored only four goals short of a hundred in the process and the new striker, Dixie Deans, brought in from Motherwell in October, ended up the top scorer with 27 goals in all competitions, including an historic hat-trick in the most convincing Scottish Cup final victory of the century when Celtic trounced Hibernian 6–1 at Hampden. Dalglish and Macari amassed 45 goals between them in their first season playing together. Celtic beat Rangers four times in total in league and League Cup. So all in all, set against the departure of established names, Stein had reinvigorated his squad, and his reputation in the eyes of his supporters remained undented. They won the league title ten points ahead of second-placed Aberdeen and sixteen in front of Rangers.

During that season, though, Stein had to contend with the death of his mentor, Sir Robert Kelly. After a long battle with cancer the Celtic chairman died on 21 September 1971. He had retired from the board because of his illness and was at the time of his death an honorary chairman. The value of the relationship between the two men cannot be overestimated. With Sir Robert in the background, Stein had developed the confidence to embark on his self-determined path as manager. Now he was on his own. By that I mean there were figures on the board who did not like Stein. With Sir Robert no longer there they would not feel the same constraints being placed on them in terms of the way they regarded and discussed Stein. At times he could barely disguise his contempt for some of them, whom he regarded as being as useful to the club as garden gnomes are to horticulture. They disapproved of some of his methods, although they respected his abilities. They had heard, too, rumours that he was a heavy gambler and that did not seem to go down well with some of them, though why that should have been of interest to them is puzzling. Certainly his immense public stature might have made him appear invulnerable, but from the moment he flirted with the notion of going to Manchester there were those on the board who felt that he was not entirely trustworthy.

In *Celtic – A Century with Honour*, a centenary history of the club, Brian Wilson refers to the minutes of a crucial meeting of that period with respect to rumours about an offer from Leeds United, as well as the approach by

Manchester, which obviously interested him. 'The chairman [Sir Robert Kelly], who was not present, was very much in agreement and very disappointed that he [Stein] should be so tempted.' Wilson then goes on to report that the meeting had recorded that 'loyalty to the club should play a very important part in his [Stein's] thinking'. With Sir Robert ailing and not taking a real part in the discussion, the others seemed not to be taking into account the vicissitudes of managerial life and the miserly sum they paid the man. So the above report in the minutes now seems gauche.

Now that Desmond White was chairman, a new form of relationship would be developed. With Sir Robert there was clear evidence of two Lanarkshire men with a fondness for a punt on the horses and other affinities that made for an instinctive blend. White was a man who, when not reading balance sheets as an accountant by trade and guardian of the Parkhead coffers, had climbed mountains as a pastime and was a kind of discreet Patrick Moore with a private but enthusiastic interest in astronomy. White may have been interested in the sharp crags of the mountains on the moon, but Stein was keener on the curved slopes of the Epsom Downs. This did not suggest incompatibility, of course, for Stein was still the provider of success which put a beam on the new chairman's face as the crowds continued to roll in, although even Stein would smile wryly at the announcement of attendances at times, such as when a 40,000 crowd did look a tad more like 55,000. However, White and Stein enjoyed no form of constructive intimacy. The absence of the man who had made the final decision to bring him back as manager produced a painful autumn, aggravated by one of the biggest upsets in Scottish football history.

This was the Scottish League Cup final on 23 October 1971. The vast majority of those who turned up at Hampden Park that day were expecting what was perceived to be the formality of Celtic lifting the cup once again. Partick Thistle, their opponents, moved from 6–1 to 7–2 against in the betting as they were backed rather heavily at the first price. But even the shrewdest insider gave them no chance. Stein surprised the dressing-room with his selection. Outside, among the supporters, the choice was accepted as holy writ, as usual. Billy McNeill was injured, but to the astonishment of his colleagues Bobby Lennox was left out; Jim Craig, who was really only a one-position player, was preferred as the only substitute. Stein was relying on his younger brigade.

It all backfired. Firstly, Thistle, accustomed to the tighter atmosphere of their home ground, suddenly discovered that Hampden, instead of being intimidating, afforded them space and even time on the ball which they seized upon greedily. Secondly, Celtic were to lose Johnstone after twenty minutes through injury, and with Craig as the only sub they became disjointed. And at that stage, unaccustomed as they were to such a situation, it was a case of all hands to the pumps, for Celtic were already two goals down. At around 3.40 that afternoon Frank Bough, in the BBC *Grandstand* studio in London, refused to read out the scoreline that was handed to him until it had been triple-checked, for he was being told that Celtic, after just 36 minutes' play, were trailing 4–0.

I have never witnessed a Celtic crowd so muted. Defeats they had witnessed against very prestigious opponents, but trailing by that score to a side from the north-west of Glasgow seemed simply surreal. My recollection is that far from being angry they seemed stupefied. Dalglish scored the only goal for Celtic with twenty minutes to go, when it was too late for a revival. Then Stein had to watch Alex Rae lift a major trophy for Partick Thistle for the first time in half a century. That was the moment Stein did not like. According to Bobby Lennox he went 'loopy' in the dressing-room afterwards and accused Lennox of a poor attitude in apparently showing resentment about being dropped for the final. About half an hour after all the presentations and interviews with Thistle players and management, Stein appeared out of the tunnel and started walking down the side of the pitch, clearly wanting to get away from his players after giving them some verbal volleys. He didn't look angry in the least, just tired, and said simply to me, 'Well, you got the result you all wanted, didn't you?' It was at that moment that you realised, because of how he perceived the media and how a great many of the public regarded Celtic, that any team playing against them in a final was in reality a surrogate Rangers.

But there was no indication then that this man was taking a pummelling inwardly, sustaining all the emotional highs and lows, which at times must have been like being a passenger on a stunt aircraft over which you had no control. He was tired, puffy around the eyes certainly, but still looking jaunty even in defeat. That night he joined friends in the Marie Stuart Hotel, just over the hill from Hampden, and ceremonially carried into the party 'a big wally water-jug', as some of his friends described it, which Stein said would have to take the place of the League Cup which he had left with some others. It brought the house down, and he ended up the life and soul of the evening as he led the community singing. Nobody detected any sign of strain. But it was there, hidden.

Later that season his constitution paid the penalty of having to withstand one of the most dramatic climaxes at Celtic Park. If there were any substance to his players' view that he broke up the Lions too soon, it would be in relation to Europe. For success in that arena was to elude them thereafter. It is difficult to refute the suggestion that if a Gemmell or a Wallace or an Auld or even a Hughes had been kept on in the squad that season, with their invaluable experience, it would have altered the course of events in the European Cup, for Celtic reached the semi-final that season and were eliminated in the cruellest way possible. It was the first penalty shoot-out in the history of the club.

It was the evening of 19 April 1972; the opponents were Inter Milan again. The first leg in Italy two weeks earlier had been goalless. In a tentative, tightly defensive display at Celtic Park, the Italians, as if their resolve were born of a revenge for what had happened in Lisbon, looked eminently watertight and gave the impression, as Italian sides often do, that if you stop the other side from scoring then something will work out in your favour eventually. It did, through the most dramatic penalty shoot-out.

It was an odd night altogether. On the other side of the city Rangers were playing Bayern Munich to try to qualify for the final of the Cup Winners' Cup. In total, 150,000 people watched football in Glasgow that night, split evenly between the two stadia. Both games were covered live on television, but since the Rangers game kicked off earlier, my contribution in commentary came only when they crossed live to Celtic Park for the later stages and I had to try to stand the test of a penalty shoot-out. For after 210 minutes of football in total, a goal had yet to be scored. If it was difficult to withstand the pressure on a television scaffold in 'The Jungle', hovering above the mass of humanity there whose very existence in life seemed dependent on the outcome, it must have been hell on the park for players quite unaccustomed to this new method of deciding a game.

It was the first kick that detached Celtic from Europe again. It fell to the splendid Dixie Deans, who was fulfilling the trust placed in him by Stein as a prolific goalscorer. He strode up to the first one and sent it over the bar. Anguish there was at that moment, but since others had to walk the plank as well there was still a chance. However, all the Italians scored, as did the other Celtic players. That one miss put Celtic out. Deans wanted the earth to swallow him up. Stein, anguished, nevertheless paid tribute to the way his players performed. It was only a day or two later that he displayed any emotion about Deans, but in a strangely commiserative way. For the player had allowed a photographer to take a picture of him standing by himself, isolated, lonely and suffering at a bus-stop, almost as if the rest of the world had 'sent him to Coventry'. His manager berated him for allowing that to happen. 'It wasn't your failure, it was a team failure,' he snapped.

The fact that in the following season, 1972/73, Celtic won only one prize, the championship, would have only partially satisfied Stein, given the dimension of success of the previous years, and around that time he was at his most volatile in terms of temperament. A problem arose in January 1973 that would not put him into a more placid frame of mind. Before then, in September 1972, Celtic had beaten Rangers so comprehensively, in a noon kick-off at Hampden (Celtic Park was being renovated), that when John Greig scored for Rangers in the last minute of the game to make Celtic's victory less painful to the few Ibrox supporters left in the crowd, the Celtic support at the other end cheered the effort in sarcastic vein. That put Stein in fine spirits, for his team built on that self-confidence as he inspired his newer, younger players to great heights. Dalglish and Macari were now making appearances for Scotland at international level as well as scoring for the club prolifically. He had nurtured them brilliantly and now they were responding in the right manner. But even as they did so they were stoking up a future problem for Stein.

They were brasher and less intimidated than some of the former players had been. Macari had been in the Scottish team that had played in a tournament in Brazil under the management of Tommy Docherty the previous summer. The Doc strongly fancied Macari as a player. When he took over as Manchester United manager in December 1972, Macari's name would not have been overlooked as a potential recruit. The little Celtic player was on fire on the field and his ambitions matched that. Macari principally wanted United, and his fellow players were fully aware of that. It was becoming so blatant. The player also absented himself from training as he became embroiled in a dispute about money, and his transfer request, around the turn of the year, was being looked upon by Stein with growing anger.

With that in mind, the manager tried to outmanoeuvre Docherty. In early January 1973 Macari was phoned by Stein one midnight and told to report to Celtic Park at eight o'clock the following morning. He was not told where he was going, but accompanied in a car by Sean Fallon he headed south and the mystery tour ended up at Anfield. Here Fallon introduced Macari to Bill Shankly. Macari had not known how close Stein and Shankly were but it was clear that Stein was trying to shunt him in Liverpool's direction. He was impressed by the Liverpool manager and was given an offer that would almost treble what he was getting at Celtic Park. It was tempting. However, there was a surprising intervention. According to Macari, later that night, while he was watching a Liverpool match in the stand, somebody came to sit beside him. It was Pat Crerand, who just happened to be the new assistant manager to Docherty at Old Trafford. It was a curious coincidence. To Stein it was material for a conspiracy theory. Macari relates what happened: 'Pat asked me what I was down for and I told him I was considering signing for Liverpool and that I probably would. He then asked me not to go ahead and asked if I would go to United instead. Of course, that appealed to me right away. I said I would. He then said he would contact the Doc right away, and after he had done that we arranged to meet at the Excelsior Hotel at Glasgow airport the following day to agree a deal.' Stein would never accept that this was a complete coincidence. He worried about 'tapping', and whether this was the case or not it was uppermost in his mind. The possibility of it enraged him. In any case, he disliked the idea of anybody getting one over on him.

All this had been festering at the same time as he was enduring the disappointment of having lost the Scottish League Cup final to Hibernian, 2–1, on 9 December. The Edinburgh side, in winning their first trophy in twenty years, had taken revenge for their Scottish Cup final humiliation the previous May. But that game also showed a Celtic vulnerability in the competition again: it was their third successive League Cup final defeat. The reputation for impregnability on these occasions which Stein had amassed was now looking suspect.

There was also a strange admission to John Clark by Stein around that time. 'He suddenly told me one day that he had to be careful about himself. I didn't quite understand what he meant by that. But he went on to tell us that every night, when he went home, he would place six pebbles carefully on the bonnet of his Mercedes and that if he came out in the morning and discovered that any of them had been moved he would know somebody was on the prowl after him. At first we thought he was joking. Why would he do such a thing? But he wasn't kidding. As you know, Jock drove back home by the same route every day in life. One day he went by a different route. He took a call from a man the following day who never introduced himself but just said, "Why did you go home a different way? I'm watching you, don't forget that!" Then he hung up. When he told us that I actually felt a chill up the spine.'

Cranks, of course, might have wanted to queue up to phone Stein, but this had been so specific that he obviously could not push it out of his mind. It had even forced him to unburden himself to others about the pebbles and the odd phone call, when by nature he was an utterly private man. To those of us who still saw him in boisterous action at that time, he seemed beyond any physical fragility. But even he could not sustain the pressures coming daily to him from many sources.

CHAPTER TWENTY-ONE
THE WARNING

In the final week of December 1972, Stein, on leaving Celtic Park one day, felt a cough coming on and a sudden breathlessness that obviously scared him, for he immediately stopped his car in the road to try to recover. He reported this immediately to the club doctor and was taken to the Victoria Infirmary in Glasgow where he lay for twelve days in the intensive care unit. Rumours began to sweep the city that he had had a heart attack. He had not. He had suffered the first symptoms of a heart condition that stemmed from an irregularity of the beat and which could ultimately cause major problems with water gathering in the lungs. He received treatment for that, and for the rest of his life had to take diuretics to prevent the build-up of water in the system, although there were occasions when for purely professional reasons he would decide not to take his pills, as we shall see later.

As he convalesced it was just as well he was in an environment with the best medical attention because he insisted on listening to the radio commentary of the New Year game on 6 January, which Rangers won 2–1 with a late goal by Alfie Conn, whom Stein would audaciously sign for Celtic four years later. Twelve days later, as Stein began to get back on his feet again, Macari was transferred to Manchester United for a fee that on Stein's insistence was £20,000 more than he would have accepted from his friend Bill Shankly. He had been beaten by Docherty over this issue nevertheless, and it sowed the seeds in some minds in the dressing-room that the manager was not invulnerable to the pressures of the market in the south, and that devotion to the club did not also entail complete servitude. Dalglish, Hay and others were taking note of all of this, and Stein steeled himself for a new era of less reverential players who would no longer act like novitiates meekly accepting an ideology, which in Celtic's case seemed to be an inflexible belief in penury.

When he left hospital with a stern warning to take life easier, he simply set about taking on a much more serious challenge from Rangers in a title race that was to go right down to the last day. Sean Fallon recalled, 'You wouldn't have thought he had been in hospital or that he had got a warning. He just dived into the job again with the same enthusiasm.' He was proving that a football club could sustain its status through the healthy provision of talent from a reserve team carefully nurtured to play to norms established from youth to senior level. It is, of course, a system that was wholly bypassed in the 1990s, to Scottish football's detriment. Today's reserve team is tomorrow's first eleven – that was the theme Stein established to great effect.

Indeed, every time you saw him in the months after his illness there was optimism in his voice when he spoke about that rare talent in his side, George Connelly, who he was sure was about to embark on a distinguished career. For Stein to be talking of him as a potential Beckenbauer was enough evidence of the special regard he had for the young player. It was as if he wanted a specific and positive aspect to talk about to deflect interest from the media's concerns about his health. When, in May, Connelly attended the Football Writers' Dinner to receive the Scottish Player of the Year award for 1973, the late Scottish actor Russell Hunter, who played Lonely in the *Callan* TV series and who was a speaker at the dinner, pointed to Stein's face as the award was handed to his young player. 'A proud faither wi' his son, that's what we're seeing here,' he said. Stein beamed with pride, and all of us who were there carry a poignant memory of that occasion because of the ultimately tragic, and mysterious, downfall of George Connelly.

Stein was never slow to admit that a major failing in his Celtic career was being unable to prevent Connelly from slipping into obscurity, a massive talent being denied its full flowering as a result. But the young player presented him with problems he had never faced before, and it is unlikely that any manager would have been able to delve into Connelly's mind and help him solve the mental strains that produced his depressions and eventually forced him simply to don his clothes after training one day and walk out on Celtic. And Connelly's personal demons were not restricted to Celtic Park, for he also walked out of Glasgow airport an hour before he was due to depart with the Scottish international team for Switzerland, shortly after he had received that award. His closest friend at the club, David Hay, had become an indomitable defender who seemed to personify the tenacious spirit Stein liked to see in his team, and Hay felt that at least part of the problem was a practical joke played on Connelly when the team was visiting the USA which spectacularly backfired in a way his colleagues simply could not have forecast, for the player took it so badly that he suffered a severe loss of self-esteem. So much so that he consulted the Celtic doctor about his mental condition soon after. Hay deeply regrets the episode to this day – to the extent that he was unwilling to go into details – and feels it lay at the heart of Connelly's problems, for the sensitive and quiet lad from Fife could not cope with the quick wit, sharp tongues and occasional crudities which are a dressing-room norm.

Stein would travel up to Fife to talk to the player and his family in various attempts to resolve Connelly's depressions, but it was beyond him. It was a complex psychological problem that remained perversely resistant to any overture. Stein bitterly regretted that the player was lost to football altogether at the age of 27. Connelly became almost a recluse and would dodge even the most experienced journalists trying to write about his dramatic lapse into obscurity.

Connelly performed in two vital games in the 1972/73 season when he showed the personal qualities which so excited his manager. On 28 April, Celtic went to Easter Road on the last day of the season needing a single point to clinch their eighth successive league title after their pursuers Rangers had dropped a point at Aberdeen. It was a triumph of self-confidence. With Connelly dominating the stage with finesse and strength, Celtic won handsomely 3–0 with goals by Deans (two) and Dalglish. The following week at Hampden Park it was a different tale. In the 'Centenary' Scottish Cup final on 5 May in front of the last six-figure attendance for a club match in Scottish football (122,714), they lost to Rangers even after Dalglish had given them the almost customary lead after 24 minutes. Connelly coolly netted a penalty in the 54th minute to put the team on equal terms after Rangers had scored twice through Parlane and Conn. The third Rangers goal was one of the most bizarre winners in the history of the final. Rangers defender Tom Forsyth, virtually on the goal-line and with no defender near him, watched the ball rebound towards him from a post and went to prod it over the line. He nearly missed, but got his studs on top of it and rolled it over from no further out than six inches to win the cup for Rangers for the first time since 1966. Stein nevertheless did walk up to the Rangers manager Jock Wallace and said simply to him, while shaking his hand, 'Well done. You deserved it.'

But for all the effort he made that night to be his gregarious self, Stein was inconsolable. He anticipated that the press would make much of Rangers' triumph, in that they could interpret it as a turning of the tide in Ibrox's favour. He was right. Ian Archer, writing in the *Glasgow Herald*, was typical of those who felt the result was portentous. 'But the first part of his [Wallace's] Ibrox task has been accomplished, and now he can expect to move towards greater triumphs,' he wrote. After all, the media pundits had seen Celtic lose two cup finals in succession, League Cup and now Scottish Cup, and watched them being eliminated in only the second round of the European Cup by the unfancied Hungarians Ujpest Dosza.

But the portents had been misinterpreted. In fact, in the following 1973/74 season Celtic enjoyed such a resurgence that comparisons with 1967 were occasionally whispered by their admirers. Stein had apparently got his second wind, his illness now so much behind him that he seemed, in public anyway, to be brimming with good health. It is true he no longer opened up Celtic Park in the mornings, but he was slightly more relaxed about that. Sleeping was still a problem, though. He could never manage more than a few hours of that. But he was still at the centre of training, his tracksuit brought out as regularly as before. And he obtained the right response from his players. It was the nine-in-a-row season.

Only two Lisbon Lions were present in the side that travelled to Brockville on 27 April 1974 to play Falkirk: McNeill and Lennox. Celtic were coasting towards the championship and had won the four previous matches in a row, so arithmetically it could all be settled at Brockville. Appropriately it was Dalglish who scored the equaliser for Celtic after Lawson had given Falkirk an early lead. It was a humble draw for such a momentous day in the history of the club. Of course, posterity makes that significant. Stein at the time attached no more significance to it other than it was simply a staging post to a tenth consecutive title, but it had equalled the world club record held by MTK Budapest of Hungary and CDNA Sofia of Bulgaria. For in beating Rangers twice in the league and losing only four league games in the whole season they were rampant, and ten in a row seemed not only possible but inevitable. It was Stein's fifth double in his reign, for Celtic also went on to win the Scottish Cup against Dundee United 3–0.

Still, they stumbled twice in cup competitions. On 15 December 1973 Stein stood with me just behind the cup-presentation area of Hampden Park surveying a bleak scene. His *bête noire*, referee Bobby Davidson, was out inspecting a very wet and soggy-looking pitch which had come under threat from the weather. It was during the period of the State of Emergency caused by the miners' strike, so the kick-off time was 1.30 to avoid the use of floodlights. Stein was in a growling, dyspeptic mood. He liked the Tory government and what they were doing to the miners about as much as he did Bobby Davidson and the way he officiated Celtic matches.

'Look at that man,' he said to me as Davidson paced out the dicey pitch. 'This game should never be played. He knows this will make it a lottery. That's what he's got in mind. He's a bloody disgrace.'

The captain of Dundee for that League Cup final, a certain rejuvenated Tommy Gemmell, transferred from Nottingham Forest, also told me he thought the pitch was unplayable. But the match did take place in front of a meagre 27,974. Celtic simply reflected Stein's reluctance to accept this as a fair decision by the referee and never looked like winning. Dundee took the cup with one fell swoop, a goal by Wallace fifteen minutes from the end of the game. Afterwards I interviewed Stein who, without mentioning Davidson by name, made it clear that the conditions had been farcical and that the game should not have gone ahead, although he was at pains to congratulate his former Lisbon Lion, who, it has to be said, was expressing his delight after putting one over the man whom he felt had freed him too soon from Parkhead. But Gemmell also knew that in better conditions Celtic would have won and tied up another treble.

But it wasn't Mother Nature that upended them in Europe. It was malice aforethought by a man who apparently not only trained footballers but allowed them licence to experiment during games with techniques normally seen in Thai kick-boxing. His name was Juan Carlos Lorenzo, the coach of Atlético Madrid, who hailed from Argentina. That in itself should have been sufficient warning to Stein, and indeed he was prepared for the worst when they squared up for the semi-final first leg at Celtic Park on 10 April 1974. Celtic had disposed of teams who were not of the highest quality: Turku from Finland, Vejle from Denmark and Basle from Switzerland, who had given them a stern test, Celtic going through on a 6–5 aggregate. But nothing was to be quite like this Atlético match.

Friends of Stein who watched the game and knew more than most of us about the health warning he had been given the year before were worried as they watched it, fearing that the Celtic manager might actually end up in hospital again as his anger soared at the tactics of the Spaniards, who went principally for Jimmy Johnstone like a pack of hounds for the stag. The first few tackles against him, when he was viciously upended, only proved what a brave player the little man was, for he simply got up and shirked nothing thereafter. That he survived without serious injury was a miracle. Amid mounting mayhem, three Atlético players were ordered off and seven were booked. In a different age UEFA would have mounted some sort of action against the Spanish side, but they did nothing of the sort. The astonishing fact was that the game produced no goals. It was a signal failure on Celtic's part not to take advantage of Atlético's depletion. Perhaps that soured Stein as much as anything else, for his post-match interviews contained denunciations as scathing as ever a manager delivered against another. Listening to Stein, you felt that Juan Carlos Lorenzo was fit only for the butcher's apron. As he spoke, you knew what was going through his head. Celtic had blown an advantage and Madrid was likely to be traumatic for all involved, because going off the field the remaining Atlético players looked as if they had won the cup itself and signals were being made to the Celtic players from the Spanish survivors that suggested a new Peninsular War was pending.

With tensions mounting prior to the replay, and warnings being issued from Madrid that their boisterous support might turn to violence against anything in green and white, a rumour circulated that Jimmy Johnstone was to be assassinated by a gunman. Celtic advised their supporters not to travel to the game. One morning the week before they left I took a call from Stein. He asked me if he could send up some of his friends to watch the game at the BBC studios because it was not being transmitted live to the nation. We agreed on a party of one hundred, with names supplied, to sit in a rehearsal room and view it all on a large screen. Something like four times that number turned up, however, and there would have been a riot had we turned anybody away. We crammed them all in, including Kenny Dalglish's father, all of them in an optimistic mood. It is doubtful if that mood was matched by the Celtic party in Madrid itself, for Jimmy Johnstone, brave though he was on the field, was also a family man and he took the threat seriously. Stein tried to joke his way through the assassination rumour and told Johnstone, just before he took the field, 'Look, you're safe enough. You can jink about the field like you usually do. They'll never get you in their sights. Think of me. I'm on the bench. I'm a sitting duck.' Nobody laughed much, though.

Even though Atlético had six of their players from Parkhead absent, they discovered that Celtic were like a team hung over, lacking any spring in their step. They were not entirely vanquished, just gradually eroded, and in the last thirteen minutes, with their legs leaden, they conceded two goals to Garate and Adelardo. The whole saga had been a blot on the sport, but Celtic, although knocked out of the tournament, had done nothing to mar their reputation for playing Stein's game, the attacking game. His personal stock remained high.

So much so that the BBC booked him to be their main pundit for the
World Cup in West Germany that summer. I worked with him there during
the whole period of Scotland's involvement, and it was an education.
Scotland had beaten England 2–0 on 18 May and had gone on to play
friendlies against Belgium and Norway, one a win, the other a loss. But the
talk was about the indiscipline of the players, their drinking and lack of
proper preparation, some of which I had observed myself on that journey
towards West Germany.

When we eventually arrived in Frankfurt to stay in the Arabella Hotel,
Stein was waiting for us. He levered himself out of his favourite hotel
Ordnance Survey point, a comfortable sofa that allowed him full view of any
exits or entrances, limped towards me, took me by the arm, guided me
through to a quieter corner and said, 'Right, tell me all about it.' I didn't tell
him everything. It would have taken hours. Stein loved to hear gossip and
tittle-tattle, but on this occasion you could tell that he did not want a Scottish
side humiliated and that he would take this seriously. He knew also that his
job was principally with the BBC network and he told me there and then that
he didn't want to give 'the bloody English' the opportunity to ridicule
Scotland. Angry though he was about what some of the players had got up to,
I could tell from what he said that when it came down to it there was no doubt
he was going to give the players his backing against the press.

His involvement became more practical days later when, along with
David Coleman, the principal BBC presenter, and Tony Queen, his
bookmaker friend, we travelled up to the Scottish training camp at a place
called Erbismuhle in the mountains. When we arrived it is no exaggeration to
say that the players in the squad were virtually queuing up to have a word in
Stein's ear. He played it very diplomatically and treated the Scotland manager
Willie Ormond with the utmost respect, but his very presence seemed to
have a galvanising effect on the players, who had arrived in West Germany in
a demoralised, bedraggled state. You could tell that Stein would have loved
to stride among them barking orders to sort out this motley crew. But he kept
his powder dry – until Dortmund that is.

It was there we travelled for the first game against Zaire. In the hotel
lounge in the city we were sitting down, idling the morning away on the day
of the game with Stein and Queen, when Billy Bremner, the Leeds and
Scotland captain, walked in. He sped across to us, shook hands warmly with
Stein, sat down beside us and then began to unburden himself to Stein about

the problems in the squad and with Ormond, but above all with the press. He got more than he bargained for. Stein lay back, allowed him to carry on for a few minutes, then sat up, his face smouldering, and unleashed his anger. He put that large fist of his just under Bremner's chin and hissed at him, 'Don't bloody well lie down to all of this. The answer is in your own hands. You're experienced enough to get things going on the park. You get your players geed up. Don't be moaning about everything, just get on with it and stick it right up the press. Get out there tonight and show us you're in a different league from these pygmies you're playing. Go on, stick it right up your critics. Think of their faces just before kick-off; think, "We're going to stuff everybody tonight." Get out there and show us.'

Bremner was visibly shaken by this. To him, until then Stein had been a distant but revered figure of patrician demeanour, as he was to so many. Here, though, was the Burnbank miner giving him a going-over for his own and his team's good. I recall him nodding meekly in assent. But although we can misinterpret things through the distortions of time, I felt there and then that Jock Stein had become the surrogate Scotland manager for the rest of the tournament. For although Willie Ormond was a likeable man who certainly knew the game well, he had no stomach for the fight. He was soft where Bremner could be hard. Just as Stein had made his mark on the Scottish captain, he was making it on the entire Scotland squad, with the little Leeds player acting as the conduit. More than that, throughout the rest of the tournament players would secretly have words with Stein, and he would prompt them diplomatically whenever he could. All this was going on as he went about his duties as analyst with the BBC, and unknown to the Scottish management team. I recall him taking a long walk with Willie Morgan, the Manchester United player, in the grounds of the team's hotel one day. Morgan had not played against Zaire and was depressed. I can still see Stein in the distance, away from us all, pointing the finger at him. It was no avuncular chat. Morgan played in the next two games and played well. Stein's influence on Scotland in West Germany in 1974, albeit from the sidelines, did, I believe, heighten the sense of commitment within the group. His role has largely been unheralded, but it was real and significant.

At the same time, his BBC producers valued him highly and he struck up a friendship with David Coleman who, although he could treat even some of the senior BBC editors with open contempt, handled Stein as if he were a precious vase from the Ming dynasty. It was his perceptions which struck home. He was not flamboyant, not too wordy, his words were plain but insightful. He summed up the final itself brilliantly. When West Germany came back to win after Holland had been in front and had started to toy with the hosts, Stein's analysis had to do with mentality, not football. 'The problem with the Dutch,' he said, 'was that they couldn't forget the Second World War. They were wanting revenge for that instead of trying to win a football match.'

He left West Germany at the end of the tournament with another dimension added to his personality, that of a football analyst who shunned egotistical verbal diarrhoea and unravelled the complexities of the modern game with transparent common sense. He was also bitten by the television bug. He hardly ever refused an offer to appear after that. This was the beginning of a long series of co-commentaries he took part in, especially on international matches. He had always used his soundbite appearances to good effect, but now, here he was being tended to hand and foot by the BBC London folk and loving every minute of it. Along with his close friend Lawrie McMenemy, the Southampton manager, Stein was one of the main providers of wisdom. To be with the pair of them as they discussed some of football's problems in various hotels around Europe was like sitting in awe at the feet of the philosophers of the School of Athens as they broke footballing life down into comprehensible detail. But while McMenemy was a considerable figure in his own right, in Stein's presence he was very much the junior partner.

Apart from his newly acquired broadcasting prowess, Stein had certainly filed away in his mind, for future reference, the inability of Willie Ormond to command the disparate egos and temperaments in a national squad. He always insisted through the years thereafter that the squad Ormond had had, with the likes of Billy Bremner, Joe Jordan, Sandy Jardine and Peter Lorimer in addition to Celtic's very own Dalglish and Hay, was better by far than that which Ally MacLeod took to Argentina four years later. So, while he tried to be as neutral in his public statements as he could about Ormond's handling of his own Celtic players, Stein returned to Scotland after the World Cup intent on trying to solve the problem of one player who was the total antithesis of a George Connelly and who, Stein admitted ruefully to his friend Tony McGuinness, without a single trace of malice, 'took five years off my life'.

CHAPTER TWENTY-TWO
PAINFUL CHANGES

Jimmy Johnstone played his last Old Firm game at Celtic Park on 14 September 1974, the same day that George Connelly announced he was quitting football. That Rangers also won 2–1 to achieve their first league victory at Celtic Park in six years lends this occasion symbolic significance. Stein, throughout his career, had built such commanding heights for himself that he could look comfortably downwards at others from almost impregnable ramparts. But now there were tremors around the foundations, slight but discernible. As he watched his side succumb to a resurgent Rangers he was looking for something special, particularly from his little winger who, although he could suffer periodic lapses in form, invariably experienced rebirths when he saw blue jerseys. Only those who would take a warped pleasure out of watching an orphanage burn to the ground could dislike Jimmy Johnstone. He exuded a pawky, charming innocence, even though at the height of his career he had gained a reputation as an incorrigible layabout with no sense of responsibility. That was Stein's problem, for he knew that Johnstone was a decent lad who would do no harm to anybody but himself. If he had been a real villain Stein would have had no qualms in booting him out of the club. In fact, he adored this little man but also believed that he must have been sent by some capricious force to try his patience to the very limits. These limits were extended from time to time, especially as he almost invariably turned out to be a scourge of Rangers.

But that day, he was substituted. That day, a darting, instinctive opening goal by Dalglish, which normally would have been the signal for the opening of the floodgates, produced merely a trickle. That day, a talent that had helped destroy Rangers in a cup final in 1969 was lost somewhere outside Glasgow, as Connelly apparently opted for oblivion rather than glory. He was in fact to return to the fold two months later, but in such an uncertain manner that nobody could be sure whether he would walk out again, and he was merely the cardboard cut-out of the player he should have been. So Johnstone and Connelly were slipping through Stein's fingers at a time when they should have been providing him with the Midas touch again.

That is not to say that either Johnstone or Celtic were entirely burnt-out forces. In the Scottish League Cup final on 26 October wee Jimmy produced his tantalising skills again to inspire his side to overwhelm Hibernian in a prolific 6–3 victory. But he seemed no longer dependable. He did not feature in Celtic's victorious Scottish Cup campaign that season. The vital spark was absent too often; he seemed shorn of his impudence and audacity. In many eyes this might not have seemed so surprising, for Johnstone had followed a lifestyle that seemed to lead him to even more late nights than Dracula could have boasted of ('Jinky', of course, was attracted to a different kind of liquid). Still, however much Johnstone drove him occasionally to despair, Stein admitted to me with affectionate exasperation that although he felt like throwing the wee man into the Clyde from time to time, he adored Johnstone. He loved him as if he were a member of his own family, albeit a dysfunctional member.

In 1969 Stein had had to deliver his first real piece of shock therapy to Jinky. Johnstone had left a train on his way to join the Scotland squad and pleaded sickness. He phoned the Scotland manager Bobby Brown from Edinburgh to tell him he could not make it; Brown told him to return home and go to bed. No sooner was he there than a phone call came in from an angry Stein, who as usual had learnt very quickly about this. He ordered him to Celtic Park and proceeded to read the riot act. Johnstone could produce a medical certificate to back up his claim that he had been sick, but Stein simply did not believe him, to such an extent that he told the press his wee winger was 'undependable' and that if he were Bobby Brown he would never pick him again for Scotland. This was Stein clearly deciding that dealing with this internally would make little difference to his winger. He had to inflict some measure of public humiliation on him to teach him a lesson. But as Stein was to learn, Jinky was as resistant to such grave warnings as an eider duck is to a shower of rain.

Only two weeks later, on 25 May, he had Stein reaching for his imaginary pistol. In the early hours of that morning police in Hamilton noticed a car speeding through town at an excessive rate of knots. After the car failed to stop at a roadblock specially put up to stop it, a chase was initiated and eventually the car was stopped further into town. Inside at the steering-wheel was Jinky Johnstone. When breathalysed, he was over the limit. Short of throwing a brick through his manager's window there was not much more he could do to incite an outright assault on himself. However, Stein approached this differently. This time the problem was serious. This would hit the newspapers, and he knew he had under his wing a man with a decided drinking problem. That he was angry was obvious, but according to Johnstone he was also helpful. 'He wasn't too happy about it, which I can understand, but he was great with me,' he said. 'Whenever I had got into a bit of bother he would sometimes tell me to take a couple of days off, or he would say, "Don't worry about things. You just think of your football. I'll handle things, I'll see about the polis." You know, I think he had the polis in his pocket. They all respected him. It was astonishing.' That respect did not go far enough to get Johnstone off a £50 fine and a year's driving ban, but it might have been much worse.

Jinky was also discovering that his manager would attempt to handle him with a degree of sensitivity and intelligence. Stein, in an attempt to demonstrate how hard he had worked to prolong the wee man's career, told me that one morning at Parkhead he was early in, as usual, and the phone went. The caller asked to speak to Mr Stein and was surprised when the manager himself answered. The caller proceeded to tell him the alarming news that he had witnessed his favourite player, the player his son adored, Jimmy Johnstone, being carried out of a pub in Cambuslang at about six o'clock in the morning, two hours earlier. The caller asked why fans should spend money on watching a team when players misbehave like that. Stein was always dubious about such calls, but the man verified that he was a season-ticket holder and that he had seen this coming home from his night-shift. When he put the phone down, Stein was utterly convinced the story was correct and, as he told me, he didn't know whether to laugh or cry.

Training was at ten a.m. He waited on Johnstone's arrival. In he came, hurrying, with his head down; as described by Stein, he was ashen-faced and fragile-looking. Stein said nothing to him as he prepared for training. Instead of launching an attack on him on the strength of a phone call, he took Willie Wallace and Bobby Lennox aside and without revealing anything told them that they would be doing ball work in threes, and since he felt that Jinky had been slipping in form of late they had to work him hard. They did. At one point during training he saw Johnstone at the far end of the pitch having a quick vomit, then getting on with it. He shirked not one exercise. He ran Lennox and Wallace into the ground, finished every routine, then walked smartly in with the rest at the end of the morning. 'What could I say?' Stein asked me. 'He had done his work. I knew what he was getting up to, but if he was performing for me then he wasn't letting me down. He came in on time, did everything that was asked of him, so I just had to let it go that time. Jinky was a marvel.' That last remark was accompanied with a regretful shake of the head, as if he could never forget that Johnstone had let so much go to waste.

Although Stein had devoted servants to his cause such as Neilly Mochan, his trainer, and Jimmy Steele, his physiotherapist, fellow punter and dressing-room morale booster *extraordinaire*, and to whom he became very close, he had three really crucial relationships within the club which he worked on to achieve the desired effect. There was, of course, Sir Robert Kelly, who backed, however tacitly, the aggressive way in which Stein tackled any issue either within or outside the club. And there was his bond with Billy McNeill, his captain, who became a confidant as a result and who I am sure was perceived by Stein, from the mid-1970s, as a future manager of the club. Finally, there was the paternal instinct that was brought to bear on his affection for Johnstone, which saw him persist in the belief that a favourite son could be saved from the damnations of drink.

Stein always claimed that what he did with the player actually kept him longer in the game than anyone else could have done. You cannot disagree with that. This was also a way of explaining to a support bemoaning the dramatic loss of form of one of the greatest players ever to wear the jersey that he could have done no more for the wee man. Indeed, given Johnstone's erratic conduct, people might have thought that Stein, a noted disciplinarian, let ultimatum succeed ultimatum in a surprisingly tolerant sequence over the years. Johnstone himself, however, has the answer to that in three words: 'He needed me.' But like some others, he did not appreciate at the time what was being done for him. 'When I think back now I know I was completely in the wrong and the Big Man did everything he could to change my ways. But it was difficult. I was my own worst enemy. If only I had listened to him. And the strange thing is, I knew I could do better if only I could buckle down and train and behave. I knew it. I felt that I would be good enough to captain the team as well. I never argued with what he was saying to me because I could never win and I knew that I was running out of time. Eventually they called me into the boardroom one day [in June 1975] and I thought I was in for another bollocking because I had had another wee drink situation. But it was to tell me the club were releasing me. Jock never said a word. He just stood there and let Desmond White tell me this. I listened, then walked out. I felt devastated. There were tears in my eyes. I didn't want to leave. But it was my own fault, not Jock's.'

One of the greatest of them all was no longer a Celt, and he was only 30. Stein's silence that day was compounded of his sadness and his disappointment that he had ultimately failed to exploit this man's talents further. They did meet at a later date. Johnstone apologised for all the difficulties he had heaped on his boss and thanked him for all the help he had given him; Stein, on the verge of showing emotion himself, simply thanked him in return and walked away. One of the most volatile, productive and highly successful relationships in the history of football was over.

But he was left with others who were just as challenging around that time. Another departure the previous July was to crystallise the main problem Stein was having in keeping Celtic at the top. Stein had first run up his flag about money with Ronnie Simpson at Hibernian. Then, in 1966 at Celtic Park, after returning from the very successful tour of the USA during which the camaraderie and the basic structures for European success were laid down, captain Billy McNeill had gone to see his boss, who was in a cheerful and buoyant mood, and asked on behalf of the squad for a basic rise in wages. 'Eff off!' was all that was said to him, and he retired from the scene a much chastened man. Rather than return to the dressing-room immediately after such a short and humiliating few seconds, McNeill hid in the toilets for about fifteen minutes, then walked back to his mates as if he had been in deep negotiation, although without success. Stein had set out his stall in the most blunt way, and it was going to take a bold man to take him on again on the issue of wages. Anybody who went into that office with that in mind went in quaking.

Negotiations on contracts were on the whole brief. As described by Bobby Lennox, there was hardly time to draw breath. 'It would just be shoved in front of you. "There it is, sign!" That was about all that was said, and of course we just did. You didn't dare to try to question things. At least I didn't. I was petrified to.'

Billy McNeill looks back on those times with great affection for his manager, but he also speaks of the wage structure at Parkhead with a distaste that might make you think he is talking about the iniquities of the Victorian child-labour tradition. 'We were completely undervalued at Celtic Park,' he said. 'When we learnt what players were earning in England we were staggered. We were paupers by comparison, yet we had won the European Cup. When I think about it, it was a disgrace. Remember, in those early days with Jock all we wanted to do was to play. The club simply exploited that. It was almost as if you were being disloyal if you had to ask for more. Jock himself was a working-class man dealing with working-class lads, and eventually, when I thought about it, it was surprising that he seemed so tight with the money, as if it was his own cash he was dispensing. But you see, the problem for the players was that they all wanted to play for Celtic; nobody wanted to go anywhere else. If you did that, as some of the players will tell you who left, it was like going down a level in life, even though you might be earning more money. There was nothing to equal the whole atmosphere of being a Celtic player. That's what kept you in their grasp. Jock knew that as well and he obliged the club by being the hardest of all men in dealing with money.'

The bonus system lay at the heart of his incentives for players, as John Hughes learnt to his detriment. 'He exercised control over you by putting you in the stand. My basic wage around the period in the couple of years before I left the club was £30 a week. I had to play and win or else I was finding it hard on that amount. So when I had a long period out of the team I suffered. No bonuses, and you were left with buttons compared to other places. And even with the bonuses it wasn't as good as it should have been. But that is what you feared and how you had to toe the line, for if you didn't then you were put in the stand and you were back to your basic. So when I had my dispute with him and had just built a new house, which he knew about, it mattered little to him that I was kept sitting in the stand with no chance of real earnings.'

On the other hand, as if to underline the nature of Stein's swings of mood or his obvious partiality when it came to rewarding players, when Willie O'Neill was replaced as full-back by Tommy Gemmell and was effectively a reserve player thereafter, Stein paid him first-team wages with bonuses out of gratitude for his previous services, and simply because he liked him. But the new generation of players, while far from being completely rebellious, were departing from the easy compliance of the Lisbon Lions generation. The player whose career is almost a microcosm of the transitional period which saw new blood, new ambitions and new effrontery in the club was Davie Hay, who learnt enough through his experiences to become Celtic manager himself. He still reveres Stein, but nevertheless had his problems. 'I walked out on the club for two weeks in 1974 in a dispute with him,' he said. 'But let me put this into perspective. I revere Jock. He was the best. He saw talent in me and he encouraged me. I can never thank him enough for that. But I began to get unsettled about the wages and in 1974 it came to a head. I decided I would have to stand up to him. That is not easy to do when you have the utmost respect for anybody. I was being paid £65 a week and I wanted £100. I had had a good World Cup in [West] Germany and people in the south knew about me now. And I was worried that if I got injured and didn't get the bonus money I would struggle financially. It was a basic wage and good in comparison with the man in the street, but it was nowhere near what we deserved. The answer, of course, was no. So I went on strike for two weeks. I was stupid enough not to make up an excuse and say I had a groin injury or something like that. George Connelly joined me a week later when he walked out. But I went back and got stuck into training, for I always gave Celtic 100 per cent.

'Now, remember, they had been prepared to let me go to Spurs previously but I just didn't want to go. I had made that clear. But another offer came in from Chelsea: £250,000, a lot of money in those days. I got a call from Stein to meet him at the ground, but since the office was closed we sat inside his Mercedes in the car park. I honestly thought he was there to tell me that he wanted me to stay, as I had made that perfectly clear that's what I now wanted to do. Instead he just said, "I think it's time you left. You've caused us some problems this season." That shattered me. The thought that he could actually dispense with me is something I found hard to live with for a while. I went to Chelsea that July and signed for £210 a week in comparison to the £65 at Celtic Park.'

Hay, like the others, wondered about Stein's parsimonious attitude and his difficulties when dealing with wages disputes. But he offers a not inappropriate interpretation which he felt at the time and is even more convinced about now: 'I just wondered if he found it awkward to deal with us because he was poorly paid himself, and if he found it hard to get money out of those at the top at Celtic Park then why should he bother all that much about our demands?'

The Celtic board at the time, in the wake of Manchester United's 1971 offer, were concerned about Stein's loyalty but nevertheless had made it clear that they would not enter an auction at any time over their manager with anybody as he was being well paid already. In comparison with whom, you would have to ask? Although the board might well have been turning a blind eye to the possibilities further afield, Stein knew what salary he could command elsewhere, but he was simply not a gold-digger. You cannot even equate his gambling habit to avarice. That was simply in the blood. In my own personal experience he never once held out for more of a fee for his broadcasting work; he simply took what was on offer and did the job. That is not to say he was not well paid by the BBC, who highly valued him. And when he undertook that series of countrywide chat-shows sponsored by a brewer, with myself as chairman, I did the negotiations for both of us and he didn't demur once about the amounts. Indeed, when a column appeared in the *Sunday Mail* at that time with a caustic remark about how we were both merrily rolling along on the gravy train, he proposed that some of the money should be given to charity. It duly was. He did gamble – he gambled heavily at times – but outside of leaving his own money to the vagaries of the racecourse it seemed to me that building a fortune for himself was foreign to his nature. Had anything approaching the opposite been the case he might have been more awkward with the board of directors at Celtic Park. For however well they might have tried to rationalise it, Stein was not well paid. His average basic salary during his managerial spell at Parkhead was £10,000. Even at that time this was a figure he could have doubled or trebled by moving down south. The fact that the Celtic board expected him to display loyalty showed that they seemed to be insensitive to the fact that his bond with the club was being demonstrated beyond any reasonable doubt by his acceptance of a relative pittance, even though he had proved to be the outstanding manager of his generation. He did have a business interest outside football with some partners including the future Lord Gordon of Strathblane, namely the Lord Darnley pub-restaurant on the south side of the Glasgow. But he took not a blind bit of interest in its running. It was a sort of financial insurance policy.

The directors were certainly concerned about him moving away from Celtic Park but did not seem to be prepared to make his position so attractive that he would not possibly consider departing. There was a report at the beginning of June 1975 that he had been offered the Scotland team manager's job again, but that came more out of a growing disenchantment with Willie Ormond, and the chairman of the SFA at the time, Rankin Grimshaw, making sure that rumours would abound by uttering public statements that were far from ringing endorsements of Ormond. The press follow-up on Grimshaw's remarks seemed to suggest that a move to Park Gardens and the SFA was inevitable for Stein. As we were to learn, he was indeed offered and almost accepted the post, but then, to the mystification of the SFA, reneged.

He had been appointed manager of the Scottish under-23 side and had led them to victory in Romania on the last day of May 1975, after which he was described by Alfie Conn, then of Tottenham Hotspur, as 'Mr Magic'. This was awkward for Ormond for the following day his job seemed to be hovering on the edge of a precipice when Scotland trailed Romania 1–0 in a European Championship qualifier, with only minutes to go. From my commentary position I could see not only the game but the press beginning to write Ormond's professional obituaries. As they hammered out what was to be the last denunciation of this pleasant little man – almost with delight, for they had not forgotten the 5–1 thrashing Scotland had received from England at Wembley only eight days earlier – a classic rescue act took place. Gordon McQueen, with only a minute remaining, came up for a corner and scored the equaliser. The press were then involved in one of the biggest rewrites in reporting history: they had to tear up the farewells to Ormond and write instead about the great reprieve. That did not last, though, for after the Grimshaw utterances they jumped on the Stein bandwagon again. But nobody was really satisfied with the outcome. Returning to Scotland from Romania on the aircraft, watching Ormond being dwarfed by the massive figure of Stein sitting beside him in the front row, you knew the rumour mill would start again. It did not seem right that Stein was simply a coach to the younger side. But anybody who knew him at that time felt that if Stein had an interest in the senior job, it was a long-term one. Presently he was making it clear he was no immediate threat to Ormond.

He was simply content to be given the contrast of work with Scotland and probably to wallow in the media gossip about his future, for the domestic season had not produced what he had intended. Rangers had won the league, thus bringing to an end that illustrious sequence of nine championships in a row which, at the time, was perceived to be a feat highly unlikely to be emulated. Rangers did equal it in 1997, of course, so now it registers, in the Scottish psyche at least, as reaching only base-camp of Everest with the elusive 'ten in a row' as the tantalising peak, still shrouded in mist. Celtic, clearly in decline as a European force by that 1974/75 season, had been eliminated in the first round of the European Cup by the Greek side Olympiakos 3–1 on aggregate, and their lapse in form and etiquette was epitomised by that most mild-mannered of players Bobby Lennox being sent off late in the second leg. Stein was also saddened to bid farewell to his great Lisbon captain Billy McNeill, who retired after winning the Scottish Cup against Airdrie – reportedly his 832nd game for the club. But to compensate, he was now seeing the majestic unfolding of the talent of Kenny Dalglish, who had been scoring goals like it was a demonstration of free will. As he watched him rain in 21 goals in all competitions that season, some of them stamped with genius, Stein knew full well that he would be dealing in the future with a lad as ambitious and as hard-headed as the others he had dealt with recently, and who would challenge the orthodoxy of nodding when the manager said 'Sign!'

But he put all of that behind him in June 1975 as he left Glasgow with Jean for the island of Menorca and a holiday that would dramatically change his life.

CHAPTER TWENTY-THREE
IF ONLY…

I t was Bunty Queen, the wife of Tony Queen, the Glasgow bookmaker, who noticed the difference in Stein on that holiday in Cala En Porter on Menorca. The Steins had been regular visitors over the years to the Queens' villa on a cliff-top above a tiny horseshoe-shaped beach. I recall vividly Tony Queen's wife telling me that while Stein enjoyed holidays, he always fidgeted to get back home whenever he went there. 'I don't know what it was,' she was to tell me, 'but that year he came out he was more relaxed than I had ever seen him. He would get us all on the beach and make us do the exercises as if he was training a team and we would all have a good laugh about it. He was in a great mood. And do you know, for the first time in all the times he had been out there he turned to me one night and said, "Ach, I feel as if I could stay a bit longer."' And I can still see Bunty's deeply tanned face as she said, almost in anguish, 'Oh, if only he had, if only he had.' She sounded guilt-ridden when she said that, as if she should have foreseen a disaster.

Others felt the same emotion, among them Paddy Crerand. Details of those days on the island and the journey there and back still linger with him. Crerand was part of a holidaying group which consisted of the Steins, the Queen family, Bob Shankly and his wife and a whole host of kids of the Glasgow families holidaying there, all of whom adored Stein. He had driven down to Manchester airport in the Queens' car and had been met there by Crerand. When Crerand, knowing the airport well, parked the car for them he was told by a watchful attendant that the road-tax disc on Queen's car was out of date. The car should have been put off the road and should never have been driven back to Scotland on their return. 'If only …' Crerand said, echoing Bunty Queen.

That last night in Menorca before they left to fly back to Manchester, Stein was in such a relaxed mood that Crerand witnessed something quite unique: he drank two glasses of red wine. But it was not as if Scotland's most famous teetotaller was about to spiral downwards into a life of dissolution, for as he struggled with the second glass he opined, 'It's absolute piss. I don't know how you could drink that stuff.' Crerand knew this was not Stein on his hobby-horse, just a slight reminder to others to enjoy a rare moment. That is etched on Crerand's mind.

When they returned to Manchester airport and went out to get the car Crerand pleaded with Stein to stay another night. He showed him the out-of-date tax disc. But then Stein advanced his reason and told Crerand that he had to get back to Glasgow because he wanted to see Arthur Ashe playing in the Wimbledon final that Saturday afternoon. Nothing Crerand could say to him could dissuade him. Ashe probably fascinated him as the black underdog against the then supremo of tennis, Jimmy Connors. He wanted to see this man win and told Crerand he thought he would. So there was no relenting. He had made up his mind. If only he had not been so stubborn.

With Stein at the steering wheel, Tony Queen in the passenger seat, and in the back Jean Stein and the two Shanklys, they set out for Glasgow in the untaxed Mercedes. At around three a.m. on the morning of Saturday, 5 July they were involved in a head-on collision with a Peugeot car driven by a Dumfries man, John Ballantyne, on a stretch of the notorious A74 Glasgow–Carlisle dual carriageway near Lockerbie. The Peugeot was travelling down the wrong side of the road and the accident was unavoidable. Later photographs of the smash left you wondering how anyone could possibly have survived. Stein told me later that he was thankful he had been driving a Mercedes. As he lay there before the ambulance arrived to take them to the new Dumfries and Galloway Royal Infirmary, which had been opened by the Queen and the Duke of Edinburgh the day before, he recalled being asked by a young policeman to take a breathalyser test. He was barely alive, let alone able to breathe into a bag. I suspect that florid image of death which he described to me during that 1982 flight across the Pacific was experienced then, at the side of the road, when life could easily have slipped away from him, for he had suffered severe head, chest and leg injuries. Ten hours after the collision he had to have an hour-long operation involving an incision in his windpipe to help his breathing, after treatment for his head and chest injuries.

Back in Menorca, language difficulties rendered the news horrific. The local police went to the villa to inform Bunty Queen, who had stayed behind on the island. Their English was virtually non-existent, and the only word she could distinguish, and which they kept repeating, was, 'Morte. Morte.' She knew what that meant and she almost collapsed in distress.

Stein and Queen, the only two who were hospitalised, were pulled gradually back from the brink. Only immediate family were allowed in to see the victims in the first couple of days, but within the week the irrepressible wit of Stein bubbled to the surface, for even though he was linked up to various drips and medical supports and was unable to speak, he nevertheless began to communicate with people by scribbled notes. Some of them, to his fellow patient Tony Queen, were quips not fit for the eyes of the prudish. They were more like shocking Glasgow graffiti than *billets-doux*.

When Billy McNeill had his first glimpse of Stein, several days after the accident, he was shocked. He began to appreciate just how close to death the man must have been. He also felt that his former boss could not possibly return to the same sort of lifestyle. But he did. Almost. It was not easy, though, and it took a considerable time. His treatment was prolonged, and the chronic ankle condition which produced the limp was exacerbated almost intolerably. He was to suffer increased pain, discomfort and further operations on it in the subsequent years.

Celtic suffered too. They seemed adrift without him. Although Stein was discharged from hospital at the beginning of August, he did not take up his post officially for the whole of that 1975/76 season, his deputy Sean Fallon taking charge of the team. On 23 August he slipped into Celtic Park to watch the reserves, including the young Tommy Burns, Roy Aitken and the enigmatic George Connelly, beat a Dumbarton side 7–0; then on Saturday, 6 September he returned to the ground to watch the first team beat Dundee 4–0. He was spotted sitting in the stand, and when the applause started there it soon spread around the ground in tumultuous acclamation of his presence. But he was suffering extreme pain in his foot and ankle, the old injury, as he put it to me, 'playing hell with me'. In March 1976 he had to travel to Manchester for specialist treatment on the aggravated injury to help ease the pain and speed up the recovery. That was his third operation on that foot.

The directors of the club were privately concerned that he might never be fit enough again to resume his duties, but they were reckoning without Stein's obdurate desire to lead again. It would be naïve, though, to believe that Stein, although not in the dug-out or purveying team talks and tactics on the day of a game, was not having an influence behind the scenes. To my surprise, he turned up with the Celtic team one day in the middle of his convalescence when they came to the studios to see a re-run of one of their games. And in the room next to us I heard his voice booming through the wall as he gave goalkeeper Peter Latchford, in particular, a real grilling. Stein not in charge?

Of course he was. But that sleight of hand could not be sustained, for Celtic were to collapse against Dundee United on 10 April, losing the match at Tannadice 3–2. They were to win only one game out of the last seven and the title went again to Rangers.

Throughout that season, with concern lessening because of heartening reports of his slow but gradual recovery, Stein's absence from the front line for all of us in the media was as if a curious calm had descended on the land. It was much like an armistice, or the silencing of what had been a constantly pealing bell. It was uncanny. We were suddenly realising what Stein had meant to us. Between his return to Celtic Park as manager and the day of that crash, Scottish sports journalism had undergone a revolution forced upon it not from within but from without. Allan Herron of the *Sunday Mail* assesses Stein in the same vein as another writer, John Rafferty, who felt that the Big Man could have been a success in any walk of life, but particularly in journalism. 'He had the mind of a newspaper editor,' Herron said. 'He knew how to catch the eye on a page with a headline backed up by a good story. He once fed us a line that against Dynamo Zagreb in a midweek friendly he was going to introduce a new revolutionary style of football. We led with it in the newspaper. It was ostensibly a 3–4–3 which he had set out, but all it seemed to us watching was nothing startling. They lost 1–0. But it put 10,000 on the gate. He was bloody marvellous at that.'

Nobody had ever experienced this sort of control before, and it used to anger Willie Waddell at Ibrox. Rangers, before Stein, had made no real efforts to manipulate the media as they felt they were the Establishment club and would get their due rewards of publicity simply because of their massive influence on readerships. Rangers sold newspapers better than any other club simply because of who they were. Stein changed the ground rules. Waddell, having been a prominent journalist himself, knew just how effectively Stein had taken a grip on the minds of the media and knew he would have to take him on. It was no contest. At the beginning of season 1972/73, after the experience Rangers had with some of their supporters misbehaving at Easter Road during a defeat by Hibs, Waddell announced that he would publicly address the crowd at Ibrox the following Saturday to denounce sectarianism among his supporters and to call for a new era of purity. This was to be on the back of the presentation of the Cup Winners' Cup medals to the players, who had won them in Barcelona but who had been denied a presentation ceremony because of the riotous scenes at the end of that match. The newspapers were alerted and editors prepared for an occasion as solemn as an adult baptism in the River Jordan. History was to be made. On Saturday, 12 August, Waddell, who was now general manager of the club, walked out on to the pitch before the game and stood in front of a microphone with his speech on a piece of paper. On that same day, Stein, some twenty miles away in Stirling at the tiny ground of the Albion, and knowing full well what was in play at Ibrox, walked round the pitch at half-time, made sure there were photographers near and then vaulted over the perimeter fence and launched himself into the terracing where an Irish tricolour was being flaunted by a group of supporters. He wrenched it from their grasp and berated them for singing IRA songs. Of the many occasions on which he could have done that, it was no coincidence he selected that very moment to intervene. Stein did not need a degree in journalism to work out who would win the publicity battle that day.

But for all that they gave him publicity, Stein rated photographers at about the same level as goalkeepers – which meant, according to him, they were not too high in the evolutionary chain. The real aggressive paparazzi were as alien in Scotland at that time as the tsetse fly. But he could not abide photographers coming on him suddenly at unexpected angles. On 30 April 1977 at Celtic Park during a PR exercise in which players went round the pitch perimeter to hand out flags and scarves to supporters around the track, there was a friendly invasion from fans who simply wanted to make sure they got a souvenir of their championship win. An angry Stein started to pull people off the pitch and one photographer snapped him in the process. So Stein attacked him. He pulled his camera from him and then swung a boot at him. The shaken cameraman retreated hastily. But this time there was to be a reaction. The Glasgow branch of the National Union of Journalists felt that whatever stature this man had, and no matter how revered he was, he had to answer for something that had gone a step too far. They asked Stein to attend a meeting of the local chapel of the union at the old Trades Union Social Club at Carlton Place in Glasgow, which he duly did, and after being threatened by the union that they would 'black' his column for the *Sunday Mirror* and cause it to disappear, he apologised and all was forgiven.

That was the only significant instance of retribution by the press. For like a skilled wrangler in a vast prairie, Stein corralled the entire Scottish media with daring swoops and dashes that brought many of them to heel from their maverick ways. Not too many mustangs got away from his lasso. Some believed you had to write his way or you might as well take up reporting on garden fêtes in the Orkneys. He was the first manager to phone individuals from the media at home, on a regular basis, to take issue with them. He would travel late at night from his home on the south side of the city to a late-night newsstand to get the first editions of the newspapers, and with that ammunition to hand he would go back home and reach for the phone. With those unsuspecting scribes or commentators who had written or said something approaching a criticism there would be conversations that could scald you to your very soul. Across the whole spectrum of the media there would be arguments, fall-outs, bannings from Celtic Park, mending of fences, ridicule, cajoling, baiting, good-natured jousting, spectacular rows and superb humour as we were all sucked into the vortex of his own making. It was a remarkable period which nobody, not even those who had been in the business since the height of the Bill Struth era at Rangers just after the war, had ever experienced before.

At the end of that 1975/76 season, when for the first time since he arrived at the club Celtic had won nothing, Stein wished to dispel any doubts that were arising, even at board level at Parkhead, that he might not be up to the important task of reviving the fortunes. He stepped out of his official convalescence and took charge of the testimonial game arranged for Jimmy Johnstone and Bobby Lennox on 17 May against Manchester United. He relished being out in the open again, breathing the ozone of adulation, which might not have eased the constant discomfort of his ankle but must have done wonders for his soul.

CHAPTER TWENTY-FOUR
THE BOY WHO
WOULD BE KING

Jock Stein and Kenny Dalglish formed a mutual admiration society that had the bearing of exclusivity. Although both held others at the club in high esteem, there was something in their relationship that at times suggested the one could not do without the other. For although they expressed their football genius in different ways, these two special men seemed joined at the hip. If Stein set out the basic notes, Dalglish was left to perform the symphonic variations. This he did with an ardour that produced one of the great scoring sprees of any generation, executed with such style and grace that Kenny's artistry could have been set on a stage and put to music. For by the beginning of season 1976/77 the lad with the bristling feet had scored 145 goals for the club in major competitions, and each one of these had convinced Stein that if Celtic Football Club were to face the future as a credible European force then they had to hold on to such a precious asset as Dalglish. The problem was that Kenny did not see it that way. For there was an obverse side to their relationship. While he deeply respected the man and his achievements, Dalglish was not overawed by his manager. Bluntly, he was not scared of him. In contrast to others who had purveyed stories of rejection in the manager's office and negotiations that turned their legs to jelly, Kenny was as icily cool and impervious to that as he was when being mauled by Rangers' fierce defender Tom Forsyth.

Dalglish's fondness for the manager began when he was a sixteen-year-old apprentice joiner on the part-time fringes of Parkhead who impressed Stein one day by telling him he would like to go full-time. Instead of rushing his player into it, for he recognised how talented he was, Stein took the trouble to phone Dalglish's father to warn him of the uncertainties of the game, that his son might not make the grade however promising he looked, and that the parent ought to intervene and perhaps talk him out of it until he had a trade. His father left it to Kenny to make up his own mind about that, and Celtic as a result were the beneficiaries. Dalglish never forgot the care he was shown at that time; Stein never forgot what results the young man eventually brought him in return. But despite all that quite genuine affection, events tore them asunder from each other.

Just before the July 1975 car accident, Dalglish had told Stein he wanted to leave the club. The manager was understandably angry. It was something he found difficult to come to terms with. His player was now such a darling of the terracings that he knew even a murmur of this would send shockwaves through the support. But Stein also knew he was dealing with someone who had a balanced and developed view of the world, which was professionally self-centred but did not diminish his love of playing for the colours, and that when Dalglish had made up his mind about anything a bulldozer could not budge him. It was the car-smash that changed the situation, because out of loyalty to Stein and with Sean Fallon in temporary charge Dalglish did sign the contract at the beginning of season 1975/76. But when Stein recovered and returned to the club in the early summer of 1976, Dalglish's mood hardened to one of greater determination to leave, even though he was close witness to his manager proving that staring death in the face had not subdued his appetite for the job. Nevertheless, Dalglish scored the first competitive goal of that 1976/77 season in the Scottish League Cup against Dundee United at Tannadice on 14 August, and although they were not to go on and win that trophy it was Dalglish who scored Celtic's only goal from the penalty spot in Aberdeen's victory over them, 2–1 in extra-time, in the final at Hampden Park on 6 November.

But other new faces were now in the dressing-room. The season was only three weeks old when Stein made one of the shrewdest signings of the latter part of his career: he brought his former player Pat Stanton from Hibernian to Celtic Park to play as a sweeper. This most intelligent and elegant of players was out of the top drawer, and his performances not only helped Celtic to more stability, they eventually showed up in poor light some of the signings Stein was to make in later months. In his first Old Firm game on 4 September it took Stanton some time to find his feet and Celtic were two down in the first half. But that same player rose to majestic heights in the second half and was able to release his forward players to an effective fight-back to earn a 2–2 draw, with two goals by Paul Wilson. Another name was soon vying for headlines. Ronnie Glavin, the former Partick Thistle player, was a natural goalscorer surging from midfield. With the Dalglish problem constantly on his mind, Stein needed to think of alternatives. That one worked: Glavin ended up top goalscorer in the league that season.

In the dug-out beside Stein was Davie McParland, the man who as Partick Thistle manager had out-thought Stein in that famous Scottish League Cup final in October 1971. He had replaced Sean Fallon as assistant manager, who, it has to be said, took none too kindly to the way Celtic dispensed with him. McParland was articulate, fresh, modern in his thinking and wholly in awe of Stein, and he took most of the training. It was working. On 24 November, Joe Craig, another new signing from Thistle, scored the only goal of the game spectacularly at Ibrox to give Celtic their first major win in more than a thousand days against their rivals. Stein's delight at that was tempered significantly by the sight of Bobby Lennox being carted off with a broken ankle after a tackle by John Greig.

Dalglish was still scoring. Stein was still anxious about the player's future. Celtic were still heading for another double. The manager's sense of dedication and conviction to the task was evident, more in attitude than in physical endeavour, for McParland did most of the heavy work on the training ground. But effective it was. By the end of February 1977 Celtic were seven points in front of Rangers. Then, as if he felt it was right at that time to show that he had lost none of the sense of audacity that had marked his early years, he transfixed the country with a ploy that took him on to the front pages again.

On the evening of 5 March I travelled with him after a league game at Pittodrie which Celtic lost 2–0 to a chat-show night in a hotel in the north of Scotland, part of the ongoing arrangement we had with a brewery sponsor. These nights attracted more than just Celtic supporters and Stein was in his element, talking in general terms about Scottish football. He was meticulous in what he said because although they were supposed to be private occasions he knew the press would soon hear of anything indiscreet. Nevertheless, he rarely shirked an issue, and people were surprised to discover that this man who sometimes came over dourly, if impressively, on television could be brilliantly witty, and he had them eating out of his hand, even Rangers supporters whom he treated with such diplomatic nicety you would have thought you were listening to the polite tea-lady in the Ibrox Blue Room. Without having said so to each other, we knew what the first question would be. And sure enough it came.

'Why did you sign Alfie Conn?'

Four days earlier, Conn, the former Rangers player who had scored for the Ibrox club in the 1973 Scottish Cup final, had joined Celtic. In some areas it was regarded with the mixed feelings that followed the first highly publicised gender swap, that of April Ashley, eliciting equal amounts of scorn and sympathy. But if anybody was expecting Stein to throw himself into an impassioned explanation of why a former idol of the Ibrox masses was now to wear green and white, they were disappointed.

'I signed Alfie because he's a good player and will do a job for us,' Stein replied.

The apparent banality of that utterance carried much more effect than had he stood on a soap-box denouncing the blinkered environment of sectarianism. The signing itself was a practical incision into the morbid body of orthodox thinking that infected the Old Firm. He knew what he was doing: he was applying common sense. It was another simple wake-up call to those of ingrained beliefs. There was a wider audience out there, including the Protestant firebrand the late Pastor Glass, with his rantings about Popery, and the various Presbyterian ministers with their sincere letters to the *Glasgow Herald* criticising Rangers for their non-Catholic agenda, who coming from different angles were either hardening sectarian views or having nil effect on the festering sore, simply making it an interesting debating point among the chattering classes. But here was Stein implementing something that would be well understood in the pubs and social clubs, if not universally applauded. It was a lesson in the practicalities of getting on with life while at the same time reminding any bigots that Rangers' policy was self-destructive. It caught the imagination of the public much more than diatribes by clerics. It was not a gesture on principle, for a successful Conn was what he wanted.

It was typical of Stein's impeccable sense of timing that Conn scored on his home debut on 9 March at Celtic Park in a 2–1 victory over Partick Thistle. By the end of the season he had become the first Old Firm player to win a Scottish Cup medal with both clubs. The day I walked up the marble staircase at Ibrox Park in July 1989 to see Maurice Johnston, the former darling of the Celtic support, swathed in an oversized Rangers blazer, I thought of Stein that night in March 1977 and of how he had blazed the trail for Graeme Souness and handed on to him the audacity to break moulds.

There was another practical aspect to the signing: Stein was supplementing his strike force as a precaution against any transfer move, for Kenny Dalglish was remaining obdurate. He still wanted away as Celtic coasted to another title and headed for another Scottish Cup final. As his contract lay there unsigned, and after Celtic had clinched the title on 16 April when Joe Craig scored the only goal of the game at Easter Road against Hibernian, Stein had a confrontation with Dalglish, as his former player recalled. 'He told me he would have to inform the SFA that I was an unsigned player. He was right, of course, given that I wanted to play in the final against Rangers. He knew I wanted that badly. I didn't want to let the support down. Whatever I felt about my own ambitions I still loved the support and all that they had given me, and I wanted to win that cup. So I signed.'

Stein, of course, was technically correct. An out-of-contract player had to be registered fourteen days before taking part in the competition. But you cannot avoid the impression that coercion was involved. He wanted the player for the final and had laid down the gauntlet. But it might have lain in the back of his mind that once pen had been put to paper he might have tamed Dalglish. If there had been subterfuge attached to that, it certainly did not work on the steely defiance of Dalglish. He played in the final, though. It was to be the last major prize Stein ever won.

On Saturday, 7 May 1977, the lowest post-war crowd for an Old Firm final attended Hampden Park – just 54,252. The crowd size was affected by two factors: the rain lashed down constantly from a dark sky, and this was the first ever live coverage of an Old Firm final on television. Even from the now high commentary position I felt, looking down on the pounding, artless surges from either side, that the sense of detachment from the proceedings came not from my altitude but the arid football. Jim Reynolds, writing in the *Glasgow Herald*, thought that 'a match which should have been bursting with flair took on a chessboard look'. Even then it was no Boris Spassky versus Bobby Fischer. It was another game downgraded by tension; it was a game of sticking points, not of fluidity; of man-marking, at which Celtic in this case excelled, the Icelandic midfielder Johannes Edvaldsson completely obliterating the threat of Derek Johnstone.

It was the latter player who was at the centre of the controversy. In the twentieth minute Conn, taking a corner, swung his cross to MacDonald who headed back across the goal. Kennedy, in Rangers' goal, only partially cleared the ball which fell to the feet of Edvaldsson. His shot, straight at Johnstone, was apparently handled by the player on the line and a penalty was awarded. To this day the player is adamant that the ball struck his chest, not his hand. There was an ensuing fracas of protest by the Rangers players while Celtic pondered who would take the penalty. The game will be remembered not only for the award of the kick but also who took it. It was not Dalglish. That season he had scored with seven penalties and the situation seemed ripe for him to step forward and take the responsibility. But the ball was grabbed by Andy Lynch, who had only ever taken two penalty kicks in his career, and missed both of them, while with Hearts. I recall being surprised by this at the time, and by the assured way in which he struck the ball beyond Kennedy for the winning goal. For a man who loved the limelight of scoring, Dalglish seemed a surprisingly docile bystander. It was perhaps an indication that he already had one foot out of the Parkhead door.

Winning is enough on such occasions, as we know, but it was a triumph without the lustre that had distinguished other occasions. And in Stein's mind there was the vexed question of Kenny and his refusal to accept terms. It was being said in the background that this was being forced on the player because of financial difficulties he had got into as a result of a failed business venture. But he simply rejected all inducements, even though Celtic were prepared to throw their traditional thrift aside and give him whatever he demanded. But the personal relationship was now at a low ebb, with Dalglish sticking in his heels to leave the club, despite having signed the contract. He had known all along that Liverpool were heavily in for him. Still, like many of the Celtic players I have talked to, he recounts his leaving Celtic Park with decidedly mixed feelings. 'He knew, and I knew, that that contract I had signed before the final wasn't worth the paper it was written on. It was signed for practical reasons. However, he still pushed me to go with the team to Australia to play in a tournament there after the final. I told Jock I didn't want to go. He argued with me about that for a spell. Then one morning I got a call from him saying he had decided not to take me because he only wanted players who really did want to play for the club. The team went out and they won there in a final against Red Star in the tournament.

'When they came back they picked up on pre-season training and we went to play a friendly against Dunfermline. I was still officially the club captain and we were in the dressing-room just before the game when Jock started to talk to us and finished up by turning to Danny McGrain and saying, "Right, Danny, lead the boys on to the park." He didn't say a word to me. That's when I knew I was finished. But I hand it to him. The following morning I got a call to say he would drive me personally down to Moffat, just off the main road to the border, where I would meet Bob Paisley and the Liverpool chairman John Smith. That's what he did. We drove down, met those two men, agreed the transfer and shook hands on it.

But before he left me that day he suddenly grabbed me in a big bear hug and just said, "Good luck, ya wee bugger." It was affectionate, and I felt quite moved by it.'

Celtic were diminished from that moment on, even though they had just broken a British transfer record in receiving £440,000 for their player. To what extent and for how long they suffered as a result of this offers grounds for argument, but it was certainly the end of a glorious partnership.

There are two photographs taken of Stein during his last year at Celtic that starkly reflect the erosion of his previous authority. One is of the boardroom tableau on the day he left his job in May 1978. The other is certainly a picture of him standing on the steps at Dunfermline on 10 August 1977, eyes firmly set on Dalglish making his way on to the pitch for his last game with the club. A father watching his son go off to the trenches of Flanders Fields could not have looked more forlorn. The sense of loss the photograph conveys might be pinpointed as the moment he seemed to be aware of the exigencies of time, that the era over which he had lorded for so long was disappearing in front of him. He had failed to retain the most outstanding talent of the decade. There is more than a hint, in that single shot, of a man deserted. He was about to enter his *annus horribilis*.

The sense of impending doom that might have seeped into him from then on could only have been heightened when Pat Stanton, upon whom he wished to build a new side, was carried off injured in the first hour of the first league game of season 1977/78, on 13 August against Dundee United; he was to retire a year later after barely kicking a ball again. Alfie Conn was also taken off in that match with a serious cartilage problem and only played a minimal part towards the end of the season. Moreover, Stein suffered the great blow to his resources of losing his captain Danny McGrain to a serious ankle injury which kept him out for the entire season. And results were disastrous by the standards expected of Stein. Six defeats, eight wins and three draws from the first seventeen league matches affected the highly expectant Celtic support like a biblical plague. Some, I remember at the time, blamed the going of Dalglish as an act of treachery from which even Stein himself could not be absolved, although much contempt was heaped on the board for not being able to match the player's demands. Dalglish has long maintained he had told everybody at Celtic Park that money was not a determining factor, that it was a new challenge he wanted. Let us also not forget that when Dalglish returned to play in Stein's testimonial game at

Celtic Park in mid-August 1978 a large element of the Celtic support treated him like a traitor and booed him.

Stein's signings for that season hardly dissuaded the doubters from believing that things were going spectacularly wrong. Only the transfer of Tom McAdam from Dundee United – as a striker, though he became a very steady defender – turned out to have any lasting value. The others were of modest talent: Joe Filippi from Ayr United, Roy Kay on a free from Hearts, John Dowie (who with Fulham spent more time watching than playing), six-feet-five-inch Ian McWilliam from Queens Park (he made only four appearances), and above all Scotland international Frank Munro from Wolves. Without wishing to disparage any of them, they were not, as we say, Celtic class. Why did Stein give them the time of day? It is true to say he still believed that he could make players better, and we can suppose he was willing to take a gamble on them. But there was a waywardness about all of this which suggests Stein was plummeting from the standards of meticulous preparation for which he had become famed. The Frank Munro situation seemed to underline this. The player admitted years later that he was sent out to captain Celtic in his first game against St Mirren, on 15 October 1977, without having been introduced to the other players. 'I spent the game calling the rest of my team-mates "Jimmy",' he told a journalist later. It's never been determined what they called him in return after he scored an own goal on his debut in the club's 2–1 defeat. He certainly must have gone to Parkhead solely on Stein's reputation because he went from £300 a week with Wolves to £85 a week with Celtic.

The talk around the howffs and the sports desks midway through that season was that the Big Man was losing his touch. An avid Celtic supporter came up to me in a pub once and actually asked the following: 'Is this man trying to run the club into the ground for some reason?' It was a preposterous thought, of course, but it reflected the bewilderment of a support that could not make any sense of what was happening. Something was wrong. When he talked about Celtic with me away from his job, Stein seemed less involved. Previously you could bring up any subject, from player selection to the cutting of the grass or the painting of the seats, and away he would go in full spate like a man healthily obsessed by his job. Not that year. He was 55, after all, and had been at Celtic Park for twelve years. But it was something you simply did not assess at the time.

Around that period until his death I got to know him well through our sponsored hotel tours of Scotland and his work with the BBC. He came as my co-commentator to Liverpool for the Wales–Scotland World Cup qualifier at Anfield on 12 October 1977. I did notice that he was experiencing heavy breathing after climbing up the steps to the commentary position, which admittedly was so high Sherpa Tensing would have suffered vertigo. He kicked every ball for Scotland that night, and as he shuffled about and twice nearly sent our table spinning I learnt what it must be like to sit in the dug-out beside him during a tense game. He actually shouted 'Penalty!' when the famous handling incident took place; it never entered our heads that it could possibly have been Joe Jordan handling and not the Welshman. The crowd was not in the festive, party mood now associated with the Tartan Army. This was more a fanatical multitude, baying like a mob on the verge of insurrection. Venom was in the air. What Stein said before the transmission, as we looked down on the scene, was chilling: 'I hope to God Scotland win. If they don't, this crowd will take Liverpool apart.' Of course the victory avoided that potential consequence. And when the former apprentice-joiner, now with Liverpool, scored with a spectacular header with three minutes to go to make it 2–0, that big Burnbank fist was clenched in the air in tribute.

That night Stein broadcast to the biggest ever audience for a Scotland international match. The gravitas he brought to that job, and particularly to that special night when Scotland qualified dramatically for the finals in Argentina, established him securely in the public's mind, including those who did not wish him well as Celtic manager, as the voice of common sense. I have not the slightest doubt that towards the end of the 1970s he began to want to appeal to a broader constituency than simply that of his own club. He was playing up his national persona and looking wisely to his future. Along with his friend Lawrie McMenemy that night, he was already expressing worries about the massive euphoria the result had engendered. He liked the Scotland manager Ally MacLeod as a man and knew he was a great promoter of the game, but it was clear in the conversations we had that he thought he was tactically an ingénue, a promoter rather than a thinker. Only hours after the dust had settled at Anfield, Stein was the first man to intimate, in as reasonable a manner as he could muster, that Scotland might be heading for a mighty fall in Argentina. And so it proved, of course.

I suspect he was then looking well ahead to what jobs might be looming on the distant horizon, for by the turn of the year Celtic, unprecedentedly in the Stein era, were in fifth place in the new ten-club championship and eight points behind leaders Rangers. They had lost twice to them in the league and Stein had already taken charge of his last Celtic European game against S.W.W. Innsbrück in Salzburg, when they were knocked out 4–2 on aggregate in the European Cup. The decline was precipitous. But he could still pump up the volume occasionally. In the aftermath of that European defeat in November 1977, Allan Herron, asking after Stein in the hotel that night, was told by Desmond White that the manager had taken some pills and gone to bed. Herron reported that factually for his Sunday paper. When next he saw Stein at Celtic Park he got the biggest roasting of his journalistic life from him as the manager had felt that mention of his sleeping difficulties was an intrusion on his privacy. So there were still embers of the younger, more volatile Stein in him that could be fanned into life. But not for long. When, on 6 March 1978, Kilmarnock, from a lower division, knocked Celtic out of the Scottish Cup after a replay at Rugby Park, it was debatably the most embarrassing defeat, albeit only by a goal to nil, of his time as manager. The end was nigh.

It is inconceivable that the shrewdest manager ever to have donned a tracksuit would not have prepared himself for the end-game to be played out with his board at Parkhead. He had. Or so he thought. For some of the directors on the board had had reservations about his style of management through the years and had had conflicts with him on various matters. Now, for them, it was payback time.

CHAPTER TWENTY-FIVE
PARADISE LOST

'If the supporters knew how I had been treated they would have burnt the place down.' So said Stein to his friend Tony McGuinness shortly after the sequence of events that led to him leaving his post as Celtic manager. That day was 28 May 1978. Many of the luminaries of the press and broadcasting were in Argentina at the time, covering the World Cup, and even amid the recurring controversies of that period centring on the Scottish national squad, the news was received by us in Cordoba as if we had missed the closing night of a much-respected box-office hit. We felt deprived. How dare they end his club career without us, we who had tried manfully to keep up with him, stride by stride, all those years! Where was the justice? You could detect professional envy smouldering among the media directed at those who had been left behind to cover this momentous event, even though we had the World Cup finals stretching in front of us.

Although there was a logic to what was happening at Celtic Park, with a new, younger man taking over from a man in his fifties who had had a dreadful final season, the news still gave us pause for considerable thought. Celtic without Stein. It hardly seemed credible. But those who had worked so near to him over the years knew he was hardly ever the slave of events and that he shaped much of his destiny himself. This is a view echoed to me by the man who took over from him on that early summer's day in 1978, Billy McNeill. Looking back to that time, McNeill stated to me quite distinctly, 'Big Jock never did anything that he hadn't planned. He never did anything on impulse.'

We must bear that statement in mind when considering the end-game he played out with the Celtic directors, like a grandmaster at the chessboard. He had known for some time that they wanted him out – some more so than others. His relationship with Desmond White, the chairman, was frigid and mechanical at a time when he needed the father-confessor figure of Sir Robert Kelly beside him. When he talked to his friends about White it was in nothing other than scornful terms. He particularly resented the chairman interfering in his handling of transfer matters with players, which sometimes led to confusion and botched-up negotiations. Whereas Sir Robert had achieved harmony by giving Stein his head to steer the club the way the manager saw fit, White tried to police him.

On 2 March 1978 the bubbling discontent below the surface was formalised at a directors' meeting to discuss the collapse in the team's form. The minutes of that meeting, as reported in *Celtic – A Century with Honour* by Brian Wilson, record the first steps in Stein's demise. 'The chairman mentioned that personnel and staff at Celtic Park were largely the same as they had been twelve years earlier. It was appreciated that long and loyal service had been given by some persons, but the welfare of the club should take priority over personal factors. Mr Stein suggested that David McParland should take control of the first team and that he, Stein, should go with the second team with a view to improving the standard of the young players coming through.' His recommendation was thrown out of court, as I feel he thought it would be. For while McParland's appointment as assistant seemed to be acceptable to him, he did not really rate the former Partick Thistle man as a future Celtic manager and he knew the board were not going to endorse him either. This was his opening gambit on the way to the exit. He had somebody else in mind. We could go all the way back to the raising of the European Cup above his head by the boy from Sir Matt Busby's town Bellshill to see that here was a potential leader of the club in a future generation. Perhaps Stein might even then have had Billy McNeill stamped out as the manager in future years. Although he certainly did have his run-ins and occasional bust-ups with McNeill, as he did with all of us over the years, particularly when it came to the club captain discussing money and the application of certain club disciplines, they were intimates. Still, that did not mean he could take advantage of Stein at any time.

After McNeill became manager of Clyde on the first day of April 1977, another thought process must have started in Stein's mind. For in May he took a call at Parkhead one morning from Dick Donald, the Aberdeen chairman and one of the most respected figures in the business. As anybody in the Parkhead office would tell you, Stein took dozens of calls from managers, chairmen and players every single day, seeking his wise counsel on a variety of problems. Aberdeen were looking for a replacement for Ally MacLeod, who was off to manage Scotland. Stein told me what took place: 'Dick said he had one man in mind for the job: Bertie Auld. He asked me what I thought about that, whether Bertie would be the right man or not. I had to tell him that I didn't think that was the right choice. I had to be honest.

I said a more suitable man would be Billy McNeill.' Donald acted promptly on that advice and made an approach to the Clyde manager. The next step for Stein was to be frank about this with Auld. He phoned his former player, since he knew that such an involvement by him would get back to Auld on the grapevine, and explained that he was being purely professional and that he had to give Aberdeen an honest opinion on this. According to Stein, Auld did not take this well and accused him of letting him down after all he had done for him in his time as a player. Auld's version, though, is somewhat different. He told me that he took his former manager's call and simply said, 'Thanks for that,' and put down the phone. However much the likeable Auld may now make light of it, he must have been hurt to the quick. But one word from Stein into the Aberdeen chairman's ear and McNeill had been re-routed to a new career. The leap from there to Celtic Park would be seen as less dramatic than if he had come straight from Clyde. Stein might not have seen the route to Celtic as straightforward thereafter for McNeill, but he knew his former captain now had a better launching pad.

On 20 April 1978, over a month after that directors' meeting when the pressure for change was discussed, Stein advised the board to move for McNeill. They in turn left it up to him to make the move, which he did at the Scottish Football Writers' dinner in Glasgow shortly after, when McNeill was being presented with the Manager of the Year award at the Macdonald Hotel in Newton Mearns. Stein made a discreet approach to McNeill and asked him to meet him outside, where he had parked his car about a couple of hundred yards away. 'I was intrigued,' McNeill recalled. 'I drove down to where his Merc was, got into his car and without hesitation he said to me, "I think it's time you were back at Celtic Park. Would you take the manager's job?" I was a little bit stunned by that but I listened to him as he laid out to me the reasons why he thought me and Celtic were made for each other. He was very persuasive.'

Stein was helping the club, not the board, for he knew at least some of them truly wanted him out of the place altogether. Therein lies the supreme irony in all of this, as clearly stated by McNeill himself. 'I accepted. I now look back on that as a major mistake I made. My wife Liz and I were very happy with our new environment up in Aberdeen. We had made new friends, the board were great to work with, especially the chairman Dick Donald, I had good players, we had been getting good results. I tell you this, if the Celtic board had approached me to take the job instead of Jock I would have rejected it. I wouldn't have gone to Celtic. But I couldn't bring myself to say no to big Jock. I just couldn't face up to turning down what he was saying. His presence was overpowering. If it hadn't been for Jock, I would never have returned.'

Of course, at that time the Celtic board were not aware of McNeill's serious reservations about the move. They had found Stein's replacement and that is all they were concerned about. Stein, of course, did not mention to McNeill his antipathy towards White, and others. Instead, a warning came from Dick Donald at Aberdeen who, too emotional about his manager's departure, informed those organising a farewell party for Billy that he would not be attending. But he did want a message passed on through someone else: 'Tell Billy, thanks for everything, but tell him I don't think he'll enjoy working with that board as much as he did with this one.' And so it turned out for the new manager.

The board now felt that everything was cut and dried. It was not. At their meeting of 20 April in the North British Hotel they had set out their intentions about Stein, minuted thus, as reported in Wilson's book: 'In view of Mr Stein's long and valued service with the club, it was agreed that at the time a new manager was appointed, Mr Stein be offered an executive directorship with the club as recognition and compensation by the club for these services. Mr Stein indicated that he would be very pleased to accept such a directorship which, presuming Mr Stein accepted the Celtic job, would take effect at the time of the club's next annual general meeting.' On the surface, that lent the impression of a benevolent board. Indeed, Stein was quoted in the *Glasgow Herald* on 1 June 1978, saying, 'I am more than pleased to be going on the board at Parkhead.' Well, he certainly was, until it was explained to him what this in fact entailed. When things became clearer he could scarcely believe what he was hearing: he was to take over the area that involved selling club lottery tickets.

His deep disillusionment was expressed firstly to his family. 'You'll never guess what they want me to do,' he said. 'They want me to sell pools tickets.' He knew then that he could not accept, even though his initial reaction to a place on the board had seemed favourable. In the face of media amazement at their stance the board tried to portray this as Stein heading a whole new commercial enterprise, but whatever spin Celtic subsequently put on their offer, the harm was done. Stein had interpreted it, as the media generally had, as a demeaning proposal that showed scant regard for the qualities he had demonstrated as a football man, and it was almost as if they were airbrushing his record of its significance. That record, incidentally, showed that under him Celtic had won 25 major trophies: the European Cup, the Scottish League Championship ten times (including nine in a row), the Scottish Cup eight times and the Scottish League Cup six times. Their full league record under Stein was: played 421, won 296, drew 66, lost 59, goals for 1,111, goals against 413. To imagine a man with a record like that being asked to head the club's then very limited commercial operations – a man, moreover, who had shown little interest in the handling of money other than when he had a punt on the horses – is like trying to imagine Michelangelo turning his creative mind to tax collection. The absurdity of it had simply not dawned on the board.

Or had it? Was it an offer they felt he could only refuse? Here was the most famous man in Scottish football, renowned throughout Europe, who could lift a phone to any player or manager in the game and be listened to with respect, being asked, at his stage in life, to become a salesman. Salesman of what? Not even that had been defined properly. Virtually everybody who worked with Stein talked about his innate intelligence and believed he would have been a success in any walk of life. But this proposal contained the inherent message that he was to be distanced from football itself, and that would have been the equivalent of exile. It is also true that a new manager might have felt oppressed by the presence of such a massive figure in the background, and McNeill might naturally have felt uneasy about this. Even though Stein had levered his captain into the post it was hardly likely that a young manager of independent mind would get on his soapbox and demand conditions of great influence for his former boss, even if he had the utmost respect for him. Knowing both men, it is difficult to see how they could have co-existed cosily in an age when the role of 'general manager' did not exist, and which, in any case, might not have suited Stein who preferred, like McNeill, to work at the coal face. On that basis alone you could conclude that an exit was inevitable for him. On that basis, too, you could hardly blame McNeill for demanding what Stein himself had argued for when he had first arrived as manager: complete, unfettered control over team matters. Furthermore, on that basis it is difficult to accept that one of the shrewdest men ever to hold a managerial post could not see a situation developing that would inevitably see him having to make a clean break with Celtic.

But if anybody doubts the depth of feeling Stein had about the way this had been handled then they should consider the effect it had on his family who were astounded at what he had to disclose to them. There was another factor hovering mischievously in the background – religious bias. This was a subject that engaged Stein's mind from time to time, as he recalled particularly to his friends Tony Queen and Tony McGuinness. He had always felt that his Protestant background still bothered some people on the board and other significant figures close to the Kelly family. Occasionally he would bring the subject up with his friends and me and other journalists, particularly towards the end. Stein claimed that one man had once boasted that 'over his dead body' would Stein become a director of the club, because he was a Protestant. By and large this did not bother Stein as much as the outright bigotry he had to face from Protestants in his home background in Burnbank when he first signed for Celtic as a player. If anything, it was more a penumbra surrounding his largely unconcerned management of the club at the centre. Success and his great bond with the Celtic support made it easy for him in the main to disregard any whispers he heard about religion. But towards the end he did express himself clearly to others that it was a factor which was engaging some minds. It is not a subject he would have fantasised about either, since because of his experiences he might have claimed to be as sensitive to the presence of bigotry as a smoke-detector would be to a burning inferno.

The Stein family did take all of this badly, and it makes clearer sense of the statement that started this chapter, although the rumours that his son George never returned to Celtic Park after that in protest are quite untrue as he has been a season-ticket holder for years. But his family could look at one photograph in particular only with distaste. It shows the trio of White, McNeill and Stein in the boardroom at the moment of transfer of power to the new man. For the first time in his life Stein, offering an awkward, almost reluctant reverse handshake to McNeill, looked like a banished and utterly inconsolable figure.

What also stung him was that in effect he was being told he was all washed up as a football manager when he knew there was a lot left in him at the age of 55. On 14 August 1978 a testimonial game was organised for his benefit at Celtic Park against Liverpool, which the visitors won 3–2. At the end of the game, as reported by *The Observer* on 20 August, Liverpool manager Bob Paisley had some stern advice for him: 'You're too young, too alert, too eager to go on being involved to think of cutting yourself off from the action. You're three years younger than I am and you're still not saturated with football. You've still got appetite.'

It aroused something in Stein. He had watched the forlorn figure that Bill Shankly had cut on his retirement: eventually he had had to be shown out of the Liverpool training ground like a vagrant, although he was shown some mercy by Everton who allowed him entry, just to keep him near a ball being kicked. And he knew the Liverpool club secretary used to travel out to the promenade at Blackpool regularly, just to keep Shankly and his wife company on a bench as they stared out to sea and talked about days gone by. It was an image of retirement desolation that scared Stein. He was on a temporary high though, having heard the adulation of the crowd at his testimonial game. From that game and the special dinner in the Glasgow City Chambers the following evening it was estimated that he grossed something in the region of £80,000 for his fund. Knowing that he was now really flush for the first time in his life, and with Sean Connery sitting beside him as a guest at the top table, his long-standing friend Lawrie McMenemy, in proposing a toast to him, began by saying, 'It's not often you get James Bond and Goldfinger at the same table.'

But being fêted by the great and the good and having unprecedented funds in the bank was no substitute for coming to terms with being out of a job. An offer of work in Kuwait, at a salary reputed to be £60,000, had come in to him, but leaving Celtic to be cast into a footballing wilderness like that did not appeal, even though there was a biblical precedent for believing that a few days in that terrain could work wonders for the soul. Then another call came. Not from a humble source like Jimmy Gribben those many years before, but from a loftier level – the millionaire chairman of Leeds, Manny Cussins, who knew Jock from his tussles with Don Revie in the past and who apparently had money to burn. The offer to become manager of Leeds United was irresistible to Stein, although Gerry Woolard, Stein's accountant who acted on his behalf in many matters, considered that his eventual move to Leeds was motivated more by anger and resentment at Celtic than anything else. He wanted to show them that he was not a burnt-out case. That seems a simple but more plausible explanation than any other.

For there were solid reasons to make anybody wonder what had possessed him. He was almost 56. He had a reputation that sometimes was dismissed by people in the south as having been achieved in a small pond. He was putting that dangerously on the line, at an advanced stage of life. His wife

Jean was still the same woman who had declined to go to Manchester, yet he grasped the opportunity without any real qualms. On Monday, 21 August he decided to accept the offer. When eventually he travelled down with Woolard to discuss terms, Stein astonished the Leeds board by sitting down only for a few moments with them before rising to his feet and declaring he was leaving everything in the good hands of his accountant and that he was going out to have a walk around the ground, to meet people and to see what state the pitch was in. A contract, meanwhile, was produced, but it was never signed, in keeping with his customary practice. Still, he struck up good personal terms with Cussins who straight away fell in love with Stein. He was simply smitten by the man's rugged sincerity in the way he talked about football. Some of Cussins' fellow directors did not share his view about Stein and felt he was too old, but Cussins was the Kelly of Leeds and that was that.

So, surrounded by distinct reservations among supporters and officials of the club, and realising he was far from being first choice – others had been in the frame, including Lawrie McMenemy, who had turned the job down – Stein took over as the thirteenth manager of Leeds United at a time when the club was in serious decline. All of which confirms his accountant's view that he took it on the rebound from the disappointment at Celtic, despite the obvious potential perils. He presided over a defeat in his first game when Manchester United came to Elland Road and won 3–2. In his second game, the local *Evening Post* referred to Stein's 'electric presence' as Leeds crushed Wolverhampton Wanderers 3–0. The correspondent went on to write, 'For the first time since Don Revie walked out [Revie had left Leeds to become England manager in the summer of 1974] Elland Road was fizzing with that unique atmosphere particular to a top soccer club. Gone was that cathedral-like quiet, the air of apparent disinterest.' But it was not all smooth running, and draws and defeats were to come in a sequence of games that showed the dimension of the task anybody would have had to take on after Revie. Stein tried to go into the transfer market to boost his resources, but even backed up by Cussins he found it was not easy. He was becoming disheartened. Then, on the wind of another change elsewhere, came salvation.

Most people, with the significant exceptions of Stein, Ernie Walker (secretary of the SFA) and Willie Harkness (the president of the association), had meanwhile forgotten that he had been offered the Scotland manager's job before Ally MacLeod, after Willie Ormond had left. He had, of course, progressed things far enough to have some people within the SFA thinking that he would accept, but he'd eventually turned it down. But this time the post was more than simply at the back of his mind, it was at the forefront, taunting him. MacLeod was in trouble. The press were after him. The public were crucifying him in letters and phone-ins to radio stations. Some of us had been writing about Stein as the only logical replacement. But the Leeds move seemed to have stemmed the flow of interest in him.

Then one morning in late September, just after the resignation of the exhausted MacLeod on the 26th of that month, I took a call at the BBC from the journalist Jim Rodger, who was still Stein's gofer. He asked me if I would phone Stein and advised me of a number at a hotel to which he had taken the Leeds team. I will always remember that when I was put through to his room that afternoon and he answered, I could hear Peter O'Sullevan's voice in the background on the television. I pictured him lying on his bed watching the racing, which was no great surprise. He asked me what I was working on that Wednesday evening. I told him I was at Ibrox doing a commentary and would make a report later on for *Sportsnight*. This was a very unhappy man I was talking to, morose, slowly spoken, husky. It was then he came up with what was on his mind. 'Tell London that you can say something about the Scotland job and me,' he said. 'You could go on and say something to the effect that you believe I would be interested in going back to Scotland. You know how to phrase these things. You can't say you've been talking to me. Just play it like you're confident that I would take the job. Make it sound like the SFA are being a bit slow on this.' I knew what he was after, and since he was in my view the man most suited, and it seemed that the SFA needed a wake-up call, I obliged. I alerted London, who were greatly excited by this revelation, and that night Harry Carpenter introduced me as the top news item. I waded into it and, as I recall, said something to the effect that all Ernie Walker needed to do was lift the phone and contact the Big Man and he would be our next manager. Although I made no mention of having had a conversation with him, it would not have been difficult to conclude that he had whispered in my ear.

The following morning I turned on my radio, and when the sports item came on the news the presenter said he had Jock Stein on the other end of the line and promptly asked him about the rather sensational claim made on *Sportsnight* the night before, that he was prepared to give up a job of only a few weeks to return to Scotland as the national manager. 'Archie Macpherson was just flying a kite,' Stein blandly replied. 'You take all these comments with a pinch of salt. I'm very content doing my job at Leeds.' I didn't fall out of the bed in surprise. I could have written the script myself. I knew exactly how he was shaping this. The bandwagon was beginning to roll, and since he was by far the most obvious choice for the post I hadn't minded putting my shoulder to the cause, as others were now doing. The Master was at work. Soon the movement became quite irresistible, and on 4 October 1978, just 44 days after joining Leeds, Stein was appointed to the Scotland post. He took up his duties a day later, on his 56th birthday.

Gerry Woolard was left to break the news to Manny Cussins that Stein was accepting the job. Cussins was distraught. He told Woolard that he would offer Stein £35,000 in his hand, there and then, and give him complete ownership of a luxurious house in Leeds. But the accountant knew there were no inducements that would make Stein change his mind. A brief episode in his life had left resentment in its wake in England, but that was of no real consequence to a man who would still pursue his aims with the same ruthlessness that characterised his early career. For he was home where he belonged.

But there were many of us who, though delighted to see him back and conscious of a nation still in a state of shock and embarrassment after the World Cup finals fiasco in Argentina, wondered how he would cope with what we all imagined to be the stifling and claustrophobic atmosphere of the Scottish Football Association. We anticipated that there was every chance his working relationship with the powerful SFA secretary Ernie Walker would resemble the irresistible force meeting the immovable object. If his relationship with the officious Desmond White was one of the reasons leading to the terminal bitterness, how on earth was he going to survive with a man who was popularly called 'The Ayatollah'? We awaited this outcome like spectators at a stock-car race anticipating the first spectacular collision.

CHAPTER TWENTY-SIX
NATIONAL SERVICE

To the surprise and delight of veteran SFA watchers, who, like the Kremlinologists of the Cold War had to be skilled in reading the subtle manoeuvres within the almost impenetrable association, Stein and Walker bonded like the coming together of long-lost brothers. Judging them, as we had, by their public images, it seemed they would blend as palatably as whisky and prussic acid. In fact both discovered that neither fitted the stereotype each had created for the other. To see Walker in a relaxed mood away from his desk, as Stein and many of us did, whisky in one hand, cigar in the other, was to witness an urbane man, witty, perceptive about people's personalities and a great raconteur. He was also a lover of the game, with as much passion as Stein himself. All that was far removed from the official persona. Stein lapped him up because he actually saw something of himself in the man. They could talk for hours, not only about football on a level Stein had never experienced before with someone outside the managerial area, but also about the ways of the strange, uncertain world they inhabited.

It was something of a shock, though, when first I went to see him at the SFA shortly after his arrival. I had to climb several flights of stairs before arriving at his tiny, garret-like room near the clouds. The scene was like a dethroned king occupying a broom cupboard. There he sat, where once he had filled every nook and cranny of Celtic Park, looking squashed by fate. That was my initial impression. And then I realised he was in fact clearly happy, relieved, and eager to tell me that it was going to be easy to adjust to a new style of life. Walker was key to this, and that relationship cannot be overstressed as a major factor in Stein's later years. It was a different sort of relationship to the one he'd had with Sir Robert Kelly, but it could not have come at a better time.

After Stein's first year in office, for example, Walker awarded all staff a cost of living increase. Going out of the door one night after a long chat about football, the secretary advised Stein that he was getting an increase in his pay-packet. 'What for?' was the puzzled response. Walker explained. The following day, Stein pushed his head round the door and said simply, 'Thanks. I was talking with Jean last night and we were discussing this. Do you know, it's the first time in my life that I have been given more money without having to fight to get it.' It did underline for Walker the fact that Stein had never been properly rewarded in his previous incarnations. His salary at the SFA, although less than that offered at Leeds, was considerably more than he'd been getting at Celtic Park. So at that juncture in his life he had developed a solid base, both personally with Walker and with his own finances.

In that respect Gerry Woolard played an important part in his career, sorting out his waywardness with money. Because he was careless in looking after his resources, and because he was widely known as a heavy gambler, rumours began to circulate about Stein's being deeply in debt. Woolard took over the running of his business affairs and effectively put a control on what money was passed on to him, almost as a salary. But all debts he ever had were eventually covered and after a while he did not owe his friend Tony Queen a single penny, although rumours persisted that he did. So his passage of time at the SFA was concurrent with a more stable background, even though the contract he had been offered, had accepted and had taken home on that first day was never signed. Walker has not seen it to this day. Stein had said to him, 'You won't need to tell me when I should give up. I'll know, and I'll tell you.' That simple arrangement was the background to final dramas.

Stein's first game in charge was against Norway at Hampden Park on 25 October 1978 in a European Championship qualifier. That day the Glasgow buses were on strike; there were no Rangers or Celtic players in the team; the rain was incessant; and the Norwegians were never great box office. Yet despite all that 65,372 people turned up. Stein's name was the main selling point. He was to admit to me that he had felt 'a wee bit edgy' about his debut, despite his great experience. Scotland won 3–2 but were twice behind to the Norwegians. Dalglish scored the two equalisers, and when Arthur Graham was fouled in the box, Archie Gemmill scored the winner from the spot with only three minutes left. So dramatic was the finish that praise was heaped upon Stein for reintroducing the crowd to the sort of climax associated with him at Celtic Park.

But two factors played on his mind. In that first game all eleven Scottish players were from English clubs. It is not that he would not have wanted to select his strongest eleven, but he did feel that, almost automatically, the players south of the border had been previously deemed to be more suitable and better prepared than their counterparts in the north. He felt he could coax performances out of more home-based Scots. He was also concerned about the 'fiery cross' atmosphere that affected the play of the national side. He had mentioned this often to us when he co-commentated on television. He had never ruled out passion in football, but he had felt that too often Scotland had surrendered all reason to emotional charges which lent thrills to the terracings but which too often were naïve and unproductive. He wanted them to be more cerebral, with the emphasis on possession and closer passing. He wanted them to be less reliant on terracing acoustics. He wanted, essentially, to modernise them.

Stein took that task to Portugal on 29 November in another qualifying game with three home-based Scots in the side: Alan Rough of Partick Thistle in goal, David Narey of Dundee United and Stuart Kennedy of Aberdeen. But the result was disappointing: they lost 1–0. Still, there was a measured reaction to this in the media. We knew what he was about and it was not even a case of giving him the benefit of the doubt. If faith could move mountains, the punters were pushing the Himalayas all the way back to the Arctic for him.

That atmosphere was maintained during the Home Championship at the end of that season, even though when we arrived in Cardiff for the first match against Wales the pitch at Ninian Park was being bulldozed and flattened out in an incredible last-minute effort to get it playable for the following day, 19 May 1979. It was the Scottish defence that received similar treatment from a man called Toshack, who scored a hat-trick and left Alan Hansen floundering in his wake as the Welsh achieved their first victory against the Scots in fifteen years.

Had the next game been a disaster there might have been the start of a rumbling of dissent, but it was not. Admittedly only one goal was scored, but that happened to be a Scottish goal against Northern Ireland at Hampden on 22 May by Arthur Graham fourteen minutes from the end of the game. Onwards then to Wembley, but in the wake of an invasion that was akin to the Visigoths' sacking of Rome. The Scottish supporters had gone on the sort of rampage on the day and evening before the game that made an innocent person's journey to central London on the tube as safe as a John Ford stagecoach trundling through Monument Valley, for they bawled, peed and vomited their way to the central point of Piccadilly. The war parties roamed at will through the streets of Soho in particular, overturning cars, breaking windows, groping women and making you want to claim you were from Lithuania. This is the phenomenon Stein had feared would be unleashed on

Liverpool two years earlier in the aftermath of a possible defeat against Wales. They were now heaping it on London in a hate-the-English eruption that sickened all of us. Stein, as we have seen, did not like any supporters' excesses, and once in Dublin at the height of his powers he had thrown some Celtic supporters from Northern Ireland out of a hotel for flaunting IRA flags and singing their anthems.

These incidents overshadowed the game, and the image I remember mostly looking down on from the commentary position was Stein walking slowly towards the Wembley tunnel from the bench, just before half-time, looking at his watch as he stood there at the top of the slope eager to get in and congratulate his men, for they were leading with a twentieth-minute John Wark goal. Just at that moment up came Peter Barnes to score an equaliser on the whistle. Stein's look of disgust as he turned down the slope was more than just disappointment at the goal given away at that vital time, because as he admitted to me afterwards he felt he knew what was in store for them in the second half. For in the stadium you would have found it difficult to play the game 'Spot the Englishman'. The massive Scottish support which had disgraced itself in town was producing an atmosphere that was effectively counter-productive. Stein knew that. He was aware, too, that Kevin Keegan had been spat on as he came out to play the game and there could be nothing more inspiring to a team than to be so blatantly rubbished on their own soil. Steve Coppell, then Keegan himself added two more goals as the English rebounded with a vengeance to win 3–1. Stein was, for the first time, uneasy in knowing that he had little in common with the herd who were then following Scotland. Previously his career had blossomed on the branch of mutual respect with the Celtic terracings. That very fact had inspired him and lifted him from depression at times. He was one of them. He certainly wanted to put a smile on the face of the genuine supporter, and in that respect nobody could have been more Scottish than he. But this was now a different relationship. It was much less emotional.

Experimentation was forced on him the following season as he was afflicted by injuries to key players. By September 1980, when he took a team to Stockholm in Sweden to play in a World Cup qualifier, he had tried out six different pairings in central defence. Other, lesser-known players were being given their chance. Iain Munro of St Mirren, for instance, had emerged almost out of the blue, and in a friendly international against Argentina, which starred Diego Maradona and which the South American visitors won

3–1, the left-back was the outstanding Scottish player. He was to succumb to long-term injury, though. Following that occasion the matches in 1979 for qualification for the 1980 European Championship proved a severe disappointment to everybody. They won handsomely in Norway 4–0, but then lost twice to Belgium and drew with Austria. Added to which on 16 May 1980 Northern Ireland won their first home international for five years by beating Scotland 1–0 at Windsor Park. A 1–0 victory over Wales five days later kept the spirits up, until on 24 May Scotland lost 2–0 to England at Hampden Park and the criticism started to surface. Stein was unsure about playing Andy Gray that day as he was still recovering from an injury that had kept him out of the previous two internationals, but in responding to the chants of 'Bring on Andy' which spread round the terracings Stein introduced the player for the last half-hour. He was palpably unfit and a flat-looking Scotland side lost 2–0. It all seemed so sloppy.

Nobody had yet attacked Stein personally, but the hints of worse to come if things did not improve floated around in the air. By the time Scotland had lost two friendlies in Poland and Hungary in the close-season summer of 1980, Stein had been in charge on eighteen occasions with eleven losses and only five wins. With a degree of trepidation we never thought we would attach to a Stein side, we watched them step foot on the road to the 1982 World Cup in Spain with that September game in Stockholm. The rising star of Aberdeen, Gordon Strachan, scored the only goal of the game, his first for his country. This was a most positive start in a group also featuring Portugal, Northern Ireland and Israel. Scotland rang up eight points from their first five games. In Israel in February 1981, Stein said to me one day while looking out over Old Jerusalem towards the Wailing Wall, 'You get a special feeling here, something different. It affects you.' He was referring to mention I had made of H.V. Morton's spiritually atmospheric travel classic on the Holy Land *In the Steps of the Master*, not to Alan Rough's wonderful goalkeeping performance or to the only goal of the game by the admirable Kenny Dalglish. This awkward fixture out of the way, Scotland eventually qualified for the finals on 9 September 1981 when Joe Jordan, as he had crucially done before, against the Czechs for example, rose to head in the first goal in a 2–0 victory against Sweden at Hampden Park. Stein's stock was high particularly as in the game prior to that, at Wembley on 23 May, a John Robertson penalty had given Scotland a 1–0 victory.

But it was a Home International game which was to dent it again, in the last match before the World Cup finals. On 29 May 1982 Scotland played England in Glasgow in the 100th match between the countries. Stein chose to downgrade the occasion by prioritising the World Cup, but the attendance of 80,529 showed how important it was to the Scottish public's mind. Stein's selection begged to differ. Aberdeen had won the Scottish Cup the previous Saturday; Willie Miller, Alex McLeish and particularly Gordon Strachan were on the crest of a significant new wave of football. The two defenders had lent the Scottish defence credibility having conceded only four goals in the eight matches played in all competitions. None of them was fielded by Stein in this match. Strachan was kept sitting on the bench even though the crowd, watching an anaemic display by the Scots, kept chanting his name for inclusion. The game was won by the only goal, scored by England's Paul Mariner. The press roared. Alex Cameron of the *Daily Record* wrote on 31 May in his most effective sarcastic vein, 'Only the pipers played well, and they selected themselves … Scotland were a yard slow on the ball and this included Kenny Dalglish and Graeme Souness.' Hugh Taylor in the Glasgow *Evening Times* the same day opined, 'Robbery! If this was just a warm-up practice game for Spain, how about giving the long-suffering fans at least some of their money back?'

A member of Stein's squad that day was the talented, elegant midfielder Tommy Burns who had made a not unreasonable contribution to some games and who had been coached by Stein at Celtic Park. 'We were in the dressing-room after the England game and Jock made an announcement about who he was taking to Spain for the finals. Now I had been with him all week for these Home Internationals and he had only spoken once to me, just to ask me how I was enjoying the experience. I felt reasonably pleased with myself. But he just said, "We're taking you all to Spain with the exception of Ray Stewart and Tommy Burns." Just that. End of story. No explanation. Nothing. He just walked out. I felt stunned enough at the time. But I have to admit that the passing years have made me angrier about that since I felt I was denied getting on to the greatest footballing platform in the world. I know he was a great manager, but why could he not have had a word about it with me? I'm 47 now and I still feel bitter about it.' As others could have told Burns, that simply was not Stein's way. In that regard he had not changed.

Despite that result, he felt he had prepared properly for Spain. I had travelled with him to Athens earlier that year to watch one of his World Cup group opponents, the Soviet Union, play Greece and did not learn all that much from a depleted side. But travelling to the other side of the world to New Zealand was another matter. This was born out of the Ally MacLeod legacy. The previous manager had neglected to scrutinise his opponents before Argentina and Stein was not going to allow himself to be exposed to the same criticism. He did not really want to go, though, and we almost did not make it.

When the BBC learnt of his intentions they decided to send me with a producer to make a TV documentary of the trip. He agreed to take part. We set off one morning from London in the spring and, after a cancellation of a flight and a re-routing via Seattle, we ended up exhausted in San Francisco. We felt as if we had come by wagon-train through the Rockies. Stein was pale and very tired-looking. I went to my hotel room, turned on the television and flopped on the bed. Within about ten seconds the famous American anchor man Dan Rather flashed on to the screen with words which went through me like a rapier: 'Good evening. The war in the South Atlantic has taken a sinister turn with the sinking of the SS *Belgrano* and the reported loss of 99 lives.'

Perhaps a minute elapsed, but not much more, then I heard the door being hammered. When I opened it Stein was there, shirtless, hair awry, seriously animated. 'Did you hear that news?' he said in amazement. 'C'mon, we're getting to hell out of here back home. Maggie'll nuke them next. I told you it could get right out of hand. Get on the phone and get us a plane back tomorrow.'

Dan Rather, or more accurately the torpedo marksman on a submarine in the depths of the South Atlantic, had given him a way out of a trip he simply did not want to undertake. It took a whole day of coaxing and a trip round San Francisco organised by a friend of Stein's who was a member of the local Celtic Supporters Club to soften his view. I pointed out that the press might get awkward about him cancelling a trip halfway through. They would make it look fishy. Eventually he gave in and we carried on. We did learn much about the origins of geysers at Rotorua and the importance of Maori culture in the Land of the Long White Cloud, but from the three games played by the New Zealanders against a League of Ireland touring side there was precious little to divine. But Stein had been politically correct, and nobody could have accused him of not being well prepared.

So when he sat in the training complex at Sotogrande in the south of Spain only a few miles from Gibraltar on 14 June, the eve of the opening group game against New Zealand, he did not look particularly stressed. The criticisms about that England match were being burnt out of our systems by a blistering sun, supplemented by the curative effect of simply being at the World Cup finals. At the time of the draw in mid-winter he had been asked by a Spanish travel agent what he thought of bullfighting. 'The bull stands no chance,' he had replied, dismissing in a sentence an entire Iberian culture. 'It's no contest. That's why it's no use.' I thought of the draw that had pitched Scotland against both Russia and Brazil and wondered if the odds against us were even longer than that of the bulls at the *corrida*.

CHAPTER TWENTY-SEVEN
THE LAST HURRAH

When on 18 June 1982 Davie Narey shot Scotland spectacularly into the lead in Seville against Brazil after only eighteen minutes, all of us from the Scottish bench through the Scottish media to the sun-dried supporters around the stadium experienced something that, in light of what was to happen afterwards might have been likened to premature ejaculation. It was just too much to expect that the other party would throw in the towel when we all felt our own climax had been reached. The Brazilians clearly wanted to prolong the encounter. Stein did not act like an ecstatic lunatic on the sidelines, which others might have done after such an exceptional strike and as he would have been entitled to do, but remained relatively restrained. Throughout his career he had tended to exclude himself from the *corps de ballet* of goal celebration. In the balmy, velvety feel of that Seville evening he must have felt a more rational response was appropriate, and that rather than accepting this was Scotland about to spring a great surprise he knew it could turn out to be a provocation.

The morning after Scotland's exit from the 1978 World Cup in Mendoza in Argentina, even though they had beaten Holland 3–2, Alan Sharp, the novelist and Hollywood screen-writer had said to me, 'We've just discovered a new way of losing.' He was more than hinting that to be a football-loving Scot you also had to be a connoisseur of defeat. The finals in Spain introduced Stein to the affliction.

Yet when the draw was first made, Stein had struck the right posture. He immediately identified the pairing with Brazil and the Soviet Union as the 'toughest' group in the earliest stages. Who in their right senses would not have billed it as that, even though in light of the fate these two countries suffered eventually in the tournament his critics thought he had completely misread this? He reflected on what he had said about Brazilian teams in the past and consequently could not have been accused of hyping the challenge artificially. He felt they had completely recast their attitude by emphasising their natural skill again, whereas in the 1974 World Cup in West Germany he had criticised them for trying to toughen up their act and become too European. Socrates, Falcão, Zico – the names from the current squad would trip off his tongue in admiration every time he was interviewed publicly, and privately you could sense his genuine exhilaration at the thought of being in the same stadium as them.

He had also insisted, just before the draw was made in Madrid, on travelling to every venue around Spain to prepare for the seizing of the best accommodation possible. Ernie Walker and Stein's exhausting trip by car around that vast country would best have been chronicled by Cervantes himself. According to Walker, Stein, sitting in the front passenger seat of the chauffeur-driven car with himself in the back, sang his way through a repertoire of songs that stretched from the 1930s right through to the Beatles, and to Walker's amazement he knew the words of everything he trilled. At one pit-stop in a hotel in the middle of somewhere, Walker recollects that he impishly challenged Stein to sample a glass of wine. 'No man comes to Spain without trying a red wine,' he told his manager. So Stein did. He drank a glass, and about half an hour later he said to Walker, 'Ernie, I can see two of you!' A *rioja* had penetrated the Burnbank man's teetotal defences, but it was never going to get a second chance.

Stein was focused on things that mattered. He had worked out that the final group game against Russia was the crucial one. He realistically did not expect to take anything from the Brazil match, anticipated beating New Zealand, and as the Russians felt exactly the same it was Malaga on 22 June he had set his sights on as the crunch. Settled in at Sotogrande, which relates to golf and indolence more than to preparation for athletic activity, he had sound professional back-up. His assistant was Jim McLean, who had worked wonders with Dundee United and was one of the shrewdest operators in the game. They had been fierce opponents at club level, but Stein respected his managerial qualities so much that in late 1983, on the very day McLean was heading for Ibrox, where he was going to be offered the Rangers job after John Greig's departure, he met him in the car park at Hampden Park to try to persuade him to take the job, which eventually McLean turned down.

Together they prepared for their first game against New Zealand in Malaga on 15 June. Many of us who had been with the side in the Algarve to watch their two friendly games against weak Portuguese opposition had noticed that Dalglish was not at his best. Indeed, there seemed to be a coolness in his relations with the manager and we wondered if he would play in that first match. He did. Allan Evans of Aston Villa, who had just won a European Cup medal with his club, was given his fourth cap alongside Alan Hansen, to the exclusion of that worthy pair Miller and McLeish. In attack there would be Alan Brazil, on his 23rd birthday, who had not played in the qualifying games and had not scored a goal in seven internationals. Steve Archibald was on the bench, and left sitting in the stand was the formidable figure of Joe Jordan, who had been recovering from injury in Serie A with Milan.

Just before the game started we noticed a banner proclaiming 'Don't worry, lads, Ally MacLeod is in Blackpool'. That annoyed Stein. The dredging up of that name by a group of supporters who before Argentina would almost certainly have been worshipping at that same man's altar only signified the hypocritically fickle nature of the terracing. But with Scotland three goals up after 32 minutes, firstly by Dalglish and then two by John Wark, the past seemed to have been well and truly buried. But like the hand of Carrie coming thrusting out of the grave, when all seemed over, the all-white-shirted New Zealanders dramatically pushed up the daisies. They scored two goals inside ten minutes in the second half to make it 3–2. Suddenly they looked fitter, bigger, stronger than the Scots even though they were about as creative as painting by numbers. The scare factor was emerging. Scotland looked nervy now and briefly unable to read the new script. But recover they did, in the last seventeen minutes, when firstly John Robertson scored with an exquisite free-kick and then Steve Archibald headed in a corner from the outstanding player on the field, Gordon Strachan. The 5–2 result led to an unsatisfactory aftermath, though. These two goals against would aggravate everybody from Stein downwards for the remainder of their stay, like that proverbial pebble in the shoe seeming to grow in size the more you trudge on. It was not ideal. At the press conferences at Sotogrande, Stein did not seem unduly put out by that hiccup, but he was now displaying a weariness and was clearly affected by the frustration that he could no longer control the opinion makers as he had of old. This was the autumnal Stein.

When the day arrived for the game against Brazil, we learnt that he had handed the captaincy to Graeme Souness in place of Danny McGrain, who was dropped, as was Dalglish. Whenever Stein spoke to me about Souness it was as if you were listening to a man purring over the joys of his shiny limousine. 'He's got class,' he had said to me by the poolside in Seville in preparation for a friendly against Spain the previous February as he watched Souness, oozing with self-confidence, stroll casually around the hotel. 'You've got to have somebody with presence around the squad. You've got to have star quality. Just look at him.'

A unified Scottish team under a new leader was eventually mauled by Brazil in the Estadio Benito Villamarin in Seville on 18 June. The Narey goal was not a product of a shock-and-awe strategy intended to produce quick submission; the Scottish plan had been one of containment, and then of moving on to the decider with the Soviet Union. But Stein had been puzzled. He had watched Russia against Brazil in Seville in the opening game of the group on an evening when broadcasts of the match were interrupted to announce the Argentine surrender in the Falklands, and had been disturbed by the fact that the Russians had dictated terms, led with a goal in the 33rd minute and only succumbed to some brilliant touches in the last fifteen minutes to lose 2–1. The Brazilians did not have a problem with technique but, as was evident in the Soviet Union game, of mentality. Socrates, the chain-smoking, guitar-playing doctor of medicine who strolled through a game looking as if he were composing iambic pentameters to accompany his meanderings, typified their languid creativity. Zico played only in spurts, as if reacting to an electric prod. Falcão did look more European and committed, but behind him Waldir Peres in goal and Junior at left-back were exposed as weaknesses by the Russians, the one nervy and unsure on his line, the other wanting to attack more than defend.

So the strike by Narey came out of nowhere. It surprised him probably as much as anybody else in the stadium. Or outside it, where, sitting on a high block of flats and watching the game on a television monitor, the BBC's Jimmy Hill famously described the strike as a 'toe-poke' and then had to head for the hills with a posse after him. The Brazilians did not immediately overwhelm Scotland out of a brilliantly flourished sense of indignity at going behind, but in a more creeping fashion. For their equaliser in the 33rd minute came from a weak decision by the referee Calderon from Costa Rica, who awarded a free-kick against Hansen for a not too life-threatening challenge on Cerezo. Zico performed his well-practised trick of finding that little space between keeper's fingertips and post. Even the goal scored by Oscar three minutes after the interval was not 'Brazilian' but a simple header from a corner-kick to a man who should have been covered.

It was really only then that flamboyance was unveiled. Alan Rough, playing in his 50th international, was left looking skywards as Eder flighted a ball in a gentle, intelligent curve beyond and above him for the third goal fifteen minutes later. Out of the closet, then, came the dummies, the flicks, the snappy inter-passing, the hip-swinging turns and twists and a goal that completely fooled many into thinking we were seeing a great Brazilian side. Falcão finished a passing movement from the well of midfield by striking a low, piercing shot past Rough for the fourth goal. It was not a result made for outright condemnation, but for decent appraisal. And that is generally what it produced.

But now the Russians only had to draw against Scotland to go through. The familiarity of that situation was taken with equanimity by Stein. The night before the game he asked his coaching assistants Jim McLean and Andy Roxburgh, a future Scotland manager himself, to discuss team matters with him. Roxburgh says that he was not only extremely relaxed but that his wit had not diminished. 'He told each of us to write down on a piece of paper what we thought the team should be for the game. We did so separately and he sat back patiently, humming, waiting as we thought it through. Then we handed him our bits of paper. He didn't even look at them. He tore them up, threw them in a basket and said, "Ach, I'll just pick the team myself."'

We travelled to Malaga largely unfazed by Scotland once again seeming to be caught between a rock and a hard place. Stein decided to bring back Joe Jordan, who had been kept on the sidelines as a spectator until that evening. The big striker had been the epitome of the style of football Stein desperately wanted to discard; now he was going to attempt to rush the methodical and largely robotic Russians off their feet. With Steve Archibald at his elbow, slipping a vital pass to him, they did just that after only fifteen minutes when Jordan, legs pumping, arms flailing, toothless gap in mouth eerily exposed, ran behind the Russian defence and deftly slipped in the opening goal. So Stein's sole change to the team paid off. Souness was now at his arrogant best and was thumping the likes of Blokhin and Shengelia with tackles that echoed snappily into the 45,000 crowd. Strachan ran tirelessly. Miller seemed secure at the back. At half-time, Stein came up to Jordan and said quietly to him, 'Keep it up. We could make history tonight.' All looked to be on an even keel.

That, of course, was the perfect basis for a disaster that arrived like a thief in the night. With half an hour remaining, Rough strayed from his line as the Russians attacked and a half-hit shot by Chivadze bounced almost comically over his shoulder for the equaliser. But that ineptness in goal was a masterpiece of visionary thinking compared to what happened next. Miller and Hansen, moving towards a ball on the right touchline, collided in a manner that would have been considered improbable in a Tom and Jerry cartoon. The ball broke to Soviet Player of the Year Ramaz Shengelia, who commendably recovered from his surprise at this unexpected gift and ran on to score, unchallenged. At 2–1 with only six minutes remaining Stein slumped on the bench. Souness's goal practically on the final whistle to make it 2–2 did little to arouse Stein. He knew it was over.

He had always been asked to be judged on how he acquitted himself in the World Cup, and although he had done no better statistically than anybody else and had failed to reach the second stage, he was very largely given the benefit of the doubt by a media which had gained some encouragement from the manner in which he and his players had gone about their tasks. There were people who grumbled about what they perceived to be his uncertainty in team selection – there was certainly an element of that – but in the final analysis, if the Laurel and Hardy defensive blunder had not occurred Stein might have made that historic breakthrough.

I did not see him again until just before the European Championship qualifying game with East Germany, only days after his 60th birthday in October 1982. He seemed in fine fettle. The summer had revived him, shaken out of him the despondency he had shown in the interview with me immediately after the Russian game, when he'd struggled to say the appropriate things and ended up in that clichéd vein of blaming the referee for not awarding a penalty at one stage in the match. Now he seemed largely at ease with the world. He had a grandson, and there was a booster-seat permanently ensconced in the back of his car. Despite his sensitivity about intrusion into his family life he did not mind being photographed with his grandson wearing the Scotland jersey. His son had graduated with a double maths degree from Glasgow University and was now working for a drugs company, as a statistician, in Switzerland. Stein was rightly proud of all of that. The strong family ties were still a source of sustenance to him.

Still, it was the usual mix of apparent contentment and impatience. For he was still swooping down to England at incredible speeds with friends, who were given only an hour's warning or so before they found themselves over the border on their way to Manchester or Liverpool. On one occasion he went through a no-entry sign in Liverpool and was stopped by the police. A nervy John Clark in the passenger seat heard the officer say, 'Oh, it's you, Mr Stein. Sorry, on you go.' Clark said the police in Lancashire would almost salute Stein as he passed by, so high was his stock there. And on one of his travels he threw protocol to the winds. One night in the boardroom at Manchester City he saw Don Howe, the Arsenal coach, coming into the room. Howe had made some criticism of how Charlie Nicholas had been treated by Stein when he was part of the Scottish squad. Although the boardroom was packed, Stein made tracks for Howe and proceeded to ridicule him so loudly and fiercely that a hush fell over the room. Howe retreated from the verbal onslaught a wiser man. The volcano was obviously not wholly dormant.

He also had to pull on his steely resilience for that European Championship qualifying campaign, for in the period between that opening game against East Germany on 13 October 1982 and the final game against them in Halle on 16 November 1983, it was a disaster. That first 2–0 victory over the Germans was to be the last. The three defeats and two draws that followed in a group also including Belgium and Switzerland was by any account a dismal record, and criticisms were becoming more blatant. But Stein seemed secure in his position, and especially in his relationship with Ernie Walker. Then, one evening, we discovered that all was not well at the SFA.

The draw for the qualifying groups for the 1986 Mexico World Cup was made in Switzerland. It was broadcast live to the UK, after which Nevin McGhee, my BBC producer, and I were invited to dinner by the official SFA party comprising Ernie Walker, the president Tom Younger of Hibernian and Stein himself. It was a pleasant evening of general football chit-chat, led principally by Walker who can steer a convivial course through any party. Drink, of course, had well and truly been partaken. Suddenly, rising above the bonhomie and without any forewarning, Younger turned to Stein as the desserts, coffees and liqueurs were being shepherded around the table and in a distinct voice that was meant to be heard by all said, 'You know, Jock, you have a worse record than Willie Ormond and Ally MacLeod, and they got the sack.'

There followed the sort of hiatus that comes from not wanting to believe what you have just heard. I looked quickly at Stein and his eyes were looking somewhere in the direction of the back of the room, his fingers slightly drumming on the white tablecloth, as if pretending he hadn't heard what had been said. Younger, after only the slightest hesitation, repeated exactly the same words, then added, 'What have you got to say about that?' But I recall that before Stein could open his mouth Younger, sitting next to Stein and leaning across him so that they were almost cheek to cheek, proceeded to recite some games during which, he said, tactical blunders had been made and that basically Stein was a lucky man still to be in the job. You could sense he was warming to his subject, as if he had been waiting for some time to let rip. Younger, let us recall, was the Hibernian goalkeeper in the side that played Celtic in the Coronation Cup final in 1953, and to that very day, like all his colleagues in that side, he'd felt that Jock Stein was a very lucky man to have lifted that trophy. Could that particular frustration have lain dormant all those years ready to be ignited almost at any time? Or was it the classic case of the boy telling the emperor he was wearing no clothes? Or a combination of both? For in truth, Younger was simply repeating much of the criticism that had been bandied about in boardrooms and pubs across the land.

Nevertheless, McGhee and I just wanted to be somewhere else, for the embarrassment escalated as Younger simply could not be shut up. Walker leant across, tapped the table in front of him and said in almost mock tones, 'Mr President, there is a time and place for everything ...' But he was immediately knocked back by Younger, who, as if pulling rank, turned back to Stein again and continued his relentless slagging. 'I'm not shutting up,' he said. 'It's about time somebody said something!' At any moment I felt the table would leave its moorings in the early stages of a Stein retaliation. Certainly the Stein of the early days at Celtic Park would already have had Younger round the throat. But he simply lowered his eyes and fidgeted with his hands, thinking things through for some sort of response. Eventually he leant forward and said quietly, 'Tam, maybe we shouldn't be talking about these things in front of our guests here.' This had an effect on Younger, who eased off and directed his talk to Walker to try to justify what had just occurred. Walker was mortified. He sped after us to request us to say nothing to the press about this, as we had been at a private dinner. Only years after the event did I report this to anybody.

It says something about this man in his early sixties, whose age was continually being brought up as if it were some natural impediment to success and who had obviously lost the confidence of his president, that he was to inspire some of the best Scotland performances in a generation, starting on 17 October 1984 and the 3–0 victory over Iceland at Hampden. He was bringing in new names. The inestimable Davie Cooper of Rangers was now entrenched in the squad, as was Maurice Johnston of Celtic, Arthur Albiston of Manchester United and Jim Bett of Lokeren. Willie Miller and Alex McLeish were getting to be inseparable for him, Paul McStay and Charlie Nicholas from Celtic were on the fringes, ready to make the breakthrough, and above all Kenny Dalglish was back in favour, as he was now reaching the best form of his career.

All this reinvigorating of the pool of players came to fruition in debatably one of Scotland's greatest performances at Hampden, when they met Spain in the second qualifying game on 14 November. *The Guardian* correspondent wrote before this match, 'Taking the opposition into account, the Scots should not regard a draw as a disaster.' The side was not damned by faint praise but rose above the customary cynicism of visitors from the south with superb football. Stein could even afford to leave out Gordon Strachan for this one. Johnston scored first after 33 minutes, diving to scoop a header no more than twelve inches from the turf into the net. He added a second nine minutes later after Miller passed to Bett who rode a wild tackle to centre for Johnston to power a header past Luis Arconada. The Spaniards' goal in the 68th minute could be put down largely to a goalkeeping gaffe by Jim Leighton, who allowed a Camacho free-kick to bounce over his shoulder. But then came Kenny. He was playing in his 96th international and had been nursing a knee injury, but with fifteen minutes left he received the ball in a crowded penalty and started to bend and hover over it as he prepared to move from the right across the box. He swivelled, confused three defenders who were unsure of his intentions, and then struck. To this day I can recall the perfect line I saw from the commentary position as the ball rose from his left foot, swerved across Arconada and then found its address in the net. The 3–1 victory could not have come in a better manner.

Stein didn't crow, he glowed. The personal satisfaction he derived from that, given the criticism he had had to endure, was obvious. But two defeats were to follow. In Seville in February 1985 they lost by a goal to nil, and then came the bitterest of pills: Wales, the so-called underdogs of the group, won 1–0 at Hampden on 27 March. Instead of being favourites to reach Mexico, Scotland were now outsiders with two away games left.

Three days after beating England 1–0 in the Rous Cup at Hampden, which boosted spirits, Scotland went to Reykjavik at the end of May and won 1–0 courtesy of a goal by Jim Bett four minutes from time. But there was still Wales in September to come. That weighed heavily on everyone concerned. Walker felt it as much as Stein. 'I knew I was not going to have a pleasant summer and that other game against the Welsh in Cardiff in September would prey on my mind, even when I was lying on the beach, and sure enough it did,' he said. 'I just couldn't settle. So you can imagine what pressure there was on Jock. We still needed three points to qualify or we could get a play-off place. It did go through my mind as to what Jock's position would be if we were to lose. I personally think he would have resigned. But I didn't want to think in those terms, yet it was difficult not to put thoughts of possible defeat out of your mind.'

That summer Stein developed a cough that refused to lift. He tried everything to get rid of it, but Walker noticed that it simply would not go away. Now, it is easy in retrospect to read much into what Stein's health was like at that period. Subsequent events tend to colour impressions, but I do recall telling people that he had looked tired and pale at a press conference I had been at two days before they left for Cardiff. It did not occur to me, though, that he was physically fragile. Old and tired he looked, but he was approaching 63 after all and he had borne incredible strain through his career, so it was hardly extraordinary that he should show some of the signs of that. We were all too concerned about a football result to ponder the matter of a man's pallor. He was Mr Indestructible after all. But the pressure was mounting as Dalglish, Hansen, Archibald and Mo Johnston were all ruled out of that game through injury, at a time when that talent would have been invaluable. Stein brought in the aggressive David Speedie, but in terms of overall experience the Welsh had the better of Scotland by 302 caps to 181. Stein knew his future would largely be moulded by the result, one way or the other.

The night before the match Roxburgh, along with Alex Ferguson, who was coach to the side, were invited into his room to talk to him. But Stein did virtually all of the talking. To their astonishment he took them right through his career as player, coach and manager; it all spun out of him as they sat transfixed by the account. When they left, late that night, Ferguson turned to Roxburgh and said, 'What was that all about? That was very strange.'

More than 12,000 Scots were in the crowd on 10 September 1985 in Ninian Park and their lusty singing was temporarily silenced when Mark Hughes scored for the Welsh in the thirteenth minute with a shot through Miller's legs and past Leighton in goal. Scotland at that stage were effectively out of the World Cup. Leighton added to the tension by coming off the field at half-time claiming he had lost one of his contact lenses. The fact that he wore them at all came as a surprise to his club manager Ferguson, who had never been aware of that. Alan Rough had to come on in his place. Cooper came on after 61 minutes for Strachan, but the Welsh were still in the ascendancy. Then, against the flow of play and just nine minutes from the end, the Scots were awarded a penalty when a Speedie shot at goal hit the Welsh defender Philip's arm. To the astonishment of the Welsh, the penalty was awarded by Dutch referee Keizer.

It is difficult now to convey the tension involved as Cooper stepped up to take the kick. Looking back, it reminded me of being in the cinema as a kid during a horror film, not wanting to watch but certainly wanting to be there. Stein watched. As the ball entered the net, low down to Welsh goalkeeper Neville Southall's left-hand side, Stein rose to his feet, acknowledged this briefly, then sat down again. There were nine minutes left. The photographers, sensing that Scotland would now go to a play-off for Mexico, shuffled across en masse, Keystone Cop style, from the Welsh dug-out to the Scots side. This annoyed Stein, and he remonstrated with them. All but one got out of the way. The man who remained lay on his back and kept taking snaps of the dug-out. Stein, incensed by this, rose to his feet and brusquely manhandled him away. He sat back down and looked at his watch. A few moments later he collapsed.

Ernie Walker, the SFA secretary, did not see the end of the game from the stand. He could not bear to watch any longer and had left his seat with a few minutes to go and headed for the directors' room in the grandstand. To his astonishment he met Graeme Souness, who was suspended for this game and who admitted that he could not bear to watch either. Walker asked him if he wanted a drink to calm the nerves, but the lady behind the bar in the boardroom refused to serve them, having been given instructions not to open up until the final whistle. Walker knew of another small VIP room where they could help themselves. Seconds later he tried to serve Souness a vodka and tonic, but his hands were shaking so much the drink was spilling all over his suit. He also made a mistake, pouring lemonade instead of tonic. He tried to rectify the mess but could not control the shakes. Then, from the television set outside, just as a curious silence had descended from above, he heard the commentator mentioning the fact that Jock Stein had collapsed and was being carried from the trackside.

Confused by this, Walker rushed out, not really knowing which way to turn. But he was quickly directed to the medical room. Stein was already in there, lying on a treatment table, holding his hands across his chest. As Walker approached he heard, 'It's all right, Ernie. It's only the cough.' A moment later, the SFA doctor, consultant cardiologist Stewart Hillis, began to inject him with a drug and heard a soft voice in his ear say, 'It's all right, doc. I'm feeling a bit better now.'

These were the last words Jock Stein spoke.

CHAPTER TWENTY-EIGHT
THE PORTRAIT

When Jock Stein collapsed on the track a few moments before the final whistle of that Wales–Scotland World Cup qualifier, there was nothing that could have been done to save his life. According to Dr Stewart Hillis, had Stein suffered this attack even in the most modern hospital with all the means of resuscitation at their disposal, they could not have intervened successfully. They had a full complement of emergency equipment inside the stadium, supplemented by an ambulance unit, which arrived quickly on the scene. They used all the conventional methods to revive him, but to no avail.

Graeme Souness, patiently waiting outside the room, eventually saw David Will of the SFA emerge and simply shake his head by way of delivering the message that it was all over. Souness had to steel himself from breaking down completely. Trembling with emotion, he managed to walk out to the press and say, with difficulty, 'He's gone.'

Ernie Walker tried to shift his organisational mind into gear as to how to deal with this officially, but in these initial moments he felt utterly powerless.

The Scottish team had initially gone back to acclaim their supporters. They had been completely unaware of the terrible drama unfolding until they returned to the dressing-room and saw the distraught figure of Jimmy Steele, the Celtic and SFA physiotherapist; then they realised something serious had occurred. Alex Ferguson spoke up: 'Right, everyone, sit down and give me a minute.' He then said, simply, 'Jock's dead.' Alex McLeish's recollection is that nobody moved for about twenty minutes after that. They had dealt with tension superbly for the whole day, but this moment lay outside their understanding.

In the streets around the stadium word spread quickly. Hundreds of Scots stood outside the ground in quiet confusion. I had left immediately after the final whistle, completely unaware of what had happened, to speak at a corporate hospitality dinner organised by Don Revie's son Duncan in Cardiff Castle. During the first course he came up behind me and whispered in my ear, 'My dad's been on the phone. Jock died just after the game. He doesn't know the details. Would you let the guests know?' He spoke to me again saying exactly the same thing, as if I was refusing to listen or believe, then I got wearily to my feet and announced the news. Later, while walking back to my hotel, I could see supporters simply standing in groups quietly talking to one another where normally they would have been carousing. It was eerie. They looked like an army that had just succumbed to a superior invisible force. I had always wondered what it must have been like looking into the stricken face of the little boy who asked of his hero 'Shoeless' Jackson, accused of cheating in the famous baseball scandal of 1919, 'Say it ain't so, Joe!' That night was as close as I would get to that experience as one bewildered tartan-clad figure loomed in front of me to say, 'It cannae be!' By that time, of course, many of them knew, but some had to ask all the same. Mass disbelief engulfed the football community in the city. Reporters were given the thankless task of reflecting the feelings of the supporters. One response stood out. In front of a garish television light, this anonymous man, dressed in the full regalia of a Scotland supporter, said quietly to the camera, 'We'd rather be out of the World Cup and have big Jock back.' A day later many supporters made a trip to Ninian Park to ask if they could see where he had died. Separate groups were allowed into the medical room, where they stood in silence for a few moments.

The shocked and weary official SFA party arrived back in Edinburgh in the early hours of the following morning, and Walker, Will and family friend Tony McGuinness drove straight to the Stein home to console Jean and daughter Rae. George, Stein's son, working then in Switzerland, had been informed. On Walker's return to his own home he became the central figure in organising the funeral arrangements and the discreet return of the body to Scotland.

The rest of us bent to the task of delivering tributes and obituaries. I found it harrowing to appear in front of a television camera, having to control my emotions as I delivered words which even as I spoke I knew were largely inadequate. Over the following days the praise poured in for the man from around Europe. The tone of editorials in Scotland reflected the feeling that a national tragedy had occurred. The minute's silence at all football grounds the following Saturday deepened the sense of loss around the country.

His funeral took place on Friday, 13 September 1985. It is estimated that 10,000 people lined the streets along the south side of the city of Glasgow, not too far from Hampden Park, to pay silent tribute to the cortège as it made its way to Linn Crematorium. As well as his family and close friends, many of the great names of football from around the UK, and Stein's Lisbon Lions side of course, crammed themselves into the chapel to hear the football-loving Church of Scotland minister the Reverend James Martin lead the service and deliver an uplifting eulogy. The impression that day was of a state funeral taking place.

An hour later, in a pub in the middle of Glasgow, with several colleagues, before we got very drunk and very possibly after that, we started quite spontaneously to swap our Stein stories. The chat distilled the essence of an era we were only just beginning to appreciate; it felt as if a much sought-after fortune in gold-dust had slipped through our fingers and was being blown back to the hills whence it came. Had we really appreciated what we had come through, and what had anybody earned out of it? They were the best of times, they were the worst of times. Now, if you were to apply the words 'Bliss was it in that dawn to be alive' to Stein's revolutionary era, it would not be because a genial environment had been created. Indeed from time to time, if you put your ear to the ground, you would hear whispers that Stein had established a Reign of Terror of which Robespierre might have been proud. To the more discerning it was like being aware of the aura of greatness the man carried and that taking any bruisings from him, as we all did, was part of a rites of passage that was indispensable to the growing-up process. It could be a tough neighbourhood. But it was undeniably exhilarating.

The give and take, the cut and thrust with him was perhaps better appreciated after its passing than in its happening. Overall, many in the media who lived through that period re-defined themselves. They appraised Celtic in a way they never had before. They typed with an eye on what reaction they would get from Parkhead where previously they could be caustic about the club with impunity. They paused before saying something which might bring down upon them a cascade of retaliation. They felt Stein's presence lurking somewhere around them, no matter where they were. It is not that he entirely stifled dissent, either within the club or in the wider world, as future generations might conclude he did when reading of his influence. The rows were evidence of his continuing battle to influence minds and his excesses in that regard became too easily recognisable, and, with no little courage, resistable. But it would be foolish to deny that a Stein culture existed which exerted a strong gravitational pull and influenced minds in extraordinary ways. He knew that Celtic had been undersold by the club itself in past generations, that it had certainly been treated, by too many, simply as a necessary adjunct to Rangers, and, worst of all for him, that it had been excruciatingly patronised. By the time of his car accident he had purged the land of such outlooks.

At the same time he was purloining from Rangers their generally accepted mantle of Establishment club. The traumatic Ibrox Stadium disaster was certainly a major force for change there, but their frequent humblings at Stein's hands gradually percolated through the rigid sectarian thinking. That club could not change overnight, but it was Stein who introduced them to the real world. Years later, when Jock Wallace sang the 'Sash' in the Ibrox boardroom in 1986 in celebration of a 4–4 draw at home against a ten-man Celtic side, a disillusioned director, David Holmes, forced the issue with the then owner Lawrence Marlborough who, fearing another decade in the wilderness, ordered change. This led to Souness, then to a new owner, David Murray, then to the unprecedented signing of ex-Celt Maurice Johnston and, ultimately, to Lorenzo Amoruso – an Italian Catholic captaining Rangers. It took a couple of decades, but it can all be traced back to a period when one man inflicted so much humiliation on them that it was something they would try to prevent from ever happening again, even at the cost of dropping that inevitable Ibrox scouting question of religion, 'What school do you go to?'

Sir Alex Ferguson developed a clear cut identity, but he also had observed at close quarters how Stein projected his influence over the entire spectrum of Scottish footballing interests. The manager's office was no longer a lair but a powerhouse, and that was a model for Sir Alex. The Manchester United manager went on to implement a personality drive that might have been drawn from a blueprint left by the master. In the dressing-room, Stein balanced absolutism with enlightenment. Others without the basic gumption that bonds the personalities of Stein and Ferguson have tried to ape them as managers and flopped. It is to Martin O'Neill's credit that at Celtic he successfully created his own milieu of work utterly different from Stein's. In season 2003/04, when Celtic broke the club record for consecutive league victories set by Stein's squad in 1967/68, O'Neill was guarded in his response to favourable comparisons being made between himself and his legendary predecessor. He wasn't merely being diplomatic and reverential; he was wise enough to know that you could not compare the generations like that. It was a different world then. There were more teams around of higher quality. Scotland abounded with talented, home-grown players; even provincial clubs were capable of stretching either of the Old Firm teams to the limit. And on the side, Stein won the European Cup.

For all these achievements he was awarded the CBE in the summer of 1970. By today's standards of official recognition, that seems paltry. It was rumoured, years later, that he had declined the offer of being knighted and had recommended that it should be offered to his chairman instead. But the honours system does not happen to work that way, and that suggestion is difficult to prove. He certainly should have been knighted, for if he did sacrifice his knighthood then Sir Robert Kelly had even more to be grateful about, over and above being saved by the Burnbank lad who came along at a time when many Celtic supporters were in the mood to scream the Cromwellian plea to the chairman in the stand, 'In the name of God, go!' In any case, despite his inclination to talk less about himself than about others, when it came to assessing his achievements I am not so sure Stein would have rejected a knighthood anyway. He had a capricious way of surprising us all from time to time, as his career has shown.

That career was based on an obsession with his work. According to Dr Hillis, on the day he died Stein did not take his diuretics, the pills designed to prevent the possibility of physical problems and the gathering of dangerously excessive water in the system. He did not do so because the effect they had on his body prevented him from carrying out his full duties: looking after the players, dealing with the press, building up the atmosphere. He could not allow that to happen because of his intense professionalism. He took the risk.

The fact that he died at pitchside offered no consolation to his family, although it struck a sentimental chord in those who saw him as a footballing warrior. They felt that expiring so close to the game he loved was to some degree heroic. In fact it was a tragically premature death. Had Stein taken his drug, had that photographer not incensed him and forced him to erupt from the bench, it is the medical view of Hillis that he would conceivably have survived the rest of the surrounding pressure. For he did not die of a heart attack in the acceptable overall description of such an incident. Because of the lack of the preventive measures he had at his disposal it was the build-up of water in his lungs that brought the end. In effect, Jock Stein drowned that night.

You do not summarise him merely by reference to that one single day in Lisbon in 1967, but it does remain the eternal flame in the mind's eye of the Celtic community. As Billy McNeill said to me of that moment when he raised the European Cup, 'He gave me my dreams.'

Two weeks after Jock's death, Tony McGuinness invited Jean Stein and her daughter Rae to his spacious villa in East Kilbride to offer consolation, for he himself was still suffering the pain of losing a dear friend and welcomed the reunion. They sat around talking for a short while, then McGuinness decided to pour them all gin and tonics. Behind them, hanging on the wall, was a life-sized photographic portrait of the virile-looking, teetotal Jock Stein, staring out at the world with that magisterial distinction. McGuinness handed the drinks around and sat down. They were about to put their glasses to their lips when the portrait suddenly slipped from the wall and slammed to the floor like a clap of thunder. There was silence for a moment. Then McGuinness spoke.

'Oh, my God! Pour the drinks down the sink. He's still watching us.'

Many of us know that feeling.

STEIN'S PLAYING AND MANAGERIAL CAREER

ALBION ROVERS: 14 November 1942 – July 1950 (player)

	P	W	D	L	F	A	Goals
Southern League	69	14	6	49	100	236	1
'B' Division	79	41	14	24	153	140	2
'A' Division	15	2	2	11	18	47	2
Southern League Cup	23	5	7	11	33	56	0
League Cup	18	6	5	7	36	40	1
Scottish Cup	5	2	0	3	6	11	0
Summer Cup	6	0	1	5	6	18	0

LLANELLY AFC: July 1950 – 3 December 1951 (player)

	P	W	D	L	F	A	Goals
Southern League	44	19	10	15	89	81	5
FA Cup (including							
qualifying matches)	13	4	7	2	29	21	1
Southern League Cup	4	1	1	2	9	10	0

CELTIC: 4 December 1951 – 29 January 1957 (player)

	P	W	D	L	F	A	Goals
League	106	56	19	31	227	151	2
League Cup	20	8	2	10	34	35	0
Scottish Cup	21	12	6	3	40	24	0

He announced his retirement, through injury, as a player on 29 January 1957 after having captained Celtic to victory in the Coronation Cup final in May 1953 and to the League and Scottish Cup 'double' in season 1953/54. He became Celtic's reserve team coach in July 1957

DUNFERMLINE ATHLETIC: 14 March 1960 – 30 March 1964 (manager)

	P	W	D	L	F	A
League	137	64	28	45	259	208
League Cup	24	10	6	8	49	40
Scottish Cup	19	13	3	3	60	15
European Cup-Winners' Cup	6	3	0	3	16	8
Inter Cities Fairs Cup	5	2	0	3	8	8

Honours: Scottish Cup 1961

HIBERNIAN: 1 April 1964 – 8 March 1965 (manager)

	P	W	D	L	F	A
League	29	18	4	7	67	40
League Cup	6	4	1	1	15	4
Scottish Cup	4	3	1	0	10	3

CELTIC: 9 March 1965 – 31 May 1978 (manager)

	P	W	D	L	F	A
League	421	296	66	59	1111	413
League Cup	127	97	16	14	350	129
Scottish Cup	71	50	16	5	192	56
European Cup	58	33	11	14	118	52
European Cup-Winners' Cup	8	6	1	1	15	3
UEFA Cup	2	0	1	1	2	4
World Club Championship	3	1	0	2	2	3

Please note that Sean Fallon, his assistant, took charge of the team for the whole of the 1975/76 season while Stein was recovering from a car crash in July 1975.

Honours won as Celtic manager

10 League titles
6 League Cup final victories
8 Scottish Cup final victories
1 European Cup final victory

LEEDS: 21 August – 3 October 1978 (manager)

	P	W	D	L	F	A
League	7	3	1	3	12	8
League Cup	3	1	2	0	1	0

SCOTLAND: 12 May – 7 December 1965 (temporary manager)

P	W	D	L	F	A
7	3	1	3	11	11

SCOTLAND: 4 October 1978 – 10 September 1985 (manager – including friendlies)

P	W	D	L	F	A
61	26	12	23	80	70

INDEX

Aberdeen football club 44, 48, 60-61, 92-93, 145, 187, 238, 248-249
AC Milan 169
Airdrie and Coatbridge Advertiser 30, 36, 38, 39
Airdrie football club 35, 102
Aitken, Roy 91
Ajax 141, 184, 195
Albion Rovers 29-30, 31-36, 38, 39, 42, 64, 158
Allan, Willie 119
Amancio (Real Madrid player) 157
Amoruso, Lorenzo 280
Anquilletti (AC Milan player) 169
Archer, Ian 213
Archibald, Steve 267, 269
Argentina, national team 260-261
Arsenal 52-53
Ashe, Arthur 232
Atlético Madrid 215-216
Auld, Bertie 12-13, 14-15, 16, 97-98, 102, 105, 106, 115, 133, 137, 151, 153, 155, 157, 161, 165, 181, 184, 189, 198, 202, 248-249

Baily, Eddie 134-135
Bari football club 188
Barnes, Peter 260
Basle football club 179, 215
Baxter, Jim 121, 122, 123
Bayern Munich 135, 207
BBC 163-164, 193, 216, 217
Beattie, Andy 61, 96
Bene, Ferenc 81
Benfica 177, 179-180
Bergkamp, Dennis 168
Bermuda, Celtic visit 134
Berwick Rangers 94
Bett, Jim 273
Bingham, Billy 82
Birmingham City 97-98
Blacklaw, Adam 123
Blantyre, Lanarkshire 22, 23, 24, 57, 65
Blantyre Celtic 22
Blantyre Victoria 20, 22, 27-28, 31, 106
Bonnar, John 54-55, 63, 158
Bothwell Castle pits 23, 25, 35
Bough, Frank 206
Brazil, Alan 267
Brazil, national team 265-266, 268-269
Brechin football club 64
Bremner, Billy 122, 182, 217-218
Bristol Rovers 40
Brogan, Jim 175
Brown, Bill 123
Brown, Bobby 222

Bruce, Donald 60
Buckley, Paddy 60
Budapest, Nep stadium 80-81
Burnbank, Lanarkshire 19-20, 21, 23, 24, 25-26, 43
Burnbank Athletic 21
Burnbank Gazette 27-28
Burns, Tommy 262
Busby, Matt 27-28, 195, 196

Calderon (referee) 268
Cameron, Alec 115, 262
Cappellini (Italian forward) 150
Cardenas (Racing Club player) 159, 161
Celtic – A Century with Honour 204-205, 248, 250
Celtic (Glasgow) *see also other clubs' entries for matches against Celtic*
training 11-12, 69-70
JS as a player 42-43, 44-45, 47-49, 50-51
Coronation Cup (1953) 31, 47, 52-55, 158
players visit World Cup finals (1954) 61-62
JS becomes manager 98, 99, 100, 101
North America and Bermuda tours 133-135, 168, 187-189, 225
European Cup (1967) 9-16, 17, 42, 149-156, 281-282
awarded Team of the Year trophy (1967) 164
European Cup (1970) 173, 183, 184-186
record under JS 165, 204, 251, 280
Celtic Park, 'Jungle' 135-136, 143, 207
Celtic Plate 135
Celtic View 135, 158
Chalmers, Steve 17, 124, 135, 140-141, 142, 154, 144, 146, 153, 171, 176, 198
Charlton Athletic 39
Chelsea football club 227
Clark, John 16-17, 69, 103, 116-117, 149, 165, 198, 209, 270-271
Clyde football club 62-63, 64, 98, 198
Coatbridge 29, 30-31, 38, 39
Coleman, David 217, 218-219
Coleraine football club 67
Collins, Bobby 53, 55, 58, 62, 63-64
Conn, Alfie 211, 229, 239-240, 241, 243
Connachan, Eddie 75, 76-77
Connelly, George 170, 171, 175, 181, 212-213, 221, 227
Connery, Sean 253
Cooper, Davie 272, 275

Cooper, Terry 181
Cormack, Peter 94-95, 96, 98-99
Craig, Jim 11-12, 14, 20, 114, 124, 125-126, 133, 144, 150, 175, 178, 193, 198, 201, 205, 206
Craig, Joe 239, 241
Craig, Mrs 201
Crerand, Pat 'Paddy' 69, 75, 77, 195, 209, 231-232
Crystal Palace football club 200
Cullis, Stan 93, 96
Cunningham, Willie 74, 75, 82, 83, 84, 89
Cussins, Manny 253, 254, 256

Daily Express 68, 77, 118
Daily Record 45, 60, 64, 71-72, 79-80, 91, 92, 101, 187, 262
Dalglish, Kenny 186, 190, 197, 198, 199-200, 204, 206, 208, 213, 214, 230, 237-238, 239, 240-244, 261, 266, 273
Daly, Glen 16
Davidson, R.H. 'Bobby' 165, 187, 214, 215
Deans, Dixie 204, 207-208
Di Stefano, Alfredo 35, 157
Dickson, Andy 72, 73
Dickson, Charlie 73, 77
Docherty, Tommy 208, 209, 211
Donald, Dick 248, 249, 250
Dowdells, Alec 68
Dowie, John 244
Dukla Prague 124, 143-145
Dumbarton football club 233
Dundee Courier and Advertiser 84
Dundee football club 34-35, 112-113, 140, 165-166, 214-215, 233-234, 238, 243
Dunfermline football club 42, 71-87, 91, 104, 105-107, 108, 109-110, 132, 140
Dynamo Kiev 125, 156, 158-159
Dynamo Zagreb 234

Earnock pit, Lanarkshire 17, 25
East Fife football club 33, 48
East Germany, national team 271
Ebbw Vale football club 38
Edinburgh Evening News 54
Edvaldsson, Johannes 241
Edwards, Alec 84, 95
Edwards, Louis 196
Elizabeth, Princess, becomes Queen 46
England, national team, 259-260, 261-262
Estoril, Palacio Hotel 9-10, 13
Eusebio 179
Evans, Allan 266-267
Evans, Bobby 45, 51, 57, 61
Evans, Kelly 39
Everton 81-83

285

INDEX